THE SMOKING NUN

ANN J TEMKIN

Editor: Wayne South Smith, www.waynesouthsmith.com
Cover design: Cristina Montesinos, www.cristinamontesinos.com
Interior design: Jera Publishing, www.self-pub.net
Author photo: Life Touch, www.lifetouch.com. Used with permission.

ISBN: 978-0-692-09528-7

Published by 4 Dimensions

This book is dedicated to women and men who have lived with a secret similar to my own, and whose stories are as yet untold. For you, I hope for healing. To you, I say, "Tell your story. It matters."

CONTENTS

Flying Bird races across the beach, her tiny feet leaving sprays of sand in her wake. Laughing, she throws herself into the lap of Deep River.

"You're watching that beautiful sunset."

The slightly older child pulls her close, rocking her gently. The ocean swells and runs away, coming in, going out, over and over and over.

"It heals my soul."

She runs her hand through Flying Bird's hair, then continues.

"Tonight the winds will rise, great rain will fall, the ocean will stand very tall, and clouds will cover the moon."

She waits, quietly, for the little one to speak.

"And then, Deep River, the sun will *burst* through the darkness, and it will be day again!"

"Yes, Flying Bird. For that is the way of things."

Is It Safe to Tell?

This is a story I thought I would never write. It was too private. People would be scandalized. Reputations could be damaged. And, most of all, I thought it was simply a story of my own foolishness.

But it was not just my story. There are others for whom I hope to speak. And I hope that reading my story will bring them some healing.

One day I decided I had no choice; I had to write about what had happened. No sooner had I come to this conclusion that I attended a book signing of a fellow writer. She knew nothing of my story or my decision. No one did.

I purchased a book and stood in line with everyone else waiting for her to sign it. When it was my turn, she wrote something rapidly, and smiling, she handed the book back to me. I looked down and saw that she had written, "Tell your story. It matters." I smiled back and chose to take her message as a sign.

But the story does not exist without context. It unfolds within another story, a deeper, wider story, a story of leaning into the ups and downs of life, a story of hope and light breaking through into darkness. This wider story is even more important to share.

I have changed most names and settings to protect privacy. I have created dialogue for moments far beyond the reach of memory.

Still, the story is true. It is true to my heart, my experience, and my lessons learned. I portray myself and others truthfully, if not exactly. The story is true to the human experience of being trapped and set free, of love, loss, betrayal, and victory. Finally, it is true to the God who delivers from slavery and brings life out of death.

Two little girls are witnesses of my story. They are truth tellers, prophets. Generally the reader neither sees nor hears them. From time to time, however, they appear, and they speak.

Flying Bird is the younger of the two. On her fifth birthday, she wore a striped cotton sun suit and jumped out of a hammock on a hot summer afternoon. Her face was open and laughing, one small tantalizing finger touching her front tooth. A large red bow held back one side of her almost-black hair. Her dark eyes danced.

Flying Bird will always remain five.

Deep River reached the age of ten. On that day, she sat very still, peaceful, for a long time. Her dark hair hung down her back to her waist, straight as a plumb line. Tiny budding breasts filled out her green dress ever so slightly. Deep River's face was serenely serious, and her dark eyes appeared to look through what they could see to something, or somewhere, beyond.

Deep River remains forever ten.

At this moment, they are dancing and chasing one another on the beach. They are excited; the story is about to begin.

Walking Backwards

"196 Lake St. It's the Cenacle convent in Brighton," I told the driver when he held the back door of the cab open for me on this bright Boston afternoon. Tossing in my suitcase, then climbing in, I could hear his tinny radio bringing the latest news from Vietnam: more Viet Cong guerrillas from the north were infiltrating South Vietnam. It was May 9, 1961, and the conflict was accelerating.

"Oh, I know that one," said the driver, turning off the radio. "My wife makes a retreat at the Cenacle every year. Says she loves it. You going for a retreat?"

"No, I'm entering the order. Going to be a nun." Adjusting my purple dress, I settled into the taxi's back seat, and pulled a fresh pack of cigarettes—Winston Longs—out of my purse, tore off the cellophane top, and began folding back the tinfoil on one side. I noticed the driver watching me in the rearview mirror as I happily tap-tap-tapped the pack against my hand and carefully extracted the first, fresh cigarette. I was smiling, excited about starting my new life.

"So how did you know you wanted to be a nun?"

I held the book of matches in my hand for a moment before lighting up. Then I inhaled slowly. I really didn't want to go into all the complicated stuff about being half Jewish, being raised without any religious experience, about that Sunday in June 1956 when I felt the Presence envelope me and my life was forever changed. I just wanted to smoke and look out the window at Boston and feel my happiness.

So I took my time watching the smoke curl upward, and then just said "Well, I found out about the Cenacle after college and got to know the sisters. The retreat house was so quiet and peaceful. The nuns all seemed to have a light inside them. They seemed close to God. And they helped people too. I volunteered at the switchboard, and I watched women arriving on Friday nights. So often their faces looked sad, and they dragged in so tired some of them could hardly carry their little suitcases."

"Sounds like my wife," the cabbie interjected, stopping at a red light. He watched me in the rearview mirror while his fingers drummed on the steering wheel impatiently.

"But by supper time on Saturday," I continued, "as I watched the women going into the dining room, their faces seemed smoothed out, and their feet lifted higher as they walked. Sometimes they would send a silent wave in my direction, and when they saw one of the sisters, so many smiled. By Sunday, when they left, a few looked serious, and I could hear them making an appointment with a nun. Some had tears in their eyes, but they seemed to be happy tears. A lot hugged one another and the sisters before breezing out to their cars." I watched the tip of my cigarette glow as I took another puff, and when the glow turned to ash, I shook them off into the ashtray in the door handle.

The light turned green, and the taxi jerked forward. "So you like to help people," the cabbie observed.

"The Cenacle nuns live a life of silence, being alone with God, and they help others sort things out with retreats and spiritual direction. I knew that combination was what I wanted. I knew I belonged there."

I hope that will satisfy him, I thought, putting the cigarette out and stuffing it into the tiny ashtray, which was already half full from other passengers.

We were moving slowly through the urban traffic. Horns honked occasionally, especially in the roundabouts. I opened the window wider to let the smoke out and watch it float out, drifting elegantly upward, then vanishing with the grace of a ballerina leaving the stage.

I am in love with God.

I certainly didn't tell him that. He would think I was a crazy.

I thought about God all the time, wanted to just sit and *be* with God without anybody disturbing us. I knew that was the real reason I was riding in this taxi, driving to this destination. But those realities were much too personal to share. Besides, I am not sure now—fifty years later—what words I would have used to explain my feelings. Perhaps the language of love would have seemed weird or too bold.

And it would be hard to explain how I, dubiously Catholic, ever became part of a Catholic religious order. It would be hard to tell him about the experience that had been so powerful it changed my life forever, the experience that transported me to a place so beautiful I never wanted to leave.

Lighting another cigarette, I thought back to that day in June 1956, just a month before my 19th birthday. My intention had simply been to give my friend a ride to church in Baltimore, where I grew up. The city streets were full of hubbub even though it was Sunday. Horns honked, car brakes screeched, streetcars rang bells as they rolled down the rails in the center of the roads, stopping every couple of blocks to disgorge streams of humanity. The occasional vendor driving a horse and cart shouted out "greens, fresh tomatoes, corn" or "ice, ice, come get your ice," weaving his way between the cars. The smell of manure mingled with car exhaust.

When we finally reached the Catholic church, I decided to stay for the service. I had had a longing for God since I was six years old, despite—or perhaps because of—my lack of religious upbringing. Walking through the large wooden doors, the sounds and smells of the streets yielded to a deep silence, and we were welcomed by the faint perfume of incense.

My friend and former music teacher Joyce chose a place close to the front. She knelt down and leaned her forehead against the back of the pew in front of her. I was looking at some marble steps that led up to a sort of stage with a large block of marble covered with linen tablecloths. Two small boys dressed in white garments with ropes around their waists came out from the side of the stage, their feet tapping lightly on the marble. They lit huge candles and quickly scurried off. The aroma of the burning candles began to filter back toward us and then Joyce stood up.

A priest came out from the side, wearing a long, green embroidered silky garment. His footsteps were heavy and echoed in the silence. A woman coughed quietly somewhere behind us. The same little boys followed the priest and stood with him around the marble block: the boys on one side, the priest in front of the block with his back to us. The three of them began to chant back and forth.

"*Dominus vobiscum...*"

"*Et cum spiritu tuo...*"

Then it was mostly the priest's turn to chant. I could tell it was in Latin because I had studied that language in school, but what he was saying or why was a complete mystery. At one point he turned toward the people and spoke briefly in English—a short talk about some person who walked on top of a lake and another man who tried to do it too but fell in—while the boys sat quietly on big chairs to the side, their hands folded in their laps, their feet dangling above the floor.

Turning his back to us again, he began what seemed very serious chanting. Joyce and everyone else knelt down, so I did too. After a few minutes, he held something white and round up in the air, a boy rang a bell, the priest knelt for a second and quickly got up. He did the same thing with some kind of gold goblet, the boy again rang the bell, the priest again knelt, bobbing down and up. After a few more Latin words, people started getting up, row by row. Joyce did too, but she motioned to me not to follow.

And then everything became new. The air became suddenly soft and made a pillow all around me, from my head to my feet. The sounds of the people moving about disappeared in a spacious quiet. I saw nothing, heard nothing. My eyes were closed, but there was much more than that. Nothing existed except the soft air and the perfect peace of the silence, a wordless awareness, a floating until my own body dissolved into what enveloped me. My mind was still, undisturbed by the usual anxious self-awareness, the habit of moving and smiling and watching myself, as if constantly accompanied by a long, high mirror.

And I simply knew—not with words, but with my whole *being*, deep down into my bones—I simply experienced a great gift, a gift of a Presence I had been seeking for many years. I was simply home. This was where I wanted to live. My search was over. I knew it the way lovers whose eyes really meet for the first time know who they are, and their destiny is to be one. Their beings merge, their senses heighten. Who can explain what they experience mirrored in one another's eyes? And who would deny it?

I had no awareness of how much time had passed when I was gently returned and opened my eyes. The priest was putting little round white disks into the mouths of the people up front. The little disks were just like the large one he had held over his head when the boy rang the first bell.

Joyce had come back to her place next to me, and I pointed to the small white disks and said, "I want that."

"You will have to be baptized first," she whispered.

"Whatever it takes," I responded readily. I had fallen in love.

After almost an hour in the taxi, my ashtray was close to overflowing. I popped open the one on the other side of the backseat which was nearly empty, and looked out the window as Boston rushed by: church steeples, neon lights, billboards advertising seafood restaurants, shoppers carrying bags of groceries, young boys jostling one another playfully.

So here I am, I mused.

Suddenly "Brighton" appeared on a large wooden sign. We were getting close. As I lit one final cigarette, my mind went to all the people who had been part of my getting here, people who had been part of my journey during those five years since I first fell in love. Joyce was the first, of course, but there were others: friends, fellow volunteers and nuns at the convent, the funny little priest at the library where I worked.

Marilyn Klein was one of those very wonderful people. I first met Marilyn when I moved to the Twin Cities after college, and Joyce introduced me to a retreat house run by the Cenacle sisters. There I became friends with a Jewish nun called Mother Klein. A native of "Chi-CAW-go," she was small and quiet with twinkling dark brown eyes. Here was someone who looked a lot like me, had a Jewish last name like mine, was smart and young, and loved God and meditation.

Meeting another person who was both Jewish and Christian meant more to me than I knew at the time. With a Jewish father and a Gentile mother, I was part of two worlds. Having been raised in neither tradition, I belonged to neither. I remember liking the fact that Mother Klein was Jewish; I just didn't realize the extent of my own need to pull together the parts of myself.

Marilyn introduced me to the writings of Edith Stein, a Jewish Carmelite nun who died in Auschwitz. She was a well-known German philosopher who became a Catholic in 1922 after reading the Carmelite nun Teresa of Avila, one of my favorite contemplative writers. In 1933, Edith herself became a Carmelite and was sent to Holland in an attempt to keep her safe. But the Nazis arrested all Jews in Holland in 1938. Edith Stein was sent to Auschwitz and died in the gas chambers in 1942.

Like many mystics, Edith Stein was a champion of justice. In 1933 she wrote to Pope Pius XI:

> As a child of the Jewish people who...has also been a child of the Catholic Church, I dare to speak...For weeks we have seen deeds perpetrated in Germany which mock any sense of justice and humanity, not to mention love of neighbor. For years the leaders of National Socialism (Nazis) have been

preaching hatred of the Jews. But the responsibility...also falls on those who keep silent in the face of such happenings. Everything that happened and continues to happen on a daily basis originates with a government that calls itself "Christian."...thousands...have been waiting and hoping for the Church of Christ to raise its voice to put a stop to this abuse of Christ's name.

My worlds were coming together, and my soul was healing. As a child, I identified so strongly with the Jewish refugees that were my parents' friends. Their eyes were so large and sad. Sitting in our living room, they often seemed to leave us for a moment to revisit terrible scenes forever recorded in their minds.

Instinctively, I identified with other abused people. As a first grader, I beat up the bully in my class, not once but several times. It was the only way I knew to fight for justice for the children he taunted and humiliated, the children who stood alone on the playground because, in some way, they were different.

And now I knew that there were other people—Edith Stein and Marilyn Klein—who were Jews and Christians, who were contemplatives and stood with the marginalized.

I had thought of entering the Carmelites, but the Cenacle drew me in with its silence, depth of spirituality, and particular type of service to others. I knew that spending time in silence with my God was as essential for me as having air to breath. I also knew that was not enough. My union with God needed to flow out to others, and for me that meant standing with those who were hurting, marginalized, or simply hungry for more meaning in their lives. The Cenacle fit me perfectly; I longed to join this order. Actually, I just happened to be Catholic. My longings had nothing at all to do with Catholic doctrine or creeds or even the details of American parish life. I was very ignorant of and had no interest in all of this. Whether the nuns were aware of this or not, my application to the order was welcomed enthusiastically by Marilyn and the local Superior. I soon received word to come to Boston on May 9 to start my new journey. It was a glorious new adventure, bold and risky and as bright as the sun shining through the taxi window on that spring day.

As the taxi lurched to a halt, I fumbled in my purse and retrieved some bills, handing them to the driver with a "thanks." I took one last, deep drag, exhaled slowly and tossed the glowing butt out the window. It was a perfect spring day, warm but not hot, the humidity uncharacteristically low for Boston. My new life was beginning.

The driver wished me well. I grabbed my small suitcase, stepped out of the taxi, stomped on the smoldering cigarette butt with the toe of my pump, and set foot up the drive leading to a large brick building with sturdy, carved wooden doors. This was where I would become a postulant, a brand new initiate. In six months I might become a "novice" and make first vows two years later. Going through those large wooden doors was exciting. I was certain God would draw me close in new ways on the other side.

A bell rang as I opened the door, and a tall slender nun rose from her chair at the switchboard and stepped quickly forward to greet me.

"I am Mother Baker, and you must be Ann," she said, smiling broadly and giving me a warm hug.

She led me into the adjoining room, and we sat down on comfortable armchairs in the library, a spacious, airy room with dark polished molding and books lining all four walls.

"We are so happy to have you with us, Ann. I'll be showing you around today, and I am the Mistress of Postulants, which means I'm responsible for you while you and the other new sisters are here in Boston. First, tell me how your trip went."

We chatted for a few minutes about airplanes and taxis and then Mother Baker said, "I'm glad it went so smoothly. Now let's get you your new clothes."

This was exciting. New clothes would change me, make me part of this new world.

"And we will be calling you 'Sister Temkin' now. From today on, you are one of us."

Mother Baker handed me a neat pile of clothing—all black—and showed me where I could change. She seemed kind, and her brown eyes were warm. I looked at the clothes in my arms. There was a long petticoat, serge skirt, both held together not by zippers or buttons, but by long, narrow white tapes or bindings. A long sleeved blouse, a cape that hung down to my hips, and a short veil completed the habit.

Mother Baker explained the nuns didn't wear bras.

That's going to be strange. No flat chested women in our family, I remembered my English mother saying.

I imagined my breasts bobbing up and down like water balloons, which made me smile as the instructions continued and I was shown me how to tie the tapes and put on the veil, leaving a little bit of my hair showing.

Once I had proudly donned my habit, Mother Baker took my few personal belongings, saying, "We will store these for you."

I happily handed them over and then followed as she invited me to go through the door into the cloister for the first time where only nuns were allowed. The process of learning basic things about living there was about to begin.

We started by having afternoon coffee. Mother Baker showed me how to take one of the small mixing bowls and grip it with the thumb and first two fingers of one hand. She indicated everyone would drink in silence while facing the wall. I found holding the bowl easy enough—I had lived in Paris and was used to café au lait—and I welcomed being able to drink my coffee in silence, feeling how my habit and veil covered me effortlessly.

Six of us arrived that day and were there along with about ten other nuns. We stood in a circle all round the small room, but there were no introductions, only an occasional cough and the small clinking of bowls placed in the nearby sink. It was a bit odd not meeting the others, but at the same time, it was a relief since introductions can be awkward. It felt very good to be part of the circle, taking in the fortifying coffee, and simply focusing inward. It had already been a long day.

Drinking my coffee in silence that first day seemed beautiful; I loved it.

Eventually we would talk, but only after learning that no personal information was to be exchanged, nothing about our earlier life, family, or work. We learned that part of humility was becoming history-less.

This feels strange. I guess it's part of letting go of things that we lose eventually anyway, like money or accomplishments, and getting closer to God who will always be there for us. So it's a good thing. And there's another advantage for me. I don't have to worry about being different and not fitting in. That helps me feel I belong.

If I had been able to talk with the other postulants, there would be conversations to remember: words, reactions, differences and similarities, surprises, a progression of understanding. There would have been movement forward, increasing clarity. We would have processed our experiences together. But there was none of this: no words said out loud, no expressions to read on the other's face, no debates to recall, no passions to ring on through the decades.

Increasingly there existed only my own rumination, round and round going nowhere. And at times the sound of my heart slamming shut. The memory of all those days lies in a formless, unarticulated space. It is only now that I try to give it shape and give the shape life.

Now I know the prohibitions against connecting, knowing what others thought and felt, and sharing my own reactions took a heavy toll. At the time, I was unaware of my feelings. My family, all academics, had never focused much on feelings. In fact, my father told me decades later that he was raised in a culture where feelings were considered barbaric, and then he married my mother who had the British stiff upper lip, and they got on wonderfully. I was not raised to know my feelings well, and I only learned years later to identify and express my emotions.

And in the convent, the emphasis on spirituality and the prohibitions regarding conversation guaranteed my oblivion.

One memory from those early days is still vivid. Mother Baker called me to her stark office about six weeks into my postulancy. She was sitting at her desk, and I saw immediately that she was holding the small picture of my father as a very solemn little Jewish boy dressed in formal European clothes. It had been among my belongings, the possessions she had promised to store for me. Now she held it out for me to see, took my hand, and put the tiny photo on my palm. Her eyes met mine, and she smiled sadly.

"Sister Temkin, I must ask you to give this up. You must give it over to me."

I remember standing and looking at the photo, staring at it in my hand. *She is going to tear it* up, I thought. *She doesn't need to say it.* My eyes brimmed with tears. *This is a big moment. How much do I really want this new life?* I stood still for a long moment gazing at the image of my heritage. It was the only photo I had of my father as a child, and my sister and I each had one of the only two copies.

Finally I reached out and placed the precious picture back in her hand. "Yes, Mother Baker. I will give this up. I give it to you to dispose of."

She placed it face down on her desk before giving me her blessing, a small sign of the cross traced on my forehead. The photo was not torn in my presence, but I left with my heart ripped in two.

This was the first time I did not welcome and could not connect with the strange ways of the convent. Why didn't I protest? Why did I simply hand over the photo? Why did I destroy a link, not only to my father but to my Jewish heritage? There didn't seem to be a choice. Leaving didn't even occur to me then and arguing with Mother Baker simply didn't exist. So I toughened my heart.

Handing over that picture did not move me toward God. It moved me away...

My five companions were history-less like myself, so I knew very little about them. One was very tall and thin and by far the oldest, maybe in her mid-40's. And one day I heard her telling Mother Baker that she had night sweats.

There was another very tall woman, but she was big-boned with a masculine face and hands. She looked very worried most of the time and was definitely older than I was. I guessed she was around 35.

The other three were closer to my age of 26. One of them was about my size with an average build and unremarkable appearance. The hair that peaked out from her veil was dark brown. I learned later that her name sounded Spanish, but she didn't look at all like someone with Latin ancestry. She was the one who distinguished herself later by having the most trouble walking backwards.

One of the sisters was very dark and pretty, and looked almost as young as I. Her vowels were mostly diphthongs, and she spoke slowly and with a pretty lilt. I decided she must be from very deep in the South.

Finally, there was the Texan. Young, blond, and small, she had a distinct accent.

And that was all I knew.

Yes, we learned to walk backwards, a necessary skill for daily recreation. Twice each day we took walks, but always in groups of three to avoid subgroups or, even worse, "particular friendships." Shhhhhhh, the intimation was those might become sexual, but of course no one ever actually said that... To fit on the narrow path and be able to see one another, one of us had to walk backwards. Fortunately, I didn't find this difficult, even though my long skirt added to the challenge. Not only could we not see where we were going, it would be easy to step on our habits and fall, especially going uphill. This actually happened to a couple of my sisters.

I'm still very good at walking backwards, probably because as a child I was fascinated by the lives of people with disabilities, learning to read lips and braille and walk around blindfolded, feeling to sense approaching walls with my skin. Anyway, walking backwards was simple.

In addition to talking impersonally at recreation, there was the possibility of occasionally speaking very briefly during work times.

"If you have a question about your work, you may go and stand under one of the crosses on the corridor wall. Someone will come to you, and you may ask your question there," Mother Baker explained. It was good that we could get information, but that was all we could obtain.

For the first two or three days we slept in separate rooms, each painted white with bare wooden floors and a window. I decided that was to make sure we didn't talk, just in case a rule seemed stupid and we wanted to find out what the others thought. But once Mother Baker decided we were properly indoctrinated about keeping silence, she moved all six of us into one room.

Our beds were separated by curtains, making the room look like an old-fashioned hospital ward. Every week or so, we all relocated to a different room with cubicles in a different configuration. Everything else was the same. Each narrow twin bed had a white cotton bedspread with a small metal crucifix we placed on the bedspread. And aside from the very small chests housing our scant wardrobe, there was no other furniture.

"We move often so that we do not become attached to any particular place," Mother Baker instructed us. "You are learning to be attached only to God, not to anything or anyone on this Earth. Later when you have made your vows, you will be moved to different convents depending on their needs. We all leave our communities and our familiar surroundings, and go whenever and wherever we are called to serve. The small moves you are making now prepare you for this."

No matter where we slept, there were no mirrors. And there were no mirrors in the bathrooms or anywhere else.

"You will learn to become detached from your appearance," Mother Baker told us. "Mirrors only encourage vanity."

So we dressed without mirrors. This was simple except for the head-gear. It had to be on straight, of course, and it was harder to tell if it was straight by feel than I would have imagined. I got pretty good at taking a quick look in a glass pane of one of the doors. We probably all did, but of course, we never talked about it...

We ate together as a group with Mother Baker, separate from the other nuns, and in silence, of course. We also walked only with our own group during recreation. During times of worship and work, we interacted with the larger community, keeping silence together with the exception of those rare work-related questions. Once a day we had a class which consisted of an instruction on Scripture or on how we were to live. We could ask a question, but there was no discussion, and most of the communication was one way only, from Mother Baker to us.

So quite soon we learned to keep silent except during recreation, avoid all personal disclosure, eat with our eyes cast down, do the simple work assigned to us, move wherever and whenever we were told, dress without mirrors, and respond to the ringing of a bell: "God calling." I still instantly drop what I'm doing when someone or something else calls. The dark side of this now is that I often stand around waiting for other people...and get irritated.

This was the postulancy, our initiation, a time of letting go of the old and coming into the new. There was a life's history to leave behind packed up in a box: the clothes I arrived in: the purple dress purchased for a special date, the stylish but uncomfortable heels, the panty hose I had always hated, the bra that reminded me of my passage to womanhood. So much had brought me and my new companions to this place together. There were many more new things to embrace. It was a time that was joyous and painful and sometimes without any apparent reasonableness.

And why learn to walk backwards to ensure we were always in three's? Why couldn't we share our histories? Why drink coffee looking at the wall and not at one another? If we had been able to see one another's faces instead of looking at the wall or the floor, we might have seen our questions reflected in each other's eyes. Perhaps if we had mirrors, we might have seen the questions etched on our own faces. But, like losing mirrors, we lost conversation. We never even shared that we had questions. We certainly never discussed them.

We never talked about anything that mattered to us, not even about God.

Jumping

Deep River tied the rope around the tree trunk and began to swing it up on one side, down on the other, round and round, touching the ground with rhythmic smacks. Flying Bird ran in and began jumping up and down, up and down, always dodging the rope. It was their favorite game, and they often added questions to make it more interesting.

"What do you want, Flying Bird?"

"Everything. I will run like the wind, my face to the sun. My feet and my mind and my soul will all have fun. I will go many new places, see many new faces."

"And what will you find, Flying Bird?"

"How different people live, how they feel, how they think. I will learn from everybody. And what about you, Deep River?"

"My way, Flying Bird, will be to look beyond what eyes can see. Deep down within myself, within others, within the night. I will listen to the wind and the thunder and the dancing rain."

"If you keep looking deeper, where will you end up?"

"Inside the heart of it all, I hope, Flying Bird. Where Love is."

Living by the Bell

Six adventurous months of postulancy rushed by, and soon it was almost time to go on to the novitiate. Our preparation was completed by Mother Baker who stood before us one morning in our study room, hands clasped at her waist while we sat silently at our desks. We were not expected to ask questions or respond in any way, only listen.

"As soon as you become novices, you will all leave Boston and go to Long Island. That's where most of our sisters start their postulancy, and it's where the novitiate is. Your group came to Boston first because of some construction going on at the convent in Lake Ronkonkoma.

"All the novices at Ronkie eat in the refectory with the nuns who have already made vows. The refectory tables are arranged like a horseshoe with a space down the middle. You will see some nuns kneeling there. They are making accusations, confessing ways they have broken the rules. We don't confess sins, only infractions of the rule book. They will say 'By holy obedience I accuse myself of...' Then after the meal, they will do some kind of penance, like kneeling and kissing the feet, actually the shoes, of the sisters as they leave the room. We learn humility by this practice, and you will learn in time to do this too. And of course, we eat in silence, listening to the readings from the *Martyrology*, which is about the lives of saints, and other spiritual books."

The next day there was a ceremony during Mass. After the first opening prayer, I knelt at the alter rail with my fellow postulants as the items of new clothing were placed in our open arms: a piece of starched linen about three inches wide, a cap, a white veil, black sleeves, and a purple cape. I left the altar rail with my sisters and retired to my room for the ten minutes we were allotted to don our new habit.

The three inch wide starched linen piece, called a bandeau, had to go on first and was the most problematic. I had to put it across my forehead and tie the tapes behind my head. Since it was stiff, prickly, and straight, and my forehead is curved. This required making little invisible creases at the top so the bandeau could lie flat. No easy task. Then there were the ends where the tapes were attached. They were triangular; the purpose of cutting and hemming them this way was to accommodate my ears, but the stiff hem jabbed my tender flesh.

The cap was more straightforward. It went on top of the bandeau, over my whole head, and around my chin. My hair was totally covered. Only my and face and throat would be visible now. And my face was surrounded by the one and a half inch fluted edges of the cap. The effect was something like a baker's paper holding a small cupcake.

The sleeves were easy. They were wide and worn over the long sleeves of our blouses, snapped on just below the elbow. I would only wear them during Mass and other times in chapel. During periods of work, I was to detach, fold, and put them into the large pockets under my skirt.

Just before it was time to return to the Mass, Mother Baker came to us one at a time, unfolding the long white veils, putting them over our caps, and snapping them securely in place. We were ready to be novices. Mother Baker was now leaving us in the hands of Mother Lowell, who was Mistress of Novices, a pleasant looking, short, rather round woman with a gentle smile and bright blue eyes that sometimes twinkled.

The six of us processed in together for the remainder of the Mass. We officially became novices at the Offertory, the part of the Mass when bread and wine are taken up to the priest as an offering. We assembled in the back of the chapel and followed the gifts up to the altar rail. We were the gift of ourselves to God for this new spiritual journey. The priest received the bread and wine and then laid his hands on each of us, giving us a special blessing. We had crossed what seemed an important threshold.

If postulancy was about being introduced to the life of the order, we were now full participants. Our studies and training would continue for two full years, and then if we still felt called to the life, and if our superiors agreed, we would take vows of poverty, chastity, and obedience.

I divide the novitiate years into two categories. There were the wonderful contemplative parts I loved. And there were the crazy things that resulted in my living in a near-constant state of anxiety.

The silence drew me into a depth of contemplative prayer I had not known before. It was like being deep in the ocean, not buffeted by waves, but caught up in the movement of what is so much larger than myself. Five times a day we glided silently into the choir loft, a long rectangular room to the right of the main sanctuary. Rows of wooden seats lined each length and faced the center of the room. We took our assigned places and stood facing our sisters about six feet away, hands clasped and hidden in our large sleeves, eyes down. Then the leader for the week began:

"*Dominus vobiscum.*" (The Lord be with you.)

"*Et cum spiritu tuo.*" (And with you spirit.)

"*Oremus.*" (Let us pray.)

Psalms were chanted back and forth until, all bowing deeply from the waist, the nuns concluded:

"*Gloria Patri et Filio, et Spiritui Sancto.*" (Glory be to the Father, and to the Son, and to the Holy Spirit.)

"*Sicut erat in principio, et nunc et semper.*" (As it was in the beginning, is now, and ever shall be.)

"*Et in saecula saeculorum. Amen.*" (World without end. Amen.)

At certain points we knelt on the wooden kneelers placed before each chair, resting our hands on a long railing or the chair in front of us.

Standing, bowing, kneeling, rising. The melody rose and fell along with our bodies. And when it was over, we left in silence.

The Mass and the meditation times took place in this same choir loft. We were taught how to meditate: to read a passage from Scripture, imagine ourselves being part of the scene, listening to the voices, seeing the people, even smelling, tasting, and feeling the food, garments, and sun. We were encouraged to ponder: what does this scene teach me? How does it touch me? And then we learned to simply rest in God. I was wrapped in the arms of the One who embraced me years before in Baltimore. Such peace came only from the Presence.

We each had work assignments as well, manual tasks like sweeping, dusting, laundering, arranging flowers for the altar, setting out vestments for the priest. Work was to be carried out peacefully, silently. We studied Scripture and the Rule Book in the novitiate room. Every order has a book of rules. There is only one thing I remember from that.

"Why is this rule in here? We never do this," I asked in a rare private meeting with the Mistress of Novices. Mother Lowell's answer was interesting.

"We don't keep that rule because it doesn't work in this country. But we want to remember the ideal even though it is not practical now."

These classes, even the ones on Scripture, didn't interest me as much as the life of silence and prayer. My focus was on the experience of the monastic life.

I learned to live by the bell. It punctuated each segment of the day. The tone was deep and full, and whenever I heard that sound, I stopped whatever I was doing instantaneously and went wherever it called me: to Mass, to a meal, to the recitation of the psalms.

Some things that happened in the novitiate were funny, but we couldn't laugh. During meals we listened to readings done by one of the sisters. As novices appointed as reader for the week, we had to look these passages over ahead of time. There was always a section from the *Martyrology*. At first, these stories of saints were read in Latin. I had studied Latin and was fairly good at figuring it out, but never bothered to figure out these meal readings. We all just read the words assigned for that day, and no one understood them.

But this was the era of the Second Vatican Council, or Vatican II, which held its opening session in October 1962. This council of Bishops was convened for the spiritual renewal of the Catholic Church and the consideration of the Church's relationship to, and role in, the modern world. One of its first goals was to reform the liturgy in order to bring it closer to the laity. Lay people were to participate more by reading Scripture, assisting in distribution of communion, and so forth. And liturgical functions were to use the language of the people, rather than Latin.

Mass and the chanting of the psalms began to be done in English. And this also held true for the refectory reading of the *Martyrology*. Where we had formerly read the stories in Latin, in blissful ignorance of their content, now we understood all too well.

One morning I went to the refectory to prepare the reading for our noon meal. It began something like, "Saint Felicida had her head cut off. It bounced on the ground three times before Saint Alphonsus arrived, reached out his hand and...the head jumped back in place." Right away I started to laugh and knew I would be in trouble when I had to read this aloud to the community. No one, especially readers, was allowed to laugh.

During the next couple of hours I tried to steel myself for the challenge of reading this presumably solemn but ridiculous piece of legend. Of course this just that made me more tense. As soon as I mounted the reader's platform and opened the book, my face started contorting, and by the time I had to say that her head bounced on the ground, I was laughing loudly and couldn't stop. It took me five long minutes to get through the next couple of sentences. By that time the whole room was losing control, even Mother Lowell.

Normally, our time in the refectory was unremarkable. We all filed in and stood erect behind our chairs, hands clasped together hidden inside our long sleeves. The superior and her assistant sat at the top of the horseshoe, the servers stood at the other end of the room. Nuns who were going to make accusations were already kneeling on the floor between the tables. Of course we looked down—"keeping custody of the eyes," it was called—and presumably did not see who they were. But of course, we did look, and we did see.

On one cloudy day we saw an old nun and three younger ones kneeling before us. Our old sister was probably in her mid-80s and tiny, some four feet eight inches tall and shrinking. The sisters kneeling with her began to speak, one by one by one.:

"By holy obedience, I accuse myself of failing to respond immediately to the bell for choir…"

"…of failing to turn out the light in the sacristy…"

They droned on.

Then, last, it was our beloved old sister's turn. I tried to keep my eyes down. We were not supposed to be curious and look. But it was too tempting to watch this saintly little nun. What could *she* possibly have done?

Blind in one eye, her voice was unimpaired, and she spoke up loud and clear.

"By holy obedience, I accuse myself of failing to keep custody of the eye."

I bent over until my face was almost in my plate, trying not to laugh. I heard my neighbor's stifled giggle.

And so the humorous occasionally dotted the beautiful contemplative landscape and enlivened the mundane. But then there were the crazy things, things that confused me, made me anxious, and set my mind spinning with attempts to understand or explain away the incomprehensible.

There were reprimands that made no sense: "Sister, we *never* leave the light on when leaving a room" and "Sister, why are you turning out the light? Others are coming behind you?"

Were we being reprimanded for no reason other than to humiliate us?

This and many other questions could not be asked.

And there were the disappearances.

In the novitiate room where we had classes, which looked like a grade school classroom, each of us had her own desk. There were fifteen of us in the room, and we knew very well where each novice sat.

The empty desk in the first row dominated the room one day. A sister was absent and paradoxically most present. Was she sick? Had something terrible happened to her? A dozen questions and fears chased each other round my mind. But I could not ask. For three days, her desk remained there, empty, and for three days, her disappearance was neither explained nor even acknowledged. Finally on the fourth day, Mother Lowell announced in a noncommittal voice, "Sister has returned to her family." No more was ever said about it. No more was ever learned.

The effect on me was intense. I assumed my sister had been thrown out. It never occurred to me that she herself might have decided not to continue. She was quiet and beautiful and seemed to flow easily into her new life. I would have described her as peaceful. I had never heard her say anything about wanting to leave, but of course, such conversations were not allowed. I really didn't know her at all, couldn't know her at all. And I was totally immersed in the new life, intent on welcoming even the disciplines like refectory accusations.

I don't always understand why certain things happen, but I draw closer to God when I have to deal with the hard things.

So it didn't occur to me that she might have felt quite differently. Therefore she must have been told to leave. But why?

She was only the first; there were five or six disappearances during my first year as a novice. I was horrified and really frightened at the thought of being thrown out myself. I began worrying, even obsessing. The imagined scene of expulsion went relentlessly round and round in my head. I engaged in interminable self-observation. And I was all alone with this torment. My thoughts grew louder because I could not use words to get them outside my own head.

Would I be thrown out? Was Mother Lowell thinking of telling me to leave? What did people do who were told to go home? How could I make sure that didn't happen to me? What would I do if it did? Who might be next?

My anxiety grew and became more constant. I didn't know whether others worried as much as I did. They couldn't tell me how they felt.

The environment of isolation, lack of communication, and mysterious disappearances was making me sick.

Adding to my anxiety was Mother Lowell's reaction. She must have been watching me, watching all of us, I suppose. I don't know what she saw; of course my body must have been stiff, my brow furrowed, and my expression grim. Probably I startled easily and walked very fast too. I certainly couldn't have looked peaceful. "Peace," we were told, "is a fruit of the Holy Spirit," and I didn't have it. So one day she stopped me in the corridor.

"Sister Temkin! If you don't relax, you're out of here," she said and stood for a moment glaring at me.

I froze. It was happening. My worst fears were coming true. She was going to expel me.

That can't happen. I will try really hard, really, really hard...to relax. I will make my face and my body go smooth. That must be the way.

Inside my head, the fears roared louder and went round and round at a faster pace.

But lovers see all things through lovers' eyes. And so one day I had an answer.

Surrender. That's what we've been learning about all along. Surrender is the core of the order's spirituality. I must surrender my desire to be allowed to stay, surrender my fears.

I took out the bookmark tucked in my Bible and reread the words of the founder of the order:

> Oh! If people could understand beforehand the sweetness
> and the peace enjoyed by those who would hold nothing
> back from the Good God! How he communicates himself

to the soul who sincerely seeks him and who knows how to surrender herself. Let them just experience it, and they will see that therein is found the true happiness which they are vainly seeking elsewhere.

(St. Therese Couderc, *To Surrender Oneself*, 1864)

I must surrender myself even to the possibility of being told to leave. That is the answer. That way I cannot lose.

Now I had a word and a process to cope with what distressed me. And so I handed these matters over to God, and this brought a great deal of peace…but not enough.

Soon the limitations of "spiritualizing away" my mounting anxieties became very concretely manifest and seriously so.

One of my many jobs was taking care of the sacristy, which included putting everything away after Mass. Since Catholics believe the bread and wine actually become the Body and Blood of Christ, the bread and wine must be consumed or stored in the proper containers kept in the small tabernacle on the altar. It was really important not to spill any wine or drop any bread.

In those days the priest walked down the row of kneeling people with an altar boy following closely. The altar boy held a gold paten, or small plate, under the chin of each person and the priest placed a piece of bread in that individual's open mouth. After Mass, the sacristan cleaned the paten and other things, guided by lots of rules.

All these rules, which made no sense at all to me but which I couldn't question, combined with the presumed horror of losing even the tiniest particle of the bread. I became terribly anxious, so anxious that I began seeing little bits of bread everywhere, especially anywhere that linen cloths with their lint were used and even on the paten itself.

One day I told Mother Lowell about this. Now she was worried. Calling me into her office, she said, with great sadness in her voice, "I am not sure you can make your vows next month. You are so anxious."

I was devastated and had no meaningful response. I knew my anxious obsessions were not rational. I awaited, with dread, whatever would come next.

Two days later, I was cleaning up the sacristy and staring at some speck on the paten. I was obsessing as usual about whether there were minute pieces of communion bread on the paten, or if the tiny specks were just pieces of lint. Mother Lowell walked down the outer corridor and saw me through the open sacristy door. She came in without my hearing her, ripped the gold paten out of my hand and hit me over the head with it—hard.

The following day she told me how terrible she felt. She looked genuinely devastated by her action, pale and drawn.

"I should never have done that," she said, offering an apology, something unheard of from a Mistresses of Novices. "Are you all right?"

"Actually," I replied, "it was *the best thing*. That was *real*. That bang on the head was *real*."

I doubt if Mother Lowell was reassured, but I got just a little less crazy from that day forward.

I actually *did* grow spiritually during those years. There was great joy. And there were struggles. I thought about Jacob, the Old Testament character. After a night of intense wrestling with a strange, mysterious man, he was given a new name, "Israel," which means the one who struggles with God and man. The Jacob in me was struggling with God and with an institution designed by human beings. Jacob struggled and was wounded but not destroyed. The struggles made me need God more, made me more desperate for the Divine, for the Presence.

Finally there were only a couple of months left before we would make our first vows, those of us who remained after seven or eight had left. But we would not all do this at Ronkie. For some of us, there would be another move. Those who had entered through a convent in the Midwest would make these vows in the new, Midwestern novitiate near Chicago.

And so my little group, along with about 25 younger novices and a few nuns who had already made vows, climbed into a chartered bus and headed for Warrenville, 30 miles west of Chicago. It was an 800 mile drive and would take about 14 hours, including stops. We would be driving all night.

Sometime around midnight, somewhere in Pennsylvania or maybe Ohio, we pulled over to an interstate rest stop. It wasn't the first stop, of course, but this time we were all half asleep and feeling grimy after hours crammed into our seats with our long habits, fluted caps, and long white veils. Silently we followed one another from the parking lot toward the door of the rest stop.

The door opened just as we approached. A bedraggled-looking young man emerged, holding a very large Styrofoam cup of coffee, wobbling and weaving on unsteady legs. Trying to sober up before returning home to his family, that was the picture. Suddenly, intoxicated, he was face to face late at night with over two dozen quite strange-looking beings. He blinked, his mouth flew wide open, and he stood totally still. His left arm stretched out behind him, still holding the door handle as if glued to it. His body swayed from right to left, the Styrofoam cup spilling coffee in a precarious arc.

Ghosts? Was that what he was seeing? Aliens from outer space perhaps? Maybe some escapees from somewhere dangerous?

He stood frozen in place, swaying, while we filed into the building, gliding in our long black skirts, our feet invisible, hovering creatures from the realm of the dead. When we came out, he had left. I hope he had determined to join AA...

A month later, on November 19, 1963, I made my first vows: promises of poverty, chastity, and obedience for one year. I pronounced my vows at the altar rail at the point in the Mass when the offering is brought up: the offering of bread and wine, the offering sometimes of money, the offering of oneself. I gave my being over to my Lover, promising to live without attachment to material goods, to live chastely, and to turn my will over to God through obedience to my superiors. I received a black veil to replace my white one, and a cross with a heart in the center to hang round my neck.

My love affair with God had deepened through the dusk and the dawn of the past two and a half years. The Presence and I had lived together, loved and struggled, thrived and persevered through hardships of the desert. Now it was time to marry.

> Let him kiss me with the kisses of his mouth!
> For your love is better than wine,
> your anointing oils are fragrant,
> your name is perfume poured out...
>
> Draw me after you, let us make haste.
> The king has brought me into his chambers.
> (Song of Solomon 1:2-4)

I was now ready for my first assignment and left for Minneapolis the following morning.

Two days later on November 22, 1963, America was changed forever.

Night Falls

My new community welcomed me with broad smiles and open arms, and I was happily settling into my new home. I already had work to do, which made me feel part of the family, not a guest or visitor. We had just finished lunch, our main meal, which was simply homemade vegetable soup with salad and crusty bread that day. A couple of the nuns carried all the dishes to the kitchen sink while I filled a large bowl with hot water and soapy suds. Peacefully, I rinsed plates and soup bowls one after another, loading them in the dishwasher, smiling as I remembered my vow ceremony, the trip to Minneapolis, and my welcome home.

The other nuns were settled in the community room, separated from the kitchen only by a waist-high counter. Amongst the sloshing sounds and water running, I heard the voices and music from the radio wafting through. My ears caught snippets like "ABC Radio" but not my mind. I heard but didn't listen, being lost in my own happy memories.

Suddenly my head jerked up and eyes flew open.

"We interrupt this program to bring you a special bulletin. Here is a special bulletin from Dallas, Texas. In Dallas, Texas, three shots were fired at President Kennedy's motorcade in downtown Dallas. The first reports say President Kennedy has been seriously wounded by the shooting."

Dropping the plate I was holding into the soapy water, I ran, hands dripping, into the community room. Someone had turned on the black and white television, and the sisters had all pulled their chairs close and were staring at the small screen.

"We now return to your usual programming," an announcer proclaimed in a dull voice. A picture appeared of a woman gazing into the mirror, smoothing her hair. "Suave enhances your natural shine..."

An elderly nun reached for my wet hand and pulled me into an empty chair next to her own. "Kennedy has been shot," she said, clutching a damp tissue in her gnarled hand. "We heard it first on the radio."

"Is he alive?" I asked, even though I knew she had no answer.

No one knew whether the young, brilliant President was alive or dead. Someone began muttering, "Hail Mary, full of grace..."

Another announcer repeated, "President Kennedy has been shot," adding that someone saw blood on the President's head, and that Jackie Kennedy had thrown herself over her husband's body after trying to dive out of the car. The President was being rushed to the nearest hospital...

And then, "We now resume our regular programming." Advertisements followed, including a discussion of the latest jackets for women, "...and very often, you will find a zippered pocket discreetly hidden in the arm," a woman tells her companion with solemnity.

None of us moved; we simply stared at the screen, occasionally clutching at one another.

The famous soap, "As the World Turns," returned after the jacket sales pitch.

An hour later, Walter Cronkite broke in. "From Dallas, Texas, the flash apparently official, President Kennedy died at 1 p.m. Central Standard Time, 2 o'clock Eastern Standard Time, some thirty-eight minutes ago." Removing his glasses, then replacing them, his voice choking up, the clearly overcome Cronkite managed to fill the airwaves with information about Vice President Johnson's whereabouts and the fact that he would presumably soon take the oath of office.

It seemed as though the world had stopped turning and come to an end. This could not happen. Unlike the novitiate, regular houses with professed nuns—those who had taken vows—had televisions, and we huddled round ours during the ensuing days. We watched as Vice President Lyndon Johnson placed his left hand on a Bible, raised his right hand, and took the highest office in the land. We were watching when the alleged assassin, Lee Harvey Oswald, was brought out under police guard, asking for legal representation. We were watching two days later when that same man was escorted through the basement of the Dallas Courthouse and then shot on live TV by a man breaking out of the crowd.

We saw the entire funeral, including the famous picture of John John on his third birthday, saluting his father's casket.

The impossible had happened, it seemed. Camelot was gone.

But for the nation and for the Cenacle, life had to go on. Retreatants came every Friday evening and stayed until Sunday. After a few weeks I was assigned a couple of them for spiritual direction.

Often I would take a woman's hand, and we would both weep over our dead President, over the death of a dream, a Camelot. I was in mourning with my fellow Americans, horrified with them at the violence that we had seen, replayed over and over, on our television sets.

And at the same time, each weekend I was admitted to cathedrals of flesh and of blood as women opened the door to their hearts, sharing very personal stories. Those moments were sacred. It was like entering one of those very old European cathedrals where the presence of God is made tangible through the men, women, and children who had come there: old and young, joyous and weeping, those who have come to love, seek solace, give thanks, or even just honor their ancestors by standing where they had stood. Through the centuries, they had lit candles, knelt in prayer, sung lustily, intoned century-old prayers. The divine Presence was there, substantial, almost "thick" in the air.

Speaking with a retreatant was such a holy experience. Every time a woman opened her heart and allowed me entrance, I could feel that same Presence, that same energy from beyond embracing us both. Here was the enveloping God I had met in the Catholic church years before.

With these women and the powerful presence of God, I felt fully alive, totally unafraid, immersed in them, and almost unaware of myself. I honored the stories the woman entrusted to me.

Many came fearfully sharing secrets. For some, the wound was fresh, the impact still knife-like. Others had suffered in silence for many years, carrying burdens until their souls were like stooped old women, bent over until they could barely breathe. Whatever they revealed, haltingly or in a flood of rushing words, I never, ever loved them less. In fact, I *always* loved them more. I knew they could read that on my face, in my smile, in my eyes. And so often that was really all they needed. At least it seemed so to me. This was work for which I was well suited.

During my times of meditation, I was caught up in the Presence. My meditations on the stories of Jesus gave me nourishment, not only for my own soul but for the hearts and souls of others. The hours spent in the choir loft with my sisters, chanting the poetry of the psalms together, were like the peaceful back and forth of a rocking chair as we floated a verse across the choir and seamlessly caught the one coming back in our direction...

"Be still and know that I am God."

"I am exalted among the nations,"

"I am exalted in the earth."

"The Lord of hosts is with us;"

"the God of Jacob is our refuge" (Psalm 46)

And in the silence of daily routines, it came easily to take the burdens of the women to God and be grateful for the joys. Daily Mass formed a frame for it all, speaking and enacting God's gift to us of Jesus, and Jesus nourishing us and drawing us close to himself, to his God and to one another.

The work detail to which I was assigned did not bring me peace however. I was sent to what we called the Order. Nothing could have been a worse match. It was sort of the building and grounds department of the convent, involving endless replacing of light bulbs and similar tasks. It wasn't just that these concrete things didn't interest me; I seemed hopelessly inept. No matter how hard I tried, I didn't even *notice* burned-out bulbs or clocks that had stopped because their batteries had died.

My boss in that ill-suited area was Mother Hanson, a tall, angular nun who also served as Assistant Superior. She was second in command to Mother O'Shannon, the Superior, who by contrast stood about four feet eleven, a pleasant, small-boned woman of Irish descent capable of great humor and considerable wisdom.

Mother O'Shannon's room—yes, we had rooms to ourselves, and no, we didn't call them by the monastic term "cells"—was directly across the corridor from my own, and so I overheard her assistant burst in and confront her. Mother Hanson shrilled at high volume, her outburst carrying across the narrow corridor to my room. Even Mother O'Shannon's voice was raised, though not histrionic.

"How can you take away my aide in the Order, Mother O'Shannon?"

"She will be much more suited to work in the retreat office, Mother Hanson."

"But I need her. I am overworked."

"You managed without her in the past, Mother Hanson. I am sure you can manage now."

I opened the door of my room and hurried away as quickly and as quietly as I could. It felt wrong to be listening in on this argument, and I was having trouble sorting out my own conflicting feelings.

Part of me was overjoyed. Leaving the Order to work in the Retreat Office would be wonderful! So much more interesting and so much more suited to my abilities. Mother O'Shannon hadn't told me yet that she was making this change. But another part of me was not enjoying overhearing their conversation. I was shocked. I needed to get to the Chapel and pray. I hated the Order but had learned in the novitiate to view such unpleasantness as opportunities to grow closer to God. Mother Hanson did not seem to be following that training, and I felt disappointed. I had not expected to find nuns clinging to such trivialities.

At the same time I was really happy at the thought of learning about organizing retreats. Contacting priests, registering women, working on the services. I would be working with people and with ideas, which I did well, rather than with things where I was hopelessly bad. I notice people. I fail to see burned-out bulbs.

I am embarrassed that I remember Mother Hanson's outburst so clearly when so many things from those early days are forgotten. I remember it because I was so shocked.

This isn't what we were taught in the novitiate. What about humility and obedience? What about putting God first?

What a naïve idealist I must have been! Had I always been this way? I don't think so. My family of origin was tended more to cynicism than naïveté. No, I think I developed it during my two and a half years of training. I wonder now whether graduates from boot camp are similarly disappointed by the conduct of officers they meet in the field.

Mother Hanson's self-centeredness was not my only disappointment. Every day at morning and evening recreation, large boxes of expensive chocolates with yummy fillings were passed around. Everyone seemed to take one and consume it with nonchalance; it was routine, expected. Often the box went round a second time. The five pound boxes seemed luxurious to me. Lying in bed at night, I wondered about these new experiences.

We didn't have all these chocolates in the novitiate. And my family only had such treats at Christmas or perhaps Thanksgiving. And the convent's car is new, not like the fourteen-year-old Chevy my mother drove with its fender still crumpled after a minor accident. How does all this fit with the vows of poverty we have taken?

And I couldn't help noticing that some of the middle-aged nuns were just lazy. There were only a couple of them, but they stood out in our community of twelve. One was tall and emaciated with a long narrow face and lots of chin hair while another was overweight with food stains on her habit. These two were securely ensconced; they had completed all the probationary periods, taken final vows, and nothing short of gross immorality could lead to expulsion.

They often sat around in the community room together, seemingly doing nothing in particular, and rose with a disgruntled expression if interrupted by a request. The message seemed clear: they had paid their dues, and now they intended to do as little as possible.

I tried not to judge but again felt disappointed and somewhat troubled. Questions about the point of this cloistered life were creeping over the horizon of my mind like a dark storm cloud barely becoming visible on the horizon. Bit by bit, very slowly but inevitably, the honeymoon period of my marriage to God was fading to a close.

On the international front, the country was entering an increasingly dark period. The communist North Vietnamese Viet Cong increased military invasions of South Vietnam. In August 1964, they allegedly fired on a US Destroyer in the Gulf of Tonkin. The US Congress, at the request of President Johnson, authorized full scale involvement of American troops and the bombing of North Vietnam.

Antiwar protests were increasing. Silently, I cheered them on.

When the nation watched horrified as four African American children were killed in a church bombing and, in March of 1965, African Americans were brutalized on Bloody Sunday, I wept. I wanted to touch the faces I saw on the television screen, wanted to sit down next to the broken bodies and shattered hearts.

My own heart was lifted when the struggle for liberty and dignity brought about needed change. The Civil Rights Act was passed in 1964 and the Voting Act in 1965. I watched new vigor seize many and hope burn brighter again. I listened as people of diverse backgrounds but deep faith linked their arms and sang "We Shall Overcome."

But we were passing through a veil of tears. God was bringing us through. There was pain, and there was some healing. There were new laws.

Many who were formerly separated had walked side by side. Many had paid with their lives but not in vain. Day was following night. Our nation had seen the valley of death, and now we were emerging into new life.

On September 9, 1965, the nation experienced a blow from nature. Hurricane Betsy smashed through the city of New Orleans, leaving devastation. A city known for its beauty seemed damaged beyond repair. Untold human lives were lost.

Our order had a convent in New Orleans. About a week after Betsy completed her rampage, Mother O'Shannon told me I was being sent there to help. I left the next day.

A screaming child would greet me.

Hope

Flying Bird and Deep River lay together under the big oak tree this moonless night, staring into the dark. Deep River wrapped her right arm around Flying Bird's shoulders. The five-year-old rested her head on Deep River's small breast and reached across to grip her other hand.

"Flying Bird, where have you been?"

"I have been among the daring dreamers, running to the land of Camelot. And you, Deep River?"

"I have held the hands of people of hope, Flying Bird. And tell me, what did your running to the beauty of Camelot cost you, Flying Bird?"

"Cost? I lost many dreams, Deep River. But my heart holds new dreams now. And you? Are you glad you held the hands of the people of hope? What have you learned?"

"Yes, I am glad, Flying Bird. I have seen the darkness of night, but look! Way up there! A star still shines."

God Lives in a Quonset Hut

The ride from the airport to the New Orleans Cenacle convent was hazardous and horrifying. A collage of felled oak trees and huge twisted lamp posts formed mighty barriers. Mangled, dirty clumps of the once graceful Spanish moss littered the lawns and gutters. Houses were ripped off foundations, and furniture, tattered photo albums, and tricycles, hurled far and wide, dotted the landscape like passed-out sailors.

The Cenacle itself—a large, gracious building on a lake in an affluent New Orleans suburb—was intact. About twenty nuns lived there, and forty to fifty retreatants were welcomed each weekend. All the nuns and retreatants were white. Mother Ewing, the Superior, greeted me. She was a beautiful, statuesque woman with very pale skin, eyes so dark they were almost black, and a walk so gracious she seemed to glide across the room. It was Mother Ewing who told me I would be serving people in an evacuation center, bringing them the love of Christ.

Early the next day I was driven to the old Algiers Naval Station. I had been told that twenty-five thousand people were being housed there. I was dropped off alone and without any information except that I would be picked up again at 5 o'clock. Facing me was a high fence topped with barbed wire.

A soldier with a rifle over his shoulder stood guard at the entrance. As I got out of the car, he was the only person I saw or heard.

Where are all the people?

Staring through the fence, I finally saw what looked like a woman and a child in the distance and a few other souls dotting the landscape. An eerie silence hung over the compound.

Dozens of Quonset huts sprawled before me. A Quonset hut looks like a huge tin can cut vertically from top to bottom, emptied of its contents, and placed, empty part down, on 720 square feet of wooden flooring. The arched sides are made of corrugated steel and have no windows. What little ventilation there is comes from the front and back ends, which have one door and two windows each. These huge half cans stretched before me in endless rows on bare, dusty ground. There was no greenery, and hence no shade in sight.

I informed the guard that I was there to help and, thanks probably to my habit and perhaps my white skin, he asked no questions.

As the gate swung open, the silence was broken by the screams of a small child.

Where are the cries coming from? I have to find the child, but how?

Endless rows of port-a-potties ran through the property. I followed the sound of the screams, and the stench grew stronger and stronger as I neared their source until I faced one of these chains of portable toilets.

When I knocked on the easily identified door, the only response was intensified screaming. I pushed the door open, and there he was: a very little African American boy, not more than four, sitting on the latrine, face screwed up, arms bracing himself, legs waving wildly as he wailed. His tiny feet couldn't reach the ground, and his buttocks were wedged inside the hole. In fact, most of him had fallen in.

Trying to speak comforting words, I pulled the child out. He wasn't afraid of me; maybe he had seen nuns before. I remember doing my best to clean him up, doing my best to keep my long sleeves up and my cape out of the way and unsoiled. Then, seeing a First Aid Station sign,

I carried him there, hoping they could bathe him and locate a parent. They took him inside, and I reluctantly entrusted him in their care, sad to leave him, and wondering what would happen to him.

Looking around, I decided to go to the nearest Quonset hut since that was all I could think to do. The sun was bright that morning. Humid air hung heavily upon me. Wiping sweat from my face with my sleeve, I opened the door and stepped inside into a very dark space.

Built during World War II as Navy warehouses and sometimes barracks, the huts now housed people driven out of their flooded homes in the eastern part of the city, which is well below sea level and therefore the most vulnerable to flooding. New Orleans's poorest and blackest lived in these barracks like prisoners behind high fences.

And so I entered #53. Coming into the darkness from the unrelenting, blinding sunlight outside, I couldn't see anything at first. But gradually forms began to emerge in what was actually the perpetual dusk of dim lights hanging from the high curved ceiling. The stench of human sweat, diapers, and despair rose in the stifling heat to envelop me. Rows of army cots lined each side of the long, narrow barracks. Each cot had only one rough, thin, brown wool blanket and one flat pillow as tokens of comfort. Each cot lay only one foot from its neighbor, even though men, women, and children were crowded together, probably one hundred inside #53. Children wandered around aimlessly. Most of the adults sat on the cots, their shoulders bent and rounded, their few belongings clutched in their hands.

To my left, a man not more than forty clung to small cigar box with his left hand and wrapped his two little girls in the circle of his very thin right arm. Even though he was sitting on his cot, I could see that his clothes hung on him loosely, and his elbows and facial bones seemed to protrude through his scant amount of flesh.

"What is your name, sir? And who are these beautiful children?"

"They call me Emile, and these here are Nicole and Renee. They's 7 and 5."

"Hello, Nicole and Renee. I am so sorry about the storm. So sorry you had to leave your home and come here. But I see your Daddy's taking good care of you. My name is Sister Ann." I Looked at Emile now. "I want to help if there's some way that I can."

The children pressed even closer into his rib cage as I knelt beside them. I didn't ask about their mother for fear that some other tragedy had taken her from them. I wondered what I might do to help. FEMA forms, ready to fill out in the faint hope of getting federal aid, were everywhere. Emile had them too, piled on his cot.

"May I see the forms they've given you, Emile?"

He nodded and handed them over. It only took me a minute to see they were full of burdensome bureaucratese.

"Would you like some help filling these out, Emile? They look complicated."

"Yes, please Sister. Ah cain't read too good."

I pulled a chair into the middle of the room, found a small table, and called out in a loud voice, "These forms look really hard. If you would like some help figuring them out, let's work on them together over here. I'll try to help." Emile came over, and I noticed he limped. He pulled up a folding chair, rubbing his head and staring at the forms, his hands on the table. The little girls stood draped around him, their arms round his chest. We put the pile of forms down, and I began leafing through them, trying to figure out where to start. Slowly, a few others began to drift over as well, hesitant at first, then leaning forward to see what I was doing.

I could barely decipher those forms, and I had the benefits of a good education, had not lived with deprivation all my life, had not just endured yet another trauma. How on earth were these people supposed to make their needs known? And why couldn't the government at least write in understandable English? I was furious. But I just bit my lip, tried to look calm and reassuring, and did my best.

However, other more urgent needs always seemed to assert themselves, like little children coming into the barracks crying, holding out bleeding hands, or limping with feet cut from the debris around the base, leaving small bloody footprints on the concrete floor. I don't know how many children I guided or carried to the First Aid stations. By the end of each day, my habit was a muddy, and sometimes bloody, mess.

But Vanessa was the first mother I met whose children had disappeared. She came into the barracks, a couple of paper bags of clothes in her arms, her eyes scanning the hut and widening with fear. Not finding whatever she was looking for, she began running from person to person, appearing to question them. And then she simply dropped to her knees, burrowed her head deep into her hands, and began to wail. I ran over, falling to my own knees beside her, and put my arms around her.

Before I could ask what was wrong, she cried out, "Mah little ones! Mah little Paulie an' Jimmy. They not in the hut where they was. They not here. Nobody know where they been took."

We sat together on the floor, and she wailed as I rocked her in my arms, until finally I said, "Come, let's get up. Let's go together and try to find out where Paulie and Jimmy are. Someone must know."

I accompanied Vanessa to the Administration barracks. Her story would be repeated by so many mothers. Vanessa had been given a day pass, allowing her to leave the naval base and go home to see whether anything could be salvaged. While she was gone, officials moved people from one Quonset hut to another, filling empty places left by the few families able to stay with a relative or friend. Those moved included unaccompanied small children like Paulie and Jimmy.

Long lines confronted Vanessa and me when we entered the Administration barracks. The lines moved slowly. Vanessa would become a bit calmer, and then more and more agitated. Sometimes she began to wail as we stood in what seemed an interminable line. Finally we reached the front. Staff persons presumably had lists with the names of everyone and their locations. But there were 25,000 people and 25,000 names. Staff hunted and hunted through the papers, through the scratched out barrack numbers and scrawled notations in margins as the lines of frantic mothers grew.

That day, Vanessa finally learned where they had taken her children. Sometimes I had to return to the convent before a child was located. I just hoped they had been ultimately reunited. Riding home, I prayed, "Oh God, Jesus had a mother. She lost him coming back from a festival at the temple. She was frightened, weeping like these mothers. Mary found Jesus at last. May these mothers all find their children. Give some peace to the hearts of these women. And strengthen the staff here. They are so overburdened by their task and by the weight of the sorrow and fear that surrounds them."

I was totally unprepared for these experiences. I was one young nun all on my own, in a community I didn't know, at a facility in the middle of a crisis with little or no organization and of course, no computers or cellphones. I had been told that other nuns from various orders had come to assist; where they were, I had no idea. They were not in this Quonset hut #53, and I never saw them. No one was giving us any direction.

I had grown up in Baltimore, but Marylanders don't consider themselves southerners. I had read *Black Like Me*, the saga of a Dallas journalist passing as a black man, a very eye-opening book but still just a book. I had been involved with projects to integrate housing but in the North. I had no hands on knowledge of the lives of African Americans in the Deep South.

But in the midst of all this raw pain, this chaos and tragedy, I felt a great peace. Day after day, I simply did whatever seemed most needed. I wasn't afraid. I had no doubts about whether I belonged there or fears that I wasn't doing the right thing. God was living in those Quonset huts, and I just wanted to be there, with God and with these people in crisis. But I had so much to learn.

One day I tried to organize a badly needed cleanup. Evacuees had been confined there for about two weeks under crowded conditions. There were lots of children, and they had found creative ways to have fun. Empty food containers, wrappers from packages of diapers and paper towels, stones, and anything else they could find were used to create makeshift games and abandoned when the children became bored. These and other unidentifiable bits of trash lay scattered around the barracks.

Cleaning this place up and establishing some order will help people feel a little better.

So I found a few trash cans and a couple of large empty boxes and pulled them into the middle of the room. Then I consolidated their contents into one big trash can and asked Emile if he would mind dumping the contents into one of the dumpsters outside, which he did, limping and moving slowly. Teenagers stared at me with fire in their eyes. I could feel their anger. Several young children followed Emile out the door excitedly and then returned bright-eyed and eager for some action.

"It's a little messy here, don't you think?" I asked the little boy whose eyes were fixed on my movements. The five-year-old nodded solemnly. Emile returned with the large trash can, setting it down next to me.

Using the loudest and deepest voice I could muster, I called out, "Let's all work together to clean this place up. It won't take long at all if we all help. Let's just start wherever we are, sitting or standing, and begin picking up trash and putting it into these boxes and trash cans." And I leaned down to be the first to pick a few things up.

The little children ran around eagerly, their eyes bright. Renee and Nicole picked up a box and decided to carry it around, collecting from the young children. Vanessa's children who had been moved away and then moved back to #53 were there; they constructed a makeshift broom with a tree branch and some cardboard they found outside.

The teenagers didn't move. Some looked down at the ground, but others stared at me defiantly. "Just try to make us," their clenched jaws seemed to say. Of course, I had no intention of trying to coerce them and really wasn't surprised by their attitude. But the fiery glare in their eyes as they sat unmoving seemed aimed not just at me but at the world. They were ablaze with anger and bent on letting the world know it.

Still, it was the faces of the adults that shook me. A short, heavyset woman sat on a cot just a few feet in front of me. Her face seemed blank, devoid of any emotion, her eyes dull.

"What is your name?" I asked, kneeling down in front of her.

Slowly her eyes met mine. After a moment she looked down again, mumbling "Alicia."

Like the teenagers, Alicia didn't move, but unlike the adolescents, her body seemed listless while theirs were tensed for a fight. Looking around the barracks, so many of the adults gazed at the floor or looked at me with those same dull eyes.

I had read about the culture of poverty, about the sense of helplessness born of generations not merely of economic poverty, but people *trapped* in poverty, inhabitants but not citizens of the land, whose every attempt to give their children a better life was met with increased oppression and often violence.

Understanding intellectually is one thing. Seeing it is quite another. Looking at Alicia, I saw Betsy had traumatized them terribly, of course. But Betsy was only the latest of a lifetime of assaults on their dignity and their very survival.

I knew about white lunch counters where blacks couldn't get a glass of water, about exclusion from voting booths, from military combat, from white jazz clubs. I knew about beatings by those sworn to "protect and serve," about the Klan, about imprisonment and lynchings. But if a picture is worth a thousand words, an encounter with a living human being is worth infinitely more. I felt overwhelmed, tremendously sad, and hopelessly inadequate.

The faces and bodies of Alicia and others seemed stomped on, crushed and torn like the family photos now tumbling in the wind, drifting homeless around the city.

"God, help me to know what to do, how to be. I'm so unprepared and so inadequate. I have not walked where they have walked. I know so little of the harshness of their lives. Still, you have put me here, and you must have a reason. So I trust you to let me know what to do, what to say."

And then I felt very peaceful again in the midst of all that chaos and turmoil. I just did the task right in front of me, and then the next and the next. I held hands of old women, prayed with them, helped with federal forms, wiped the tears of children. It was so easy, so natural. God was present in every face, and God was present in my hands. They brought God close to me, and I touched them with the love of that same God. They were my teachers. We were priests for one another in the sanctuary of the Quonset hut. And the children and Emile and I made the barracks a little cleaner, just a little less chaotic.

That night when I returned to the convent in the evening with the nuns, I brought with me that little boy stuck in the latrine, all the bruised and bleeding children, the despairing men and the weeping mothers, the little ones making games out of stones and bits of paper. I didn't just pray for them; I was part of them, and they were part of me.

"Hasten, O God, to save me; come quickly, Lord, to help me." (Psalm 70:1, NIV)

I had been chanting those words every night for almost three years. My lips formed the words as usual, but they were now the cry of the desperate.

That night I was not tormented by any doubts about whether my life had meaning, whether it counted for anything. I was where I needed to be: present with desperate people.

Jesus showed up; he shared life with all of us. He stood with us and helped. "The word was made flesh and dwelt among us." (John 1) He told us to do the same for one another.

> I was hungry and you gave me food, I was thirsty and you gave me something to drink, I was a stranger and you welcomed me, I was naked and you gave me clothing, I was sick

and you took care of me, I was in prison and you visited me. (Jesus, Matthew 25:35-36)

The evacuation center made a profound impact on me, but I didn't spend my whole six months in New Orleans there. After about two months, most people were resettled or at least released. I resumed the usual routines of prayer and seeing retreatants, who were all white. New Orleans was a very segregated city.

"God, I miss the black faces. We have taken a vow of poverty, but what does that mean? I have seen poverty, and we are not poor," I prayed. "We white nuns sit here in great comfort and security surrounded by other white people, very well-to-do white people. Some of them are ostracized by their family members because they stand for integration. But we sit and talk about this in a place where those living in the Quonset hut cannot come. This has to change!"

I talked to God a lot like that as I ran from one responsibility to another. I was in charge of the library, which was easy, and an aide in the sacristy, which meant I had to get up around 5 a.m. to prepare for Mass, setting out the communion vessels and the priest's vestment.

I had to play the organ even though I had never played an organ. I'm a pianist, and the instruments are absolutely not the same. Not only was I ignorant of organs in general, this particular one was a *pump* organ. Of course, no one gave me any instructions. I knew organs use pipes to make their sounds. Pipes need air, and if there was no mechanical system to supply the air, someone had to pump it in. In this case, that someone was me. I had to use the huge, sloping pedals to blow air into those pipes.

My assumption was that my feet had to pump rapidly in order to keep the instrument fully inflated. So I pumped as fast as I could. The result was that these overly energetic movements pushed me further and further away from the keyboard, but I didn't know what else to do.

So when I could no longer reach the keys, I yanked the bench forward in between notes, a jerky occurrence required about every 30 seconds.

After a few experiences of this frantic activity, I learned that a more sedate pace was sufficient to accomplish the task and, in fact, worked much better.

And then there was the depense, where all the food is prepared except the meat and potatoes. All the breads had to be set on plates, desserts made, butter sliced, and so forth. I had to prepare these things for the community, the priests, the lay employees, the volunteers, and the fifty retreatants. All these groups ate separately, and they ate different things. As soon as everything was in place in the sacristy, I ran to the depense to make all the breakfasts for the nuns and our priest, then to the chapel to play the organ for the community Mass, back to the depense to prepare everybody else's breakfast, back to the organ to play the second Mass, and finally to the depense again to start lunch...

I am really, really not gifted in the kitchen and knew nothing about baking. And everything had to be made from scratch. And it was New Orleans—below sea level—where baked goods just collapse. The first desserts I made were eleven flat, mushy cakes.

When the nun in charge saw them, she shook her head and said, "You may use a cake mix."

This was a huge exception; she clearly saw me as hopeless and decided to take pity on me. I remember her kindness.

Even though I now spent most of my time in the convent, I had encounters with the outside world and have memories of despair and hope. I remember the 60-year-old black man, bent over and hobbling a bit as he moved behind his vegetable stand. It was my turn to do some shopping.

Sir, may I have a basket of those beautiful tomatoes and some green beans please?"

Tears began to roll down his wrinkled face. I wondered whether that was the first time he had heard the word "please" from a white person or been addressed as "Sir." I tried to imagine what it must have been like to be "hey boy."

I remember the story one of the nuns told me when she came home from a conference. She was a slightly plump and smiling nun in her early 40's and had always been very warm and friendly toward me. She worked in the retreat office and occasionally, at recreation time, she and I would talk about spirituality, how we might better meet the needs of women who came to us for retreats, what books she had just read on the topic. But that day as we walked by ourselves alongside the lake near the property, she was not smiling.

"I was downtown yesterday. There was a conference there on spiritual direction."

"Yes, we missed you at recreation. How was it?"

"Did you know that I invited Yolanda to come with me?" she asked, turning to look at me.

I told her I had not known that, but commented it was "a great idea." Of course, I knew Yolanda was a student and Yolanda was black.

"Well, on the way home we were both feeling tired and decided to stop for a cup of coffee. We pulled over at a Howard Johnsons near the expressway. The place was pretty deserted, and the only car in the parking lot was a police car."

She paused and turned to look out at the lake for a minute, not saying anything.

"Well," she continued slowly, "when we came out, someone had spray painted 'the Klan is watching you' on our car. And the police car was gone. The parking lot was totally empty."

I pulled my cape around me even though it was a warm day. I was frightened. "Did you see them after you drove out? Weren't you afraid?"

She had been afraid. She was still afraid. The police could, of course, know where she lived from the license plate.

There are many reasons to be afraid in New Orleans these days.

One day Mother Shelley came. She was the Provincial, which meant she was in charge of the whole Midwestern region. Tall, large-boned, with the kind of face the British sometimes call "horsey," I had always like her. The arrival of the Provincial was an important event, and we were quickly summoned to a community meeting.

"Mothers and Sisters, I have come here myself to tell you about an important decision your Superior, Mother Ewing, and I have made. As you know, New Orleans has always been a very segregated city. Therefore, when we built our retreat house a few years ago, we knew it had to be segregated, even though we don't believe in such things. The Jesuit retreat house has been here for a long time and has always been segregated.

"Well, we have decided to integrate our retreat house, starting tomorrow. We will send letters to all the women who have come here announcing our new policy. We will explain that Jesus taught we are all children of God and that we believe segregation to be wrong. The Bishop knows our intention and is fully supportive. I will stay here with you for a week or maybe two to be with Mother Ewing. We do not know what the reaction may be."

We all sat very still, taking the news in. I felt so proud of Mother Shelley, Mother Ewing, and my order. I was smiling as she spoke. Looking at the faces of the other nuns, they looked determined, ready to do what was right. Some looked fearful, hands fidgeting in their laps. I only saw one nun who seemed to have a raised eyebrow.

"Please be in prayer for peace and for reconciliation. And if you have questions, please feel free to speak to either Mother Ewing or myself. Also, if women who see you for retreats have questions or objections, it is best that you refer them to us as well. New Orleans is a much divided city right now. As you know, many white families are breaking up over the issue of segregation. Some very influential and wealthy men have been excommunicated by our Bishop for their public support of segregation. Some relatives of those men come to us for retreats. They are standing up against these powerful patriarchs, and that takes a lot of courage. We must support them. It does not help us that the Jesuits are not choosing to integrate. Nonetheless, we must do the right thing."

With that we were dismissed. I was so happy. We were taking a stand for justice! This was what the Gospel was all about.

We did indeed receive threats. I never heard any of them myself, but Mother Shelley told us of them. She also told us that some people had tried to bribe us. Here she was more specific. Our retreat house was new and had a sizeable mortgage. At least one person had come to her saying, "The Jesuits are not integrating. We will pay off your entire million dollar mortgage if you will do likewise."

Mother Shelley stood very straight, her hands clasped together at her waist, and declared in her deep voice, "I told the gentleman, 'We shall integrate. It is the right thing to do.'"

I felt proud that day. But on other days I felt ashamed, not of our order, but of our city. Powerful voices opposed justice and change. I remember that New Orleans had a hate telephone number. If you dialed this number, you got a hate message against Jews, blacks, and anyone else that wasn't white and Catholic or Protestant. The message changed every week as I recall. I remember when a black Assistant Bishop was about to be assigned to New Orleans. The message that week was about the "n-----" who would be putting his hands on their children when he baptized or confirmed them.

I was horrified and felt nauseated. This was the United States. How could this be happening here?

And I remember that the Archbishop slammed closed the doors of a parish after people walked away from the communion rail when a black missionary approached to help with communion. And that same Archbishop had the courage to publicly excommunicate four very wealthy business men, heads of some of the most prominent families in New Orleans, because those men publicly advocated segregation. This was wonderful. The church was standing up to power as Jesus did himself. I again felt proud to be part of this diocese.

And I wanted to do more. I wanted to march in Selma, but the nuns wouldn't let me; it wasn't "our work." That made me very, very sad. I was cut off from my brothers and sisters with whom I wanted to link arms and sing and risk the worst.

I suppose it is understandable. Our work is retreats, and that means integrating our building, supporting devastated women whose pro-segregation husbands had been excommunicated. These women do not agree with their husbands. But they are powerless, and we are probably the only people in a position to help them work through their terrible conflicts. At least we try to do that.

And then one spring day, after only six months, my sojourn in New Orleans ended abruptly, and my world tilted upside down again.

Mother Ewing called me into her office. "Sister Temkin, I have some news for you. Good news, I think. You are ready for the juniorate, which will prepare you to make your permanent vows. The juniorate is in Chicago. You will study and pray. This is an important time of discernment. I will let you know the time of your flight. You have done good work here, Sister. We will miss you. I am happy to recommend you for final vows."

Just two days later, I found myself in a taxi headed for the airport. The rubble in evidence upon my arrival was now largely cleaned up, although we passed trucks and workmen still laboring to bring back the once beautiful city. I was very sad to be leaving.

Sitting in the airport, I thought back over my days in this unusual city. I saw the faces from the Quonset huts and the tears of the vegetable vendor. I still see all these faces today. I loved the work I had done among the poor. I loved being part of a group that was doing the right thing: integrating our retreat house, and supporting others who chose justice despite the price they paid from some family and friends. I was just "in my own skin" with no self-consciousness, no fear. My relationship with God was full and true.

The plane took me to O'Hare airport where I immediately got a cab and gave the driver the address. I wasn't familiar with Chicago, and I knew nothing about the house where the juniorate was. I only knew that the juniors were a distinct group but within a larger community. I wondered who might be there that I knew from the novitiate.

I was surprised when the taxi got on the expressway and appeared to be heading away from town. Three quarters of an hour later I found myself abruptly deposited, not in the city, but in an upscale suburb outside of Chicago.

I thought of my arrival in New Orleans with its streets flooded and full of wreckage left by Hurricane Betsy. In my new city, the properties were large and imposing. The lawns all well-manicured. This was not what I had signed up for. My heart was battered and bruised by a hailstorm of luxury.

Starving on Steak

The familiar aroma enveloped me as soon as I opened the taxi door: steak. Thick, juicy steak, grilling on hot charcoal coals! It had been over five years since I had smelled them, and I had never been a steak person. Nevertheless there was no mistaking that rich, smoky smell that caused my mouth to experience the flavor of a chargrilled, medium rare steak. Memories flooded back too. Not memories of my childhood home—we couldn't afford steak—but of parties with friends, Fourth of July picnics by a lake, and similar extravagant moments.

The convent building seemed bigger than the others I had seen, and the taxi had taken me up the long drive that wound through the estate. I thought about the three years that had passed since my first vows. It was time for the final training period, the juniorate, which would prepare me for my lifelong vows. There would be other juniors; I wouldn't be alone. But beyond that, I didn't really know what to expect, something like a second novitiate I supposed, a return to a more rigorous cloistered life of prayer and study. The steak aroma was definitely not what I imagined.

Today must be just some special celebration.

Voices wafted toward me along with the aroma. I followed their ringing tones along the path circling the huge Tudor manor and found myself in a large garden behind the retreat house. A tall, quite beautiful nun in her late 30's came to me right away and introduced herself as Mother Livingston. Her smile was warm and broad. There was a twinkle in her eye, and her whole manner exuded friendliness.

She explained that she was in charge of the juniorate but was not the Superior of the community, whose name was Mother Henry. "I will introduce you," she said, leading me across the lush lawn to a much older woman, short and decidedly dumpy.

As I was introduced, Mother Henry turned very slightly to acknowledge my presence with a nod and then returned to watch a procession of salads, potatoes, breads, vegetables, and desserts arriving to accompany the huge steaks sizzling on the grill.

"What's the occasion, Mother?" I asked Mother Livingston.

"There's no special occasion, Sister," she said, smilingly slightly. "Mother Henry loves these dinners."

What about our vows of poverty?

I hadn't seen steak in any other house and found such luxury very confusing and troubling. But of course, I didn't say this. Expressing such thoughts wasn't "the way we do things." And my mouth was definitely watering. Instinctively, therefore, I stuffed the question down inside, shoving it down so far that even I didn't notice it lodged there.

"Come, Sister. Bring that suitcase, and we'll get you settled. Then we'll come back down and join the community for dinner."

Ten minutes later, we were back in the garden, which was beautiful in the early evening. Brightly colored flowering bushes surrounded us, leafy trees stood firm and provided ample shade, everything was very neatly maintained, and, above all, the temperature was a perfect 75 degrees with low humidity. Everything was very different from tropical New Orleans.

Mother Livingston and I joined the food line and then sat down in a small circle of chairs with a half dozen other nuns. Once people were settled and Mother Henry had offered a brief prayer, we all began eating our steaks, sides, and dessert. I was introduced to the nuns in the circle as well as others who came by to greet me. Eight were juniors like me; I recognized some from the novitiate. We were happy to see one another, but reserved. No one hugged me; that wasn't our way either. All the other nuns present had made final vows. It was a big community, maybe 30 altogether.

Mother Henry sat talking with a massively overweight nun who looked about 65. Her face was blotchy, pasty white with red patches. She sat proudly in a wheelchair. The two held themselves regally, and the five nuns standing silently behind them only added to the impression of royalty holding court. At the same time, Mother Henry and her companion conveyed a sense of intimacy, their eyes on one another only, their conversation shrouded in an expectation of privacy. They were together; everyone else was separate.

Expecting some imperial decree, I managed to catch snatches of their conversation.

"Tomorrow we shall have very beautiful flowers on the altar," Mother Henry sang out, beaming at her companion, whose name, I learned later, was Mother McLarney.

"Yes, the new florist is proving himself a real artist. You have chosen well," replied Mother McLarney from her wheelchair, and then she seemed to go on to make some disparaging comments about the former florist.

I thought again about New Orleans. We didn't have florists there. We bought some flowers in the market and arranged them ourselves.

The nuns standing around Mother Henry and her companion continued their respectful silence, expressing no opinion, demonstrating no reactions of any kind.

The entire scene struck me as outlandish. In my experience of convent life, no nun made herself the center of attention. Nor did any two nuns display a special bond. And the way other nuns stood around them, as though in attendance, seemed not only strange but out of place.

This seems more like a royal court than a convent, and Mother Henry even looks somewhat like Queen Victoria. But I shouldn't make judgments.

I looked around at other nuns and turned my attention to getting acquainted with the other juniors.

The younger nuns seemed nice. Most of them were a little closer to final vows than I. One of them, Sister Strong, walked with a very noticeable limp. Later, I always knew when she was coming because her foot landed heavily on the wooden floors. Later still, I learned she was from Boston and had polio as a child.

There was one woman I knew. She was from Minneapolis. We had volunteered together at the switchboard until she entered the order just six months before me. We were together in the novitiate too. It was really good to see her; she was nice and we used to talk about lots of things while working the switchboard. But of course, it would be important to keep a certain distance now. We learned that back in the novitiate. So we smiled and greeted one another warmly, but there were no hugs.

When the sun went down, we picked up the dishes and a lot of left-over food, carried them inside, loaded them into the refrigerator and the industrial type dishwasher, dug into our pockets to retrieve and attach our wide sleeves, and walked into the choir, hands in sleeves and head down. I was stuffed by this time and a little sleepy, but I found my place easily because Mother Livingston had showed me the chart before dinner, and I had already put my prayer book in the rack in front of my kneeler.

It was the hour for Compline, the last prayer of the day. This was a new and very different community for me, a new chapel, but as we began chanting the psalms, I felt totally at home. It was as though we breathed as one—in and out—our breath floating the familiar words back and forth between us. Our bodies moved easily and smoothly: standing, bowing, kneeling as one body.

"May the all-powerful Lord grant us a peaceful night and a perfect end. Amen."

"In you O Lord, I take refuge…for you are my rock and my fortress." (Psalm 70:1,3)

Here my soul was indeed at peace. Troubling questions were set aside. And as I stood and bowed and knelt with my sisters, my body also was whole.

I looked at the bookmark Mother Shelley gave me in New Orleans.

"If we are to be fully ourselves,
We must advance in the opposite direction
Towards a convergence with all other beings.
Towards a union with what is other than ourselves."
(Teilhard de Chardin, *The Phenomenon of Man*)

Back in my room, I picked up my crucifix lying on the plain white bedspread. It was small enough to fit in my hand, but substantial. I stood there for a moment feeling its weightiness. It had substance. The crucifix made me feel alive and seemed to lift the heaviness of the meal and the strangeness of the evening from my soul. I placed it on the small wooden nightstand, undressed, and slipped into the narrow bed. I would sleep well after all that night.

Malnourished

It was dusk. Night was moving in. Supper was over. The two children leaned against the tree, their legs stretched out, sprawling. Deep River's hand lay limply on Flying Bird's clenched fist. They seemed thin. Quiet, their jump rope on the ground, discarded for days.

Flying Bird's eyes seemed strangely dull, while Deep River's frame was limp, her eyes closed. Was she asleep or looking inside for something?

There was no laughter. Neither child spoke.

The Art of Surrendering

I woke up the next day in the middle of a dream about New Orleans and the faces in the shelter. I hate waking in the middle of a dream. Emotions run through my body like the themes of a Beethoven symphony or a mad jazz jam, and I'm left with no way to arrive at closure. And although the dream itself usually disappears, the feelings linger, like lots of dissonant dominant 7th chords longing for resolution and repose but stuck hanging in midair.

But there was no time to think about my dream or my emotions. I had to quickly wash up, put on all the layers of my habit—petticoat, pockets, skirt, blouse, collar, cape, bandeau, cap, and veil—and silently hurry down the corridors to the chapel. That morning after the psalm chanting of Divine Office, Mass, some more chanting of psalms and finally breakfast, I learned that all the juniors were going to school, myself included. Classes would begin in one hour.

The school was a small Catholic college in southwest Chicago. Someone had already registered me. I was to study theology. I remember nothing at all of those courses, which says more about my lack of interest in theology at the time than about the quality of the teaching. I do remember, however, being very bored.

For a few months, however, I plodded along compliantly, and perhaps looked as though I was settling in to my new circumstances. Maybe it was fortunate that school was not demanding because my mind could not focus there. My mind and, even more, my heart became increasingly troubled.

It started with the steaks, which turned out to be a weekly event. Life became more unexpected the following Sunday evening. That night we ate indoors and didn't have steak, but we had wine with dinner and then adjourned to a large room to watch a movie.

In 1966, movies were reel to reel, and I had never known of anyone renting them. Back then a movie would have cost a minimum of $100, which is about $700 in today's economy.

I have absolutely no idea what we saw that night, but I can still hear the whirring of the reels. The sound they made didn't belong there. It was more like cars rushing past our windows than the gentle chatter I expected at recreation. I began to experience a kind of motion sickness. I was stunned, very confused, and I was beginning to feel ashamed.

With all the filth and all the stench in the evacuation center, I never felt sick like this.

Obsessions began to take hold of my mind, whirring round and round like the rolls of film.

What is our vow of poverty all about?

Well, it must somehow be all right.

Maybe I just don't understand. But this makes no sense.

What about all the hungry people?

I guess it's like marching at Selma. The nuns said that wasn't our work.

But why this meaningless extravagance?

Don't judge and you won't be judged...

Round and round. Round and round the thoughts chased one another, obsessions creating a groove, a loop in my brain.

And then, maybe a week later, we watched another movie. This time, halfway through, very abruptly, the film broke. The reels whined slowly to a halt. I was relieved.

And just that quick—Presto!—more whirring, flashes of light, studio theme song, a roaring lion, and a second film appeared. I pleaded illness. It was true actually; I felt nauseated. I excused myself and left.

At recreation the day after that evening, a time when we could talk, I sat at a table where one of the nuns was working on a puzzle. She was probably in her late 50's and had been at that Chicago convent for several years at least.

"Did you like the movie last night, Mother?" I asked, pulling my chair close to the table.

"Well, you know, Sister, I'm not a big fan of movies, but I did think the acting was good." She picked up a puzzle piece, turning it over in her hand, pondering where it might fit.

"The one that started first seemed interesting, until the film broke. I was really surprised when one of the nuns quickly left the room, returning five minutes later with another one."

"Well, there are always two in the can, Sister. Movies are Mother McLarney's favorite thing, and Mother Henry likes to give Mother McLarney every happiness she can...because of her illness." The puzzle piece was placed successfully between its neighbors, where it fit perfectly.

"Mother McLarney is ill?" I kept my eyes on the pieces of puzzle, studying them carefully, my voice casual. I picked up a piece myself, having spotted a matching space, and dropped it into place, remembering that Mother McLarney was the older nun sitting with Mother Henry that first evening.

"Yes, Sister. She has a heart condition. Angina. She is sometimes in terrible pain." She looked directly at me, and I felt her gaze. Looking up, I found her looking deep into my eyes, seeming to search for what lay behind them.

Just then the bell rang, the call of God, so without another word, we all rose, pulled our large sleeves out of our pockets, and moved silently toward the choir, eyes already cast down.

What do I do with these steaks, sides, desserts, and movies? With these thoughts? I think I feel angry. Is that a sin?

The only thing I knew to do was to surrender — surrender my opinions, my feelings, my judgments about it all.

That is the way to peace.

The overarching, all encompassing spiritual mantra of the order was Surrender. That is the legacy of our mystic founder, Mother Therese Couderc (1805-1885), originally Marie Victoire Couderc, daughter of a farmer in southeast France. She developed a spirituality around Surrender, taught it to the nuns, wrote about it.

...what does it mean to surrender oneself?

...I only know that it is very vast, that it embraces both the present and the future.

To surrender oneself is more than to devote oneself, more than to give oneself, it is even something more than to abandon oneself to God. In a word, to surrender oneself is to die to everything and to self...

...to surrender oneself is also to follow that spirit of detachment which clings to nothing, neither to persons nor to things, neither to time nor to place. It means to adhere to everything, to accept everything, to submit to everything.

(*Se livrer* [Surrender] manuscript, June 26, 1864)

I worked hard at surrendering myself, letting go of my judgments and my feelings. Still, my prayer life began to suffer. The beautiful psalms began to slowly lose their power, their passion. They became routine, increasingly lifeless. My meditation times were often full of distractions, dry. God began to seem far away. But I had a way of explaining that to myself.

St. John of the Cross wrote a whole book about the 'Dark Night of the Soul.' All contemplatives go through times like this. It's normal. Being close to God isn't about warm feelings...

I said these things to myself often.

Weeks later, I approached Mother Livingston on another subject. I was terribly disinterested in the theology classes we had to attend. They were simplistic and superficial, not challenging at all. This was something I felt I could talk about. I did not think I could talk about the steaks and movies.

"I am bored at the school we've been attending this summer, Mother Livingston," I admitted. "If I have to study theology, can I go somewhere more challenging?"

Mother Livingston didn't seem shocked or even surprised by my unusual and not very surrendered request. She reached into the long slit in the side of her skirt and produced a pen and a pad of paper from the large pocket underneath.

"Where would you like to go?" she asked, pen poised to write.

I hadn't expected this response, was a bit flustered, but made a quick recovery.

"I would like to go to a university to take graduate courses and get a Master's degree."

Mother Livingston proceeded to make some notes, which I tried unsuccessfully to read, and then she looked up at me. "I will get back to you with an answer quite soon." She then left the room.

True to her word, Mother Livingston called me to her office about a week later.

"I've brought you the application for Marquette University. Fill it out," she said smiling. "If you are admitted, you will move to the Milwaukee between Christmas and New Year's, and begin your Master's program in January. And in the meantime, this fall you can audit a course in counseling at Loyola with me."

The bell rang, so I mumbled "Thank you," took the papers, shoved them into my pocket, took out my wide sleeves, and began to hurry to choir.

This is really amazing! I will be going to Marquette and leaving the juniorate. I thought I had to spend two years here! Instead it will be only a little more than three months. I'll be out of these classes and away from all the steaks and movies. Just a few more months and I'll be able to go to this counseling course at Loyola. Thank you, God!"

Entering the choir loft with my hands folded inside my wide sleeves and my eyes cast down, I was relieved and excited and so surprised all at once. I could hardly believe that speaking up had gotten me a ticket out of this Chicago convent.

A week later that thought of escape seemed even better. Sister Strong disappeared.

She was nowhere to be seen for two days, and no one said anything about her whereabouts. When I did see her again, she was coming down the stairs, limping. She always dragged one leg a bit because of the polio, but this was different. Now she was limping badly. And she was obviously in pain.

It was then that surrender reached its limits for the first time.

Dawn Breaks

It was on a Tuesday that Sister Strong disappeared.

On Monday, I had seen Sister Strong clutching the staircase railing with her right hand, descending each step very slowly, putting her weight on her right leg, then swinging her left leg stiffly out to the side. Sister Strong winced like a person trying unsuccessfully to hide her pain. Barely allowing her left foot to make contact with the step, her face nevertheless pinched together with each inevitable contact. Her left leg was the one with the rod in it, a rod placed there years ago because of polio. Usually its stiffness resulted only in a subtle unevenness of stride. Today something was different and obviously wrong.

And then the next day, and the next, and the next she was absent from the refectory, from the choir, from our study room.

Before the convent, I would have run up to her, asked if she could use some help, inquired about the trouble. I would have done that without a second thought. That's the person I was in New Orleans, in the Quonset hut. I listened and asked questions and put my arms around people. But here? Would I do that despite our rules? The rules which allowed us to chatter on at recreation and laugh at movies but left us silent at important moments? I am ashamed that I did nothing, simply stood there voiceless, abiding by our rules and customs.

Finally on Saturday, Mother Livingston, looking tired and tense, called all the juniors together and explained what had happened to our sister. She had fallen a week ago and injured her leg. This happened in the kitchen when she slipped carrying a heavy sack of potatoes. She was in considerable pain, went to the convent infirmarian, and should have been taken to the doctor immediately. In fact she would have been, but Mother Henry did not allow it.

I also learned that it was Mother McLarney who persuaded Mother Henry to deny permission. I had sensed the night of my arrival that there was something very strange about the relationship between the ailing Mother McLarney and Mother Henry. In fact, Mother McLarney apparently often used her angina to manipulate our Superior, clutching her chest and threatening heart attack when she didn't get her way.

I was shocked and furious. This was evil! The relationship between Mothers McLarney and Henry was toxic and totally contrary to our way of life. Now I suspected that steaks and movies and other extravagances were Mother McLarney's doing as well. Did she demand them, feigning chest pain until she got her way? After all, although Mother McLarney's illness kept her confined to her room through most community activities, it never seemed to prevent her attendance at movies...

The wrong done to Sister Strong had pushed me quickly beyond my abilities to explain away my reactions. Luxuries were one thing, and I neither wanted nor liked them. But surrender to injustice? Injustice toward myself? Probably. Injustice toward another? No. I could not surrender to what had been done to Sister Strong and was unwilling to acquire the ability to do so.

I was angry at God as well. "How could you let this happen?" I prayed. "How long will the wicked prosper? That's what the psalm asks. I don't know why you allow so much suffering. We need your help here. Help me know what to do."

But what could I do? Almost immediately an opportunity presented itself. Our Provincial, Mother Shelley was coming the next day. She was the woman I met in New Orleans when she declared that our retreat house would integrate. Mother Shelley did the right thing, defying threats and attempted bribes by the wealthy and powerful while disregarding the Jesuits' decision to keep their retreat house segregated. She would understand the injustice and evil we witnessed here.

Mother Shelley arrived, smiling with her unique blend of compassion and no nonsense, a woman of courage and wisdom. It appeared that her hastily planned visit resulted from a phone call from Mother Livingston, a kind woman who had responsibility for Sister Strong. She was also well aware that what happened to Sister Strong affected all the juniors. I am sure this is what happened because every junior was scheduled to speak with the Provincial privately.

When it was my turn, I entered the room without hesitation. I am sure Mother Shelley sensed my agitation as I walked into the room rapidly and stood stiffly before her. Still, I was greeted by Mother Shelley's expansive smile. There was beauty about this uncomely woman. There was a light in her face that is only seen in the faces of the very spiritual, the ones who have spent many years loving, rising beyond the demands of their own egos, being courageous and steadfast.

"Please sit down, Sister. Now, tell me what you have found in this house," she invited. Her voice was very calm, and she looked deeply into my eyes, wrapping me in kindness.

"Something is very wrong, Mother," I began almost in a whisper, but my voice quickly escalated. "Sister Strong needs to see a doctor and has not been allowed to. And there are other things here too, things happen that are just not right." Now my voice was raised and the words tumbled out angrily.

I was nervous. We were not used to being asked to share our opinions and feelings. Despite Mother Shelley's gentle and open invitation, I was not sure this would end well. Nevertheless, I had to speak up, had to do something. This was my opportunity, and there might not be another.

Mother Shelley leaned forward so that our faces were quite close as she listened intently to every word I said, continuing to gaze into my eyes. "You are correct, Sister. Thank you for your concern. That problem has been corrected, and Sister Strong left for Dr. Zimmerman's office half an hour ago. Now tell me what else you have found in this house."

I poured out my consternation over the extravagances: the steaks, sides, desserts, movies, expensive floral arrangements, and all the other luxuries. Somewhat hesitantly I divulged my information about the relationship between Mothers McLarney and Henry.

"This is not the way I thought we lived, Mother." I leaned forward, my hands clenched tightly as I spoke. "It is not what I came to the order to find. Maybe there are things I do not understand, but these luxuries trouble me greatly. And if it is true that Mother Henry acquiesces to the wishes of Mother McLarney, who rules from her sickbed, I do not believe that is godly."

"Thank you, Sister. I appreciate your forthrightness and your spirit. I believe you will see changes in the house. I hope you will always feel free to communicate with me."

Now for the first time during our meeting, Mother Shelley leaned back a bit in her chair.

"And how are your parents? Your father is Jewish, I believe, and your mother's father was an English Methodist lay minister? The Catholic Church has not treated either of those groups well, so it is very understandable that they were very deeply disturbed when you entered the order. I know that was very painful for you. Perhaps you know that mine were also? My father in particular, who was not Catholic, was adamantly opposed to my decision, which was very painful for me."

"My parents are still very disturbed. They see the Catholic Church's history of persecution of others. And on top of that, as academics, they can't believe their daughter has joined a religion that tells her how to think. I guess for them it's as though I became a prostitute." I shifted in my chair, twisting my hands, trying not to cry. "They came to visit me once in New York at Ronkie. We write letters. Thank you for telling me about your own experience, Mother."

"Kneel down so that I may give you my blessing, Sister," the older woman said, smiling kindly.

I knelt while she made the sign of the cross gently yet firmly on my forehead and said a quiet prayer. As I rose, she thanked me again for speaking and asked me to send in the next junior. I found her pacing up and down the corridor. She was a shy nun, older than I was, and looking nervous at the prospect of meeting with the Provincial. I let her know it was her turn.

"It will go well," I whispered, trying to convey through my smile some of the comfort I myself had experienced.

The following day, Mother Henry was not at breakfast.

At the end of the meal, Mother Shelley stood, her large hands clasped quietly at her waist.

"Mothers and Sisters," she began in a steady voice, "I ask for your prayers. Mother Henry left us early this morning to join the community in St. Louis. Mother Livingston will now assume the role of Superior while continuing her work with the juniors."

She then gave a nod, and we began to file out of the refectory. I was amazed and smiling all over on the inside while trying to maintain decorum and custody of the eyes on the outside. It wouldn't do to skip down the refectory aisle, although that was exactly what my heart was doing. I tried to look up to sneak a peek at the faces of my sisters while keeping my head down. I couldn't see anything though, because of their caps with the starched, fluted piece that encircled and hid their faces like the petals of a Black-eyed Susan. But still I knew they were all smiling too, inside at least.

The good news continued later in the day. We had all filed in for the evening meal and were lined up in front of our places, hands in our large sleeves. Before beginning grace, Mother Shelley began to speak again. Looking up, I saw she had raised her eyes and was looking at the assembly. Again, her voice was strong yet quiet and gentle.

"Again, I must ask for your prayers, Mothers and Sisters. Mother McLarney left this afternoon, accompanied by your infirmarian who will return once Mother McLarney is settled in one of our Chicago houses. The larger infirmary and community of elderly nuns will be of assistance to her there."

This time I was able to get a look at Mother Livingston's face as she stood directly across from me. Her face seemed rather pale and drawn, and her hands, though clasped at her waist, seemed to cling to one another, as though twisting without moving.

She must have experienced enormous stress about all this.

Grace was then said, led by Mother Shelley, and we took our seats. There were no steaks, sides, or dessert that night; rather we ate a good but simple and nutritious supper of beef stew and homemade bread. When all had finished their meal, Mother Shelley rose, informed us that she herself would be leaving in the morning, said grace, and led us out of the refectory into the community room.

It was time for recreation, half an hour when we could talk or watch the news on the black-and-white television. Of course we wanted to have excited conversations about all the news of the day, but we didn't. No one told us not to talk about it; we just knew that wasn't wise. It was best to simply pray for all those involved. Conversation would surely lead to unkind words, even rejoicing at another's pain, since our relief at the departure of Mothers Henry and McLarney was enormous. I, for one, felt no compassion for them, and was in fact delighted that they had gotten what they deserved.

So we gathered around our hero, making a tight circle of our chairs. We all wanted to be close to her, our brave and wise Provincial Mother Shelley. She sat tall and seemed to look round and take note of each of our faces, more relaxed than the day before with relief and pride evident in our smiles. But there was still tension, diffidence, perhaps fear that too much joy would invite more disappointment. Mother Shelley saw in our haunted eyes unanswered questions, unhealed wounds, and lingering fears of reprisal. She responded to all of these feelings, not talking about the women who had left, about the ugliness we had seen, but by reaching deep down into something else.

"I wonder how much you have been told, my dear Mothers and Sisters, of the brave women on whose shoulders we all stand today, the Cenacle nuns who first came to this country in the 1920s. They were French...of course, you know that...and arrived in New York knowing little about our country or about Catholicism in the United States. It is so different here. Most American Catholics were poor, quite illiterate immigrants in the early days, escaping from famine and misery. The priests were often the only educated members of the community, and so they were leaders and gained great authority. This is all quite different in France, at least it has been since the Revolution.

"Anyway, we were quite a surprise to American priests and bishops. 'What! Women leading retreats? Providing spiritual direction? Why they must think they are priests!'"

I laughed, and so did another sister.

"But our sisters quietly continued their work and gained many friends among influential women. They were in New York, as you know, and those early days were quite lively I understand. They hosted poets, justice advocates...I am sure Dorothy Day must have spent many hours at the Cenacle."

"Who is Dorothy Day, Mother?" one of the juniors asked.

"Why my child, you must read about that great woman." Mother Shelley looked around at us. "You must all read about Dorothy Day who founded the Catholic Workers Movement and stood for the dignity of all the working class. She was a Socialist, and that has become a bad word today. But Dorothy Day was committed to the idea that we all do better when the least of us do well." Mother Shelley's face was smiling and radiant. She looked around, gazing at each of our faces, into our eyes. "Dorothy Day was a great woman. I urge you all to learn about her."

Mother Shelley went on to tell stories of those early days. "And did you know that the house on Long Island, Lake Ronkonkoma, where all of you lived during most or all of your novitiate, was given to us by Maude Ewing Adams? If you don't know that name, she is the famous actress who played Peter Pan on Broadway. Yes, she was a great benefactor of the Cenacle.

"And of course, since money and influence always speak loudly, bene-factors of this sort helped our dear brother priests to become reconciled to our presence and our work." Mother Shelley chuckled slightly at this thought, shifting in her chair.

"So, my Mothers and Sisters, never forget that you have a proud history. A history of strong women who have taken on great challenges, great adventures. Women who have stood up for what is right, sometimes against the powerful. Women who have stood with other women and have often been their only support and confidante. Be proud of your heritage. Try to live up to this heritage but always surrendering to the will of God. Be proud and 'walk humbly before your God' (Micah 6:8). And now, my dear ones, I must retire. Tomorrow I must leave you, and my flight is early. My body will leave you, but I will hold each one of you in my heart. Pray for one another. Pray for Mother Livingston. Pray for Mother Henry and Mother McLarney. And pray for me as well."

She looked round the room once more, smiling at each of us. Then she rose, lowered her eyes to focus exclusively on the God she bore within, and disappeared quickly from the room.

I sat there not wanting to move, basking in the grace that had flowed out from her and that still flowed around us like tiny bubbling brooks.

Now I feel at peace, here, with women devoting their lives to love of God and the others, not afraid to stand for something, to challenge the powerful.

Smiling, I felt exhilarated.

Mother Shelley made it clear we were not about steaks and movies, not about manipulation by powerful people.

I could have stayed sitting there for a very long time, but the bell rang, and we all rose and went into the chapel to recite the evening psalms of Compline. It had been a very good day.

There were, in fact, no more steaks or movies. And more changes soon followed.

Sister Strong returned after receiving the medical care she badly needed. She still limped somewhat more than before, but her foot was bearing weight without pain, and a smile replaced her former grimace.

Civil rights activists were marching in cities across the nation. The Cenacle offered their grounds to downtown Chicago marchers in need of places to set up tents for rest, food, water, first aid, and supplies.

A wealthy, middle aged woman, Mrs.Elizabeth Gundersen, phoned the nun in charge of retreats to express her outrage. The conversation escalated, and the woman threatened to come and tear all the sheets she had donated off the retreat house beds.

The nun, rosy cheeked, was unmoved.

Finally, raising her voice still further, Mrs. Gundersen concluded, "I have made retreats for twenty years, and I shall never make another, never darken the doors of the Cenacle again."

"Well, it is probably just as well, Mrs. Gundersen," replied the nun very calmly. "It seems you didn't get too much from the first twenty!"

Picking up the crucifix on my bed and placing it on the nightstand, I prayed, "Thank you, God, for bringing me to this community of women. Thank you."

I crawled into bed and fell fast asleep.

Deep River was teaching Flying Bird that day. They sat at a blue, wooden kitchen table in their home in the small village called LaVie.

"LaVie is here, on this brown ball which is called Earth. Earth is going slowing around the yellow ball called the sun, and at the same time it's twirling quickly, round and round. As LaVie gets closer to the sun, it gets more and more light. That's called day. And then LaVie moves further away from the yellow ball, and it gets dark. We call that night."

"I like the day best," Flying Bird said, clapping her hands.

"I like the day too, Flying Bird, but I also love the night. It pushes me deep."

Flying Bird thought for a minute. Then, standing up and grabbing Deep River's hand, she called out, "Let's dance," pulling Deep River up and moving them round the table.

"There is day," Flying Bird sang out, going round faster and faster. She nodded to Deep River, who responded, "There is night."

"There is day...And there is night...There is day...And there is night..."

Round and round, they danced.

"And together they are good," Flying Bird finally shouted.

Laughing, the two children collapsed.

People Divided

The wind blowing up from Lake Michigan grew cold and piercing. Leaves turned deep red and shimmering orange. They fell to the ground, and snowflakes drifted down from the heavens. Soon Chicago was blanketed in white, crystals glittering in the sun. Strings of lights appeared on trees, and carolers sang in the streets, their breath visible in the cold air. It was Christmas in the suburbs of Chicago.

And then it was time to go. I would start 1967 in a new city: Milwaukee.

Packing up my things, I thought back to the day when we were still eating steak and watching movies, and I was so bored with the classes all the juniors had to take. But that day I had been bold enough to say to Mother Livingston, "If I have to study theology, can I at least get a degree?"

I had my own mother to thank for putting this question to Mother Livingston. Without her I would have kept on surrendering: keeping silence, putting my needs and my pain in God's hands. My mother must have said to me five hundred times, "Open your mouth, dear. That's what God gave it to you for." And so I had broken silence and spoken. And Mother Livingston had listened. And Marquette, the Jesuit University in Milwaukee, had accepted me to their graduate program in theology.

Since the day when I had dared ask my question, I had also learned from Mother Shelley that there was a time and place for outspokenness in the convent too.

I am with brave women.

Closing my suitcase, taking a quick look around at my room to make sure nothing was forgotten, I hurried down to the chapel.

After Mass I had coffee and some oatmeal, said a last goodbye to all the sisters, lingering longer with Sister Strong, and went to my room to get my things. Then I walked out the front door.

Mother Livingston, who wanted to drive me to Milwaukee herself, brought the car around. Slipping in next to her, I waved to some of the nuns looking out the library window. It was sad to leave yet very exciting.

And so we began the hour and a half ride down the Dan Ryan expressway. Fresh snowflakes drifted lazily through the air, melting when they met the highway. The skyline of my new city appeared a little more than an hour later. We passed the Allen-Bradley clock with its biggest-in-the-world four-faced clock, drove along the shore of Lake Michigan lined with large stately houses, and finally up the drive to a stone mansion overlooking the ocean-like lake waters, my new convent. I expected great things.

Milwaukee was a divided city in 1967, divided geographically, politically, culturally, and especially racially. The Milwaukee River divided the trendy and artistic East Side from the more conservative West Side. The Menomonee River Valley divided the North Side from the South Side.

The famous 16th Street Viaduct, the bridge over the Menomonee River Valley, was built in 1929. It was more than three quarters of a mile long, traversing railroad tracks, factories making heavy farm and construction equipment, and a ribbon of the river. The rank, sour brewery smell hung heavy in the air. "The Mason-Dixon line of Milwaukee" is what they called the viaduct. African Americans lived on the North Side, and working class ethnic whites on the South Side. Many went down into the valley to work. Virtually no one crossed over the Viaduct to the other side.

The North Side was a hand-me-down neighborhood. Germans lived there first. The houses were brick and very solid. As the Germans prospered, they moved further from the city, leaving the neighborhood to a Jewish population. Jews prospered and left the neighborhood to blacks. The houses were still brick and still appeared solid — from the outside. But inside, renters lived in slum conditions with collapsing stairways, vermin, and crumbling structures hidden from passersby. This was a community of very poor people forced to live in an infested ghetto.

The South Side looked quite different. At that end of the Viaduct lay a working class neighborhood. The houses were more modest in appearance but generally newer and owned by their inhabitants. The neighborhood had been settled by Polish immigrants in 1850 and was still largely Polish. Many of the houses were bungalows with wooden exteriors or siding. Lawns were precisely mowed. Other ethnic groups, particularly Italians, also lived in South Side communities. No blacks lived there; the assumption was that they never would.

While there were no written Jim Crow laws in Milwaukee, that did not stop the practice of segregation. A white visitor spending time in a residential area might never see a black person. There was almost no African American middle class. Racism affected virtually every aspect of the lives of the black community, but the majority of whites were oblivious to such realities. Working class whites were intent on maintaining their jobs and living spaces. More upper-middle class whites traditionally tended to think of their community as progressive and would probably have claimed no prejudice.

When I arrived in December 1966, racial tensions, which had existed for generations, had risen to the level of open conflict visible to all citizens. Harold Breier was Chief of Police. He refused to admit anyone with a college degree to the Police Academy, forbade his subordinates to meet with any organized black group, and turned down free federally-sponsored police-community relations programs. And Breier was a lifetime appointee, so there was no hope of voting him out of office.

Father James Groppi, a young priest raised in an Italian, South Side neighborhood, was assigned to an African American parish on the North Side. The realities of his parishioners' lives—poverty, joblessness, poor schools, and all the other effects of systemic racism—took him by surprise. He quickly recognized the results of entrenched injustice and resolved to do something to organize and help his flock and their neighbors. Not everyone liked him, and I would soon learn that.

"That little dago's a thug his own self. Nothin' but a n----- lover." The short overweight man dropping into the bus seat next to his friend began.

"And the Bishop? Doin' nothin'! Any decent bishop would tell that Groppi to get off the streets and go say Mass, stop all these marches and stirring up trouble. Not our guy."

"'Course Groppi would probably just ignore him anyway. Guy has no respect for authority."

"All this is gonna lead to riots."

"Troublemaker. That's what I call him."

"What's a priest doing out on the street with a bunch of thugs?"

In fact, the Italian American priest was a rather short, slight man, a scholarly man more comfortable in a library than in a protest march. He did not expect or ask for the role of leader in the Movement. But he was also a brave man of conscience who had the courage to do what he deemed necessary as a disciple of Jesus of Nazareth. And he found himself pastoring an oppressed people; he was, in fact, in the right place at the right time.

But I knew nothing about either Chief Breier or Father Groppi as Mother Livingston and I arrived at the stately convent on Lake Drive. The large stone mansion was situated in an upscale neighborhood. We proceeded up the drive and parked under the portico of the entrance. Retrieving my suitcase from the car's trunk, Mother Livingston and I mounted the few stone steps to the small porch and entered the retreat house. It was a beautiful building with dark wood and high ceilings, a classic early twentieth century Midwestern estate on the vast lake.

A wide, carpeted staircase wound its way up to the second floor rooms for retreatants. Several large oil paintings of landscapes adorned the walls of the staircase. The small chapel lay to its left, and a library, replete with wall-to-wall bookcases, heavy comfortable arm chairs, and a mahogany table, was on the right. From the entry way, I could also see the retreatants' dining room, set with enough small, linen-covered tables to accommodate more than fifty people.

We were greeted warmly by several nuns including Mother Walker, the Superior. It was suppertime, and we were led downstairs to the area where the nuns lived and worked. The rooms below were simple; I saw a dining room, or refectory, and a community room with the usual simple chairs and small tables. Later I was taken to my bedroom in a much smaller house, connected by a short breezeway to the main building.

My third day in the city I was driven downtown to register for courses at Marquette. The red brick buildings of the University stood tall along Wisconsin Avenue, the main thoroughfare. A highly respected Jesuit school, the Department of Theology and its Jesuit chair Father Bernard Cook were well known beyond both the city and the world of Catholicism.

It was a cold winter day, and the line of students waiting to register spilled out of the building and down the block. Taking my place at the end of the queue, I was happy to see other nuns and priests. I stared at the list of possible courses, marching in place and rubbing my free hand up and down my arm, grateful for the insulation provided by my voluminous, long habit. Old and New Testament studies seemed required of first semester graduate theology students, and I selected a course in sacramental theology as well. The semester began the following day, and I dutifully embarked on my studies, riding the bus five times a week down Lake Drive and Wisconsin Avenue.

From that moment on, my life was no longer lived solely inside the convent walls. Four or five days a week, I was outside where things were changing rapidly. This was 1967. The outside world I re-entered was very different from the world I had left that day in 1961 when I threw my last cigarette out the taxi window. This new world was colorful and loud, full of passion, conflict, activity. The Civil Rights Movement, Vietnam War protests, and the War on Poverty were in full swing.

Pope John XXIII convened the Second Vatican Council in 1962, advising the bishops from around the world to attend to pastoral needs of the church. Final sessions were completed in 1965 and the effects of Vatican II were now becoming manifest in parishes all over the country and the world. Catholics and Protestants of many different denominations were having conversations, finding common ground like fighting poverty and racism rather than focusing on differences. Masses were in English. Priests and nuns participated increasingly in all aspects of the life of the community.

The church was trying to become relevant, and as graduate students, we were enthusiastic. We wanted to bring about change, and I, of course, wanted to bring reforms back to the convent, my other world.

I asked Mother Walker, "All the students are fasting next Thursday and donating the cost of food they didn't purchase to the poor. Can we join with them and do the same?"

"Well, Sister, it's a major feast day, March 19th is the Feast of St. Joseph. We fast during Lent, not on a feast day."

"A feast day seems like a great time for a fast. A real sacrifice! Plus, we would have eaten more expensive food and probably had wine for dinner. There would be more to give away."

After a lot of reasons not to fast and rebuttals of said reasons, I was given permission to make the day of fasting happen. Now for Catholics, fasting doesn't mean not eating; it means eating less.

"So we will abstain from the usual feast day wine," Mother Walker told me, "as well as the candy we generally have on the table."

"And can we leave the crust on the bread?" I had always found the habit of cutting off the crusts wasteful and therefore offensive.

"Yes, Sister. We can leave the bread untrimmed," Mother Walker sighed wearily. "Now, go and prepare things in the sacristy."

Victory! Encouraged by this small step, I became a little bolder two months later as we approached the feast of Pentecost in mid-May, the celebration of the Spirit descending, people speaking in different languages, and appearing drunk or just plain crazy, according to Scripture. To me it seemed time for another move for justice. The sacristy was one of my jobs, so I would suggest a change there.

"We spend a lot of money on flowers for the altar for Pentecost," I began my speech to Mother Walker. "I would like to use some of the beautiful peonies we have in our garden instead. They are red, like the tongues of fire, the color we always use for Pentecost. We could save several hundred dollars, and give the money away to the hungry."

It would take a long time to persuade Mother Walker of this. Pentecost is a huge feast day, almost as important as Christmas and Easter. We would have six very tall vases full of flowers, rising majestically behind the marble altar. My Superior twisted her hands slightly in her lap. Such a break in tradition would be huge...

"But I can make bouquets that are just as beautiful with our peonies," I insisted.

Finally she agreed, and that evening I cut the peonies. After supper and Compline, around 8:30, I went to the sacristy to create my masterpiece. Filling the six huge vases with water, I picked up the first peony and placed it in the vase. The flower's heavy head hung down limply over the side.

Well, I need to put in a bunch so they can hold one another up.

Confidently I picked up about ten peonies and put them all in the vase, which resulted in ten red flowers drooping down the sides of the brass vase, all looking quite dead.

By 10 o'clock I was sitting on the sacristy floor, surrounded by vases, spilled water, and floppy flowers. Peonies stood so straight in the garden. What was wrong with them? I started to cry.

What am I going to do? This has to work! I have to show we can share more with the poor. How long did it take me to persuade the Superior? I will find a way!

Then my mother's spirit began to move in me. She used to tell me as a child, "If you don't have a hammer, use a shoe." What could I use?

Necessity is indeed the mother of invention. The whole trick was to believe my mother: if you have to do it, you will find a way.

A-ha. I rushed into the community room and pulled open the cabinet. There was the big, fat roll of masking tape. Grabbing it, I ran back into the sacristy, stuck all 60 peonies in the six vases, wrapped masking tape around each bunch, carefully putting it lower than the lip of the vase, put in some more water, but not enough to reach and unstick the tape. And then I dragged the vases onto the altar one by one.

There. Hopefully that would hold till the next day. Then all I would have to do was play the organ for two Masses and two late afternoon Benediction services and cook for 50 people.

But more important things were going on in Milwaukee that year. The fight against housing discrimination would soon gain national attention. This struggle was not new. As early as 1962, Alderwoman Vel Phillips had proposed a bill outlawing racial discrimination in mortgage, lending, and rental practices, and three times the bill had been defeated.

On August 28, 1967, I watched on television as Father Groppi, working with the NAACP, led hundreds of African Americans and some whites in a march across the 16th Street Viaduct. Sitting there in the community room with the other nuns that hot August day, I could feel my feet imperceptibly moving, quietly marching in place with my brothers and sisters, surrounded by God's presence in the people. The marchers went all the way through the South Side to Kosciuszko Park. Over three thousand white South Side residents hurled insults, bricks, and other objects at the marchers. For 200 consecutive days, they marched demanding fair housing practices. This was the famous Open Housing March. Victory did not come until the passage of federal legislation in April 1968.

Memories of faces in the Quonset hut in New Orleans flashed before me. I was flooded by the awareness of how much I wanted to be out there, on the street, shoulder to shoulder.

I longed to be there with those living our faith with their bodies as well as their minds. Jesus would be out on the street, not sitting safely watching on the convent television.

Isn't this the incarnation you have in mind, God? Not just the Jesus who lived 2,000 years ago, but us, the Body of Christ, marching today?

I felt sad when the bell rang and we all moved into the chapel. When I was honest with myself, I admitted that I felt dead more and more often during times of prayer. This was especially true in the mornings during the time for silent meditation. My prayer life had been floundering for over a year when I was still in Chicago. At first I assumed that it was just a stage. But often I cried out to God in a lament:

I can't focus....

God, you seem so far away...

I love you, God. Why don't you let me know you are here?

I hold my arms out to you, and...nothing.

You don't take my hands, don't hold me, don't speak.

I feel rejected. I feel a fool, holding myself out to a lover who is stony silent.

I went to Mass. I took communion.

That has always meant so much. Now...

I know this won't last. This is just part of the contemplative journey. I've read about this.

But the distance lengthened, and in the chapel the silences grew louder. As the days stretched, I felt more and more abandoned.

And silence was no longer rich; it was now an empty void, an abyss. And at the same time it began to have a sound: a thin, tinny sound like a cheap child's toy.

There was a small crack in my heart.

Occasionally, I began to hear a tiny voice whisper, *Is this the life I am meant to live...?*

Bread, Wine, and Cigarettes

"Go to the sacristy, Sister Temkin. Father DeLuca has been sent over to help us during Holy Week."

Entering the chapel and starting up the center aisle, I saw light coming from the small room to the left of the altar where we kept all the vestments, altar linens, vessels, and prayer books for Mass. I spent a lot of time in that sacristy each week, working with the different priests who appeared to lead services or preach retreats. Sometimes I knew them, sometimes not.

Reaching the front of the chapel, I could see a man dressed in black pants and a sports shirt through the open sacristy door. Well over six feet, he braced himself with both hands on the table, bending over from the waist to study the big red-covered book containing the liturgies for the coming week, the most sacred week of the church calendar.

"Hello, Father. You must be Father DeLuca," I greeted him with deference as I entered the small room.

"And you must be Sister Temkin," he responded, straightening up and turning to face me.

His blue eyes looked at me directly, shining brightly beneath his wavy dark hair. His face lifted in a broad smile as he reached out his large, strong hand to shake mine.

And so we reviewed the week's ceremonies together, day by day: Holy Thursday when the Last Supper is celebrated, Good Friday with its focus on Jesus' death, and of course, the grand Easter Liturgy. I found it easy to work with him. More than easy. We talked about the liturgy, which made my day brighter and lighter while my appreciation of the texts and the liturgical pageantry deepened. Working collaboratively like this rather than doing rote tasks was exciting.

Every day that Holy Week, I laid out Father DeLuca's vestments, arranged the markers in the large altar books, put out the carafe of wine, box of bread, and chalices into which the wine would be poured, as well as the paten for the bread, all the little cloths, and a flask of water. Before Mass, I chanted the psalms with the other nuns in our separate chapel. We faced the raised altar from the left side and could see the front pews of the retreatants' chapel to our right.

Each morning as we finished chanting, I entered the adjoining sacristy and picked up the long, brass candle lighter. The morning Father DeLuca arrived, I climbed the three marble steps up to the altar as usual, while my mind wandered back to a morning the week before. That day, too, the altar was draped with linens and flanked on either side by three tall, majestic, sentinel-like candles. Lighting them was my last task before Mass. And that day as always, I could feel the eyes of the fifty women, sitting or kneeling in the retreatants' chapel. I would go to the center of the altar and bow before the gold tabernacle, which contained bread consecrated at a previous Mass. Then I would take a step to the right, light the candles there, cross back to the center, bow, light those on the left, return to the tabernacle, and make one final bow before descending the steps on my way back to the sacristy.

The week before, everything had begun as usual. The retreatants watched my every move as they always did. But as I stood ready to make my final bow, I felt my petticoat come unfastened and slide down to form a heap around my ankles. It was long and fell in deep folds; I knew there was no way I could keep walking with it around my feet. For a second, I contemplated kicking it ahead of me all the way back to the sacristy, but that would inevitably lead to an undignified fall. There seemed no alternative, so I put one hand on the altar to keep my balance, stepped out of the folds of long black cotton, picked the petticoat up, put it over my arm, bowed once more, and exited. I was glad my cap and veil hid my red face.

But the day Father DeLuca arrived, there was no such embarrassing experience. I topped all six candles with bright, steady flames, exited as usual through the sacristy, and walked with hurried dignity to the back of the retreatants' chapel. There I took my place at the organ. I could see Father DeLuca standing in the sacristy, clad in his vestments, poised, hands clasped at his waist, ready to move ceremoniously to the altar. I took a breath and hit the first chord of the procession hymn, "O Bread of Life from Heaven."

I really liked working with Father DeLuca that week. He was a kind man and very smart, and the first priest who reviewed all the Scriptures of each liturgy with me, even expressing interest in my impressions of the texts.

"I know you're a graduate student at Marquette and that you are studying theology there, but I'm impressed with the depth of your understanding of the texts. I don't think you got that from school. My experience is that it takes hours of soaking up the Scriptures plus an awareness of what life is like for real people."

I thanked him and was genuinely touched.

He isn't just commenting on my intellectual understanding. He seemed to be talking about me as a person, to understand things about my prayer life and my interest in people. My professors don't talk like this.

At the end of Holy Week on Easter morning, he asked whether I could meet him in the convent library so he could show me something.

"If I tell Mother Walker that you have asked to speak with me, I'm sure I can take a half hour after breakfast."

We consumed our breakfasts in separate rooms, I with the community and he alone in the priest's dining room. When I got to the library, I saw Father DeLuca was already there, standing looking out the window, a book in his hand. He sat down and held out an edition of some of the writings of Edith Stein, the Jewish contemplative nun who was killed during the Holocaust.

"Did you know I'm half Jewish?" I asked, taking a seat facing him. I was amazed; I hadn't told him about my background.

"No, not when we met. But your name, Temkin, is unusual. I've never heard it before. So I did a little research and discovered it's a Russian Jewish name. Didn't know if you knew about Edith Stein. Would you like to borrow the book? You could have it, but I don't suppose you're allowed to own books." He crossed his legs and smiled.

He was right about owning books, and although I was familiar with some works of Edith Stein, I had not read her *Essays On Woman.* I was thrilled to have the opportunity and began reading it that very afternoon, finding it fascinating. Written in between the two world wars, Stein explored the roles of women both at home and everywhere in the world. And she did this as a Catholic deeply rooted in contemplative literature. Father DeLuca had touched on my need to bring my varied backgrounds together, and this Jewish contemplative definitely served as a bridge helping me to do so.

Reading Edith Stein led to other conversations with Father DeLuca. I quickly began to open up about my own spiritual life and my doubts, about feeling so alive marching with people in the streets, some things about my life before the convent. When he discovered I had been a smoker, he brought me a pack of Winstons which I hid in my pocket until late at night when I could be alone in the retreatants' lounge. It was very private there when there were no retreats going on, and, having no fear of discovery, I luxuriously pulled nicotine deep into my lungs for the first time in seven years. For about 10 seconds, I felt a bit light headed. Then I was fully re-acclimated and smoked the cigarette down to the butt.

Some days later, finishing up in the sacristy, I remarked, "That was really nice of you to bring the cigarettes, Father. Do you think I could have another pack?"

A quick nod indicated his assent, and as I was walking away through the now empty chapel, he called "Sister Temkin." I turned just in time to see him grin, reach into his pocket, and toss a second pack through the air, sailing it over the pews. I caught it, laughing and plunging it into my own pocket.

Father DeLuca told me he had been asked to stay on and help out at the convent for another month or two. Good news!

"Sister, do you think you could come to my office so we could discuss the liturgies? It's somewhat of a distance, but the bus runs that way. I'll give you directions."

"I think so. I will ask Mother Walker," I replied and smiled.

One day not more than a month after Easter, I found myself ringing the bell at the priests' house. I was admitted by a small, elderly Brother James, who introduced himself and directed me up the winding staircase to Father DeLuca's office on the second floor.

The sun shone brightly, lighting the colorful modern stained glass windows lining the staircase. The bannister of polished dark wood curved around the landing where fresh flowers in a ceramic vase sat on a small wooden table. One of the windows on the staircase was open, revealing a budding tree. Birds perched on its branches filled the stairway with melodies. I looked up the flight of stairs. He stood waiting at the top, smiling, holding an open book in one hand.

View from the Window

Some men are larger than life. Father DeLuca was one of them.

It wasn't just his height—six foot four inches—nor his dark wavy hair and startlingly blue eyes. I had already realized from working with him that he was brilliant, progressive, and creative. Equipped by advanced degrees and training not only in theology, but in physics and counseling, he was in charge of hundreds of priests. He was in a position to exert a great deal of influence at a time when change was possible. Father DeLuca had already told me how excited he was about supporting and authorizing new ventures, and described some things, like priests living among the homeless or working in factories. He impressed me as deeply spiritual and concerned about people.

And he smiled as he waited for me at the top of the stairs, stairs I mounted eagerly.

"I am so glad you could make it today, Sister. Welcome to my office," he said, motioning for me to go in before him to the large, comfortable room where he worked. A sofa, easy chairs, and a small table formed a living room effect in one end of the room, while four tall bookcases and a large mahogany desk topped with more or less neatly arranged open books, papers, typewriter, and a black phone consumed the remainder. Two straight back chairs were placed in front of the desk.

"Sit wherever you like," he offered, indicating the comfortable furniture and lowering himself into a large armchair.

"Thanks," I said, but I turned toward one of the bookcases instead. "This is a great office you have. And I love that the walls have enormous windows and built in bookcases. Can I take a look at your books?"

"Go ahead. You can borrow some if you find something interesting."

"Thank you. I don't dare distract myself; there's so much reading to be done for my Master's thesis, but I can't resist looking... Oh, I see you have all of Karl Rahner's works. I love his emphasis on mysticism and his theology of the church. I've built my thesis on the groundwork he layed. Took it a little further though. We'll see what the profs say about that."

Father DeLuca waited as I browsed for a few more minutes, picking up a book or two and looking inside, and then walked over to the sofa and sat down.

I've been just rummaging through his books and keeping him waiting.

"I'm sorry, Father. Books are like magnets for me. But I'm sure you had something else you wanted to discuss."

"Tell me about your thesis. Rahner is an adventurous theologian. I'm very interested in where you are taking his ideas."

I was amazed and thrilled; nobody had ever asked me about my thesis. "Well," I declared excitedly, my voice strong and emphatic, "Jesus surely does not welcome just a small portion of humanity fortunate enough to be born in a Christian country. Surely God has good news for everyone, not just a select few. All people of good will are connected to God, and so as Christians we must see them as connected with Jesus."

Father DeLuca nodded affirmatively, and I hurried on.

"From there I develop the idea of baptism by sincerity of heart as the doorway into community with God, which I call 'church,' the great worldwide church. It's not just about people who believe a certain list of things or go to a certain place to pray. Everybody who sincerely wants to connect with God *is connected*, to God and each other."

"It's not just knowing *about* Jesus," Father DeLuca interjected. "Maybe it's about knowing deep in one's heart, more direct knowing than doctrines can give, and maybe with different kinds of words...or no words at all. Do you know that Lakota prayer to the Great Spirit?" He spoke slowly and solemnly. "'Oh, Great Spirit, whose voice I hear in the wind, whose breath gives life to the entire world. Hear me. I need your strength and wisdom.'"

"Yes, I do. Isn't it beautiful?" I grew more and more animated as I spoke, leaning forward and gesturing. "God speaks differently to different people. So people have different ideas about God, who is so much bigger than any of our puny ideas." I threw my arms open wide, thinking about God who is always more than we can imagine.

This unusual priest watched me closely as I spoke and gestured. I could tell he understood my ideas, and not just on an intellectual level. He understood my passion for God and for people. He nodded and interjected his own thoughts. When did I ever get to have this kind of conversation? At the convent we didn't talk. And besides, not many would have been interested in such a heady conversation. Graduate students and professors, on the other hand, had plenty of intellectual discussions, but sharing from the heart was less common. This was exciting! Father DeLuca also seemed to find it so. He uncrossed his legs, leaned forward, reaching for a pack of cigarettes and a silver lighter.

"You have a creative mind, Sister," he said, handing me one of the cigarettes and stretching forward to light mine before his own. "I've noticed that in our conversations we've been having about liturgy these past months, which I've enjoyed so much. In fact, I invited you here because I would very much like your reaction to some ideas I'm working on." He leaned in toward me just slightly. "And please call me Carter."

Our eyes locked for a moment, and I hesitated. Then I relaxed into the new informality.

"Oh, and please just call me Ann," I responded smiling.

Carter then began to discuss his work as leader and his desire to use his influence to encourage innovative expressions of the Gospels through the arts. There were talented men under him, and he wanted to free them from the restraints of the usual priestly work and give them lots of room to explore new ways of reaching people.

I became totally caught up in our conversation. I could see so many opportunities for furthering the cause of social justice through music, drama, maybe street art. He responded enthusiastically, and I didn't know when I had felt so alive!

The housekeeper knocked, and Carter invited her in.

"Father Bridges called about half an hour ago, Father. I thought you would want to know. He asked that you call him back."

Carter thanked her, and she closed the door.

I looked at the clock over the desk and saw it was after 4:30. I had been here more than two hours. Vespers would be starting soon. Being late wouldn't be a good idea, especially since I hoped Carter would invite me again.

"Oh my. I hadn't realized how late it's gotten. I have to go, or I'll be late. We chant Vespers at 5:30."

"Well, I don't want you to get into trouble with Mother Walker," he said, smiling. "But before you go, let me show you something."

I followed him over to one of the large, floor to ceiling windows where we stood side by side looking down on a busy street.

"All those people rushing by in their cars? I sit and just look at them every day and wonder about their lives. I don't want us to stand inside the walls of a church hoping they may wander in. I want the church to go where they are, and I want us to have conversation, to listen, to find out what their hearts long for."

He put his hand on my shoulder as he spoke. It felt natural, reassuring and warm.

"Think about that, and let's talk more," he added, removing his hand and turning to look into my eyes. "I need to know what you think, Ann."

I thanked him but with restraint, not showing how good it felt to be seen as valuable. After more than five years of practicing humility, being valued like this was unfamiliar—wonderful and just a little scary—exciting-scary. But there wasn't time to process all those feelings, so I allowed my anxiety to sweep me rapidly toward the door.

"Wait just a second." Carter caught my hand and held me back just long enough to take time to arrange another conversation. I would come at the same time the following week.

"See you at the convent Sunday," I said, nervous and eager to leave now.

The stairs seemed much shorter going down, and I was glad the housekeeper was not there as I exited the building. Bursting through the door into the soft air and warm sun, I felt what seemed like freedom. Unfettered, I walked quickly, my cape flopping up and down, my veil blowing in the wind. Crossing the street, unable to resist looking up at Carter's window, I found him standing there watching me, and we both waved. I hurried on toward the bus stop, not wanting to be late but filled with excitement, our conversation whirling round in my mind and ideas leaping up to be expressed next time. The light changed, and the usual rush hour traffic began racing by.

Where are all those people coming from? And did they like what they were doing all day?

The traffic thinned just a bit, and then I could hear guitar playing and chanting coming from Wisconsin Avenue. Protests against senseless killing in Vietnam were loud and angry and happening all over the country. Young men were leaving the US to avoid the draft; those sent to Vietnam returned in caskets or terribly changed.

I boarded the bus, hoping I would get to the convent in time for Vespers. Replaying my conversation with Carter about taking the church out into the streets, I opened my window. Voices began to rise like steam from the Avenue blocks away.

"Hell, no! We won't go! Hell, no! We won't go! Hell, no! We won't go!"

"Hey, hey, LBJ! How many kids did you kill today?"

Something tugged at my heart. I didn't really want to go to Vespers. I wanted to get off this bus and turn down toward the Avenue where the people were gathered. I wanted to march and chant with them, join my footsteps to theirs, my voice with theirs.

But the bus moved closer to the convent, and the voices faded. I soon pulled the bus' bell cord, got off, and started up the Cenacle drive. I could feel Carter's hand on my shoulder still, and at least that seemed right.

A week is a long time to wait to go to his office...

I pulled open the heavy door, entering.

...but in between there will be Sunday.

Holding On

Flying Bird dropped Deep River's hand and began to run, racing toward the heart of the city. Toward the music, always the music. And the voices that birthed it in pain and in sweetness.

Deep River knew her zealous sister would be back, perhaps returning with a skinned knee and a sad tale of a mother's son. She would be back, a light in her eye, a tear on her cheek.

She knew Flying Bird would run to her as the light waned and darkness descended. And she, Deep River, would take her in her arms. Simply to hold her.

Be still my soul, be still. The night is long, but dawn shines bright. Hold on, my love, hold on.

Clothes Make the Woman

After Mass the next morning, I went straight to my place of freedom, running up the steps up to my third floor room. My emotions mounted as rapidly as my feet. Far from the eyes and ears of my sisters, I felt free to be myself, whatever that meant on any given day. Today my heart was light. Carter's enthusiasm about my thesis would make my mind and fingers fly as I wrote this morning.

The three-story stone house was old, stately, and connected to the main convent by a breezeway. The tall, narrow building was the container of my special space. Large roughly hewn stones magically held together what had been a private home but now housed those nuns for whom there were no available rooms in the main building. I was young and loved to climb stairs, and so I got to live there, in the only room on the third floor.

Each narrow wooden step climbed increased my distance from both nuns and retreatants, from the routine, the custody of the eyes, the triviality of conversations emptied of forbidden personal disclosures. And with each step I climbed, I changed clothes.

First I removed the wide sleeves that attached at my elbows, unsnapping the left one, and then the right, stuffing them in my pockets, and leaving only the slim, light sleeves beneath. This process took place as soon as I began my ascent because it would attract no attention at all. To anyone I might pass on the stairs, it would simply look as though I were working, which indeed I would be. Just before the second floor landing, I would risk removing the purple cape that hung from my shoulders to my waist, slowly undoing the buttons that ran all down the front, leaving only the simple, black blouse.

It wasn't until the second floor landing was safely behind me that I undertook to free my head. I climbed the first step to the magical third floor, reached up—pop—the tab holding my veil on the right side of my cap sprang up. On the second, the one on the left was freed. Reaching the glorious third step, I swirled off my long black veil, swishing it through the air before casting it carelessly over my shoulder. At four and five, I untied the tiny bow under my chin, lifting from my head and round my face the starched cap with its rigid cupcake frame. Coming close now to the final steps, I liberated my forehead from the stiff linen piece that covered and scratched at it and hid my hairline.

The landing was now mine; I could touch my door, shake out my long dark hair, turn the knob, and enter my sanctuary. Tossing garments on my narrow bed, I twirled my purple cape in the air like a matador in the ring.

My place of freedom was a large room, not at all like the small spaces I had inhabited in previous convents. The dormer windows let in the sun and put me in the treetops. But there was something more amazing waiting for me there. I had discovered that the previous owner, who donated the house to us, had left a few things in the closet. Among them was a record player and a few precious vinyl records. Beethoven was my favorite. The sweeping violins, bold brass, deep resonate cellos, and dramatic drums crescendoing higher and higher to drop into delicate, even fragile, melodies seemed to take all raging passions of my heart, hurl them wildly through the air, bounce them off the sloping roof, and return them at last to resolve into calm and peace.

And so the first movement of the symphony crashed in as I lifted the cover off my typewriter to continue the work on my Master's thesis in Theology. Armed with documents on the church from the Second

Vatican Council, I wrote with passion about my vision of a church large enough for all.

"Your thesis must be original," we had been told. And I had reason to write something original. Immersed in first Beethoven's 5th Symphony, which opens with the bold, rhythmic, four note motif—da da da dahh—and then sweeps into whirling, luscious phrases, I wanted to state my theme boldly and support it with sweeping bow strokes from violins and cellos.

Jesus gathers all people of goodwill into his new world. Salvation is for all—not just those with a certain set of beliefs or membership in some ecclesial organization. Jesus included everybody who wished to participate. Evil had not had the last word, life had won over death, and he brought with him all who sought love and justice.

The smooth, soaring legato section seemed to sing out, "Blessed are the poor in spirit, for theirs is the kingdom of heaven." Membership in the church is through the baptism of sincerity, the water poured out to all who seek the vast ground of their being. The percussion section arrived, starting softly as if from a distant place, crescendoing, joined by cellos and trumpets. "Blessed are those who hunger and thirst for righteousness, for they will be filled. Blessed are the merciful...the peacemakers... Blessed are those who are persecuted because of righteousness, for theirs is the kingdom of heaven." I typed quickly, passionately.

When the symphony ended, my mind and fingers shifted to sounds I had heard coming from the street. "We shall overcome." I could imagine the marchers—black, white, Asian, nuns, ministers, priests, rabbis—see them holding hands and going forward.

"Deep in my heart, I do believe, that we shall overcome some day."

I could hear the cry of hope from every Mass, "Christ has died. Christ is risen. Christ will come again."

I longed to free it from the murmur of pious lips and shout it on the streets. Hatred and death are not the end.

"We shall overcome."

"Christ will come again"

Love will have the final word.

My heart was open; blood flowed freely through my veins, beating to the rhythm of the music and the marchers that I knew were out there. I was sitting in one room but part of the whole world. And as I looked up at the tree waving to me from outside my window, I heard the voice of my heart more clearly than the week before, even more clearly than the day before.

High up in the room with the music and the treetops, I heard it, *I belong outside. I cannot breathe inside the convent. I need to run free down the main street of this city, my hair blowing in the breeze, my feet lightly shod, the music of lament, of hope, of love in my every breath. I must leave the convent. To stay is death. Life for me lies outside. It was pure and clear. Surely I must leave.*

That day I allowed myself to hear it louder and louder—until the bell rang.

My fingers froze in mid-flight at the first sound of the large, resonant hand bell. I rose quietly, walked away from my typewriter, paper still rolled round the platen, and resolutely turned off the record player. And then I repeated every movement I had made with my clothing when ascending the stairs, only this time it was all in reverse. First, the linen strip went back, carefully folded so it could lie smoothly on my rounded forehead. Then the cap, covering my hair and surrounding my face with its rigid cupcake-like fluted linen. Next, I began descending the stairs slowly, and with decorum now, I placed the cape back over my shoulders and buttoned it down the front. Now I was passing through the breezeway, entering the main building, and approaching the chapel. I snapped my wide sleeves over the narrow ones. I was fully covered.

These pieces of cloth were so familiar, and I moved underneath them all, hoping to be transported beyond them. I hoped the music and rhythm of the chanting would make a safe place where I might open to the Presence, where I might grow still enough to let go and allow myself to be carried where neither my legs nor my thoughts nor my emotions were able to carry me. To let go of "me" and be lifted over and beyond the edge of the world into the Unknowable.

Taking my book from the shelf by the choir door and gripping it under my arm, I put my hands in my big sleeves, lowered my eyes, went deep inside myself, and passed through the door into the silent choir.

The Presence, my Beloved, would meet me there. On some days, increasingly rare days, the Presence would embrace me, enfold me in warmth and peace. On other days, more common now, I was met only by a great, distant silence.

Bowing to the altar, I took my place in the wooden choir benches and stood, book open to Vespers.

"The Lord be with you," the leader's voice sang out.

"And with your spirit," we sang in unison.

"Let us pray."

Back and forth we chanted the psalms. Gregorian chant has its own rhythm, its own tonal shifts up and down. Peaceful. Even. Calm. It lulls the soul.

One side calling, "God is our refuge and strength, a very present help in trouble."

The other responding, "Therefore we will not fear, Though the earth should change,"

Then, "Though the mountains shake in the heart of the sea; Though its waters roar and foam,"

And then, "Though the mountains tremble with its tumult. The lord of hosts is with us. The God of Jacob is our refuge." (Psalm 46:1-3,7)

Back and forth. Back and forth the rhythm goes.

And finally from the leader, "The Lord bless you and keep you; The Lord make his face to shine upon you, and be gracious to you; The Lord lift up his countenance upon you, and give you peace." (Numbers 6:24-26)

Now the voice in my heart sent a different message.

I feel sure I must stay. I am sure I must stay...

Day after day, I had climbed up the stairs and descended down the stairs, up into freedom and passion, and then down into the womb of peace. At first, my heart and my mind had been clear and content in each place. This same Presence that met me in the psalms was the well that gave strength for my marching and my small attempts to bring the struggles of the streets inside the convent walls.

But little by little, deep down in my soul, I came to admit to myself that I could not have it all, could not have it both ways. The day was coming when I would not be able to live both on the streets and in the chapel.

Mother Walker knew how much I loved the marches, the struggle for justice. She had said, "You are in school now. Soon you will make your final vows. Protesting, struggling for justice, are very good works. But they are not our work."

Her words rang in my mind like a bell that called "Stop!" They were institutional, practical, limiting. Her words divided prayer from action, spirit from body. I couldn't not say "Amen."

The Presence does not divide. God's presence inhabits Quonset huts and streets, mansions and chapels. Institutions divide, create walls making some men and women inside and others out. The Presence always unites when we are willing.

I had become as divided as the city in which I lived. There was a North Side and a South Side in Milwaukee, and conflict between the two. There was a bridge, but people did not to cross over it, and no one lived on that bridge.

I too had two sides: the longing to be on the streets with the people and the love of the convent with its chanting. In my heart there was no conflict; the Presence bridged it all, made everything one. The two parts of myself were in conflict only because of an institution. I would not be allowed to live on the bridge that united the two.

I shall have to choose. I feel it. I know it.

Cry of the Street

"I told one of our priests this week that he could go to Hollywood and audition for a movie," Carter said, laughing as he dropped his long body into one of the easy chairs in the convent library. "It's a new Hitchcock suspense. Probably be another hit. What do you think?" He crossed his legs and waited for my response.

"I love it." I was smiling broadly and leaning forward in my chair, lifting my hands as I spoke. "Experimenting. It's great."

"Yes, why not after all?" Carter mused, stroking his chin. "I want to see what he does with this. He is very talented. Could be a whole new way to reach people."

"I don't know why some people are so afraid of new things," I puzzled. "It's the only way to really find out what touches people."

"Ah, but Ann, you are assuming the church *wants* to touch people," Carter sighed. "I wish that were more often the case." He shifted in his chair, uncrossing and re-crossing his legs. "But let's not start down that depressing route. I thank God for your spirit of adventure, Ann."

I glanced at the library clock, making sure I wouldn't be late preparing things for the next Mass. It was nearing 10:30, so I pulled my big sleeves out of my pocket and began fastening the snaps.

"I would like to tell you about something else too, Ann, before your leave. Do you think we have time before the retreatants' Mass?"

He looked at me inquiringly, and I leaned back nodding, one of my sleeves still in my hand.

"It's something my fellow priests talked about at our convention last year. It's called the 'Third Way.'"

I began fastening my sleeve. Convention business was not of much interest to me.

Carter pressed on. "It's a way for priests to be much more human and effective." Carter paused and looked down for a moment, and then raised his eyes to meet mine. "It's about being neither married nor celibate." He looked at his watch now. His voice grew tense, and his words were hurried. "But maybe we should leave that for next time. Thursday, when you would come to my office again. Otherwise, we will be late, and Mother Walker will be upset."

I suddenly felt nervous and jumped up. "Yes, let's go. We can talk about this another time."

I didn't want to risk being late and didn't know what to make of what I had just heard. Carter rose as well. Then Father DeLuca and I walked in tandem from the library into the chapel and the sacristy, where I began carrying things onto the altar and he donned the vestments for the next Mass. We were like any couple preparing for a dinner party.

It would be evening and it would be morning four more times before we met again. Carter's strange words about the Third Way went round my brain in circles, and I tried to push them away, feeling buffeted by too many thoughts, too many questions, too many feelings. I couldn't tell whether I was excited or afraid, and I didn't have time or space to figure it out. I was busy preparing for final exams, climbing up the stairs to my third floor room, listening to Beethoven, finishing my thesis, hurrying back down to the Choir. All the while *I must leave...I must stay...leave... stay...leave...stay...*, played on, colliding and separating, coming together and wrestling again like symphonic leitmotifs.

My feet were not only climbing up and down stairs at the convent, I was also marching on the streets. The basketball team at Marquette had a triumphant season under the famous coach Al McGuire and planned a big party to celebrate. The celebration became a scandal, however, because it was scheduled at a club that did not allow African Americans to become members. This in itself merited a boycott of the club. Shameful irony added to this fundamental injustice: there were African American players on the championship team. Students were incensed, especially my fellow graduate students in theology. What was the Gospel all about anyway? Students and some professors would take to the streets. I would stay late at school that day, and I would be there along with all the others.

We lined up outside the Theology Department. Instructions were very clear: absolutely no talking, and no blocking of intersections or driveways. We would march to the location of the party, about half a mile, and then stand vigil outside the doors. We were not to prevent anyone from entering the hall under any circumstances. We were the perfectly disciplined nonviolent protest marchers, trained and monitored by the young men of Groppi's Commando Project 1.

We all understood. The occasion was a solemn one.

And so we began our silent march down Wisconsin Avenue, the main drag of Milwaukee. We were a very long line of men and women, black and white, nuns and priests, stretching several blocks, walking in pairs carrying signs saying, "We are all God's children" and "Marquette: Boycott segregated club."

Cars slowed to a crawl to stare. Most of those driving past were white because Milwaukee was largely white.

"Thugs!"

"Go home, N..... lovers!"

"Get out of our town!"

"If you come over the Viaduct again, we'll beat your ass!"

We stopped at every traffic light. So did they, giving them more time to read our signs and react. Some just kept driving. Others, many others, were all too clear about their feelings. We stood at the red light unable to move forward while they threw things at us and shouted obscenities. My fluted cap prevented an apple core from hitting my face.

"Commies." A rock flew quickly toward us, dropping to the ground just before hitting my classmate Josh.

"Criminals!"

"Dirty liberals!"

Bottles and trash came hurling at us from several cars. My habit protected me from getting bruised, but my cape and skirt were full of stains, and I wondered if they smelled of the beer which sloshed out of some of the cans.

We could try to shield ourselves from the debris flying through the air. There was no way to shield ourselves from the words.

Soon police appeared with night sticks, helmets, and guns on their hips. Since Chief Harold Breier was famous for rejecting reforms that would improve police relationships with minority communities, police presence did not make me feel protected. In fact, I felt more at risk. For whom were the billy clubs meant?

I was afraid. How would this end? Would we get hurt? Arrested? But my fear lessened as I felt more and more emboldened, connected with the other students, with the Commandoes, with my God.

Jesus is here.

Soon I was no longer afraid at all, only determined and somehow real.

I know God is everywhere. But here I can touch God's presence.

Finally we arrived at the hall where basketball players were entering for their celebration. African American players were allowed to enter; apparently their celebrity status trumped their color...for tonight. But some chose not to, either staying away or joining us. Making a semi-circle in front of the door, but leaving a space for players to get through, we sang "We Shall Overcome" and "If I Had a Hammer" and prayed for civil rights for all citizens, for justice and racial harmony. And then after about an hour, we dispersed, feeling we had changed nothing but had at least stood up for what's right. Someday things would change. "We *shall* overcome." We believed that.

All this—the marching, the preparation for tests, the exciting conversation about my thesis—whirled around in my head and my heart as I made my way again to Carter's office that following Thursday. Again I mounted the long staircase, and again he stood at the top smiling.

This time I didn't stop to look at books but went right to the chair I always used. He took his. Carter just looked at me for a few minutes. I resisted the impulse to fill the silence with casual words of greeting because I could tell he was about to say something of importance.

But he got up, brought two cups of coffee over, and sank again into his ample chair, his long legs crossed tight and flat one over the other. Only then did he begin to speak.

"I am so glad you have come again, Ann," he began, a bit of hesitation in his voice. "I said last Sunday that I wanted to share something about the Third Way. One of our priests read a paper about it at our meeting. It generated a lot of discussion." His voice trailed off.

"Yes, I remember," I hastened to interject. "I had been wondering since Sunday what this is about."

"The paper was written as a contribution to our ongoing discussion of the role of priests in the world. We've been talking about this for several years. Most of us are very conscious of being too isolated, living too much in an ivory tower, too far from the lives and challenges of our people. Those people come to us with their problems. Real problems." He paused for a moment before continuing. "We know almost nothing about one of the most important things in the lives of the laity, those things that bring the most challenges as well as the greatest joys. They come for advice, comfort, perhaps to be challenged or encouraged. Truth is, we often don't know what to say."

I was listening attentively, nodding seriously but not understanding any more about this Third Way. Carter seemed to be circling around it.

What was he talking about? And why this tone of hesitation in his voice, this somewhat halting speech so unlike his usual ways? I waited.

Carter took some time to drink more than a sip of coffee, keeping his eyes lowered and focused on the dark, steaming brew. He uncrossed and re-crossed his legs, put his coffee down, and finally continued.

"I am talking about relationships between men and women."

His words rushed out now while he searched my face, encased in its fluted cap, for reactions.

"Relationships between men and women are the greatest sign of the love of God for his people. Also they are the occasion both of much joy and of many of the greatest difficulties and heartbreak. In the confessional, we hear more about these things than anything else. We are expected to dispense some kind of advice..." He looked down. "...and we have little to offer because we know little of these things." He reached for his coffee and then thought better of it.

"The paper read at the convention proposed that priests cannot fully respond to their call to serve without experiencing such relationships." He stopped, looked at me as though trying to judge my reaction, rising nervously, walking again toward the coffee pot. "This must sound very strange to you," he added, and cast a quick look in my direction.

I still didn't know what he was really saying. He was nervous and beating around the bush. I wondered whether he expected to see me fleeing the room.

"No," I answered with deliberation. "It doesn't sound strange. Actually I think the priest who gave the paper was right. I just don't know what that means since Rome doesn't seem to see things this way."

"No, Rome certainly doesn't." Carter sat down again, wearily this time. He rubbed his chin and then cupped it in the palm of his hand. "I think we cannot wait for Rome. My call to be a priest is from God, not Rome, and I want to live it to the fullest. I cannot do so sitting alone in this office."

He stood. "Come." He reached out and pulled me up and led me over to the window behind his desk, the window overlooking the busy street. "Look there. So many needs. So much pain. And celebrations too. I want to be part of them. I want to serve from among the people, not from a distant castle."

Our clothes were touching, although our bodies were separate. Then he placed his arm around my shoulder. Standing very close to one another, I could feel the warmth of his body and his breath on my skin. And I could feel his eyes upon me.

Then Carter sat down in his large desk chair, pulling me with him until I was sitting on his lap. Slowly he turned my face toward his and kissed me, first on the forehead, then both cheeks, and then finally on the lips.

We looked at one another for a long moment. Then I reached up, untied my cap and veil, allowing them to slip to the floor.

I shook out my long, dark hair.

Beloved

"God is a lover," Deep River told Flying Bird.

They were sitting side by side, warm sun streaming in through the kitchen window, and her arm circled the younger child's shoulders.

"A lover shows us the face of God, a lover is 'God with flesh on.' You must not be afraid to love, to be loved." She opened the Bible, which lay before them on the blue table. "Listen, Flying Bird...

> As an apple tree among the trees of the wood,
> so is my beloved among young men.
>
> With great delight I sat in his shadow,
> and his fruit was sweet to my taste.
>
> He brought me to the banqueting house,
> and his intention toward me was love.
>
> Sustain me with raisins,
> refresh me with apples;
> for I am faint with love.
> (Song of Songs 2:3-5)

The Storm

I threw all my books down the library's book drop. There were a lot of them, and they beat a triumphant percussive roll as they tumbled down. The first ones created a resounding whack against the metal shoot; gradually books began to land on top of other books and the sound softened.

Done! All the courses with their papers and exams: passed. The feared comprehensive exams that reviewed my entire graduate school program: survived! And most of all, my thesis—"Membership in the Church by Baptism of Sincerity"—was written and only needed to be reviewed by my thesis committee, which was, of course, made up of three white men with collars. That wouldn't happen in time for graduation this spring, but by December I expected to be wearing my cap and gown and walking across the stage to receive my Master of Arts.

I guess the gown will fit over my habit, but the cap? On top of my fluted one? Oh well, I'll worry about that later, and maybe by that time we will be wearing the new modified habits the superiors were talking about. Or maybe I won't be wearing a habit at all...

Climbing on the bus, I saw two middle-aged women, heads together, looking my way, lips moving, obviously about me.

"Well, I don't mean to make judgments, but I don't know what she's doing down here. But at least, thank God, she's not one of those mini nuns," she pontificated in a hoarse voice that suggested too many years of too much beer. She was referring to one of the other orders whose nuns had adapted contemporary short '60s skirt lengths. Evidently she believed nuns belonged not only in long skirts but behind convent walls, not out in buses, whatever their attire.

"Yes, the ones parading around in miniskirts are just disgusting. It's a scandal, and the bishops should set them straight. They look as though they're just advertising themselves to every man around," her neighbor sniffed and both women nodded sagely.

I'm so tired of being an advertisement for nuns today. People stare at me everywhere. Everything I say or do is taken as what nuns are doing or not doing, wearing or not wearing, saying or not these days. I hate it! All I want is to walk down Wisconsin Avenue anonymous, one of the nameless crowd, unnoticed by everyone.

But of course, it wasn't all I wanted. Maybe my mind, which for over a month had been going up and down, back and forth like arpeggios chasing one another up and down the keyboard, would settle in one or another direction. Maybe my heart would find a resting place as well. I supposed it would have to, because by the end of the summer I was supposed to go to Rome, make a 30-day retreat, and then make vows for life!

And now it was all so complicated because of Carter. So much had happened since that day when our lips first touched. Last week Carter was sitting at his desk, the big window overlooking the street behind him, when I came in and jumped into his lap. He laughed and seemed totally relaxed as he slowly kissed me. When he lifted off my cap and cape and tossed them on the floor, and he passionately kissed me again.

I was nervous though, and looked over his shoulder at the door. It wasn't locked; locked doors made people suspicious.

Anyone looking for Carter will surely knock. Besides, his office isn't in a church where people can just wander in, and no one can see us from the street. Unscheduled visitors are rare, and they would have to be announced by his housekeeper. And she always knocks.

Still, unlike Carter, I kept one eye on the door and both ears cocked, which distracted me a little from what we were doing and made it more exciting at the same time. We were touching a lot more than lips now. Arms and legs wrapped round each other, and hands roamed freely under his shirt and my blouse.

For a moment I forgot where I was. Then I remembered and pulled back just enough to look toward the door and listen.

Had I heard footsteps? If someone knocked and opened the door...

But I decided I was mistaken and turned my attention back to Carter's muscular back, meeting his lips with mine.

Carter seemed so relaxed, but he was not really free. Our bodies were constrained by the awareness that a knock on his office door could send us scrambling at any moment. And it would be quite a trick to get my cape and cap in place before someone saw us. And we certainly could not risk removing any more clothing. Carter's shirt and pants were all in place. I still had on my long skirts and blouse and all the layers underneath.

When a light shone under the door, we both jumped apart, turning still as stones. It was nothing. But the spell was broken.

He cannot be caught doing this. It would ruin his future. He has too many important things to do.

And, concerned only about him, I reached for my scattered clothing.

Our hearts and minds knew no such hindrances, however, and we spent hours sharing hopes and ideas. We would work together and do great things to restore the marginalized, heal broken hearts, and "set prisoners free." Yards of cloth confined us, yet we spoke of freeing the spiritual prisoners of the American church.

"Catholics here are afraid to think for themselves. They have been told it is a sin to even question what they've been taught." I was angry. "And they think they have to ask priests about everything."

"Yes," Carter responded, "we priests have used our authority to make the people weak. We insist on practices that keep people shackled, like our prohibitions against divorce, against birth control."

"It isn't like that in France, where I first experienced Catholicism. For Americans, church laws are like red lights and green lights. When the Pope condemned birth control, there was a huge crisis here. In France, the bishops just read the Pope's letter and added, 'Non-contraceptive intercourse is the ideal, but of course, in reality it is often not the best.' End of story. Birth control peacefully carried on in France."

I continued heatedly. "Vatican II has led to a lot of changes, it's true. But how many of those have to do with superficial things like the altar being turned around the face the people? Women on retreat tell me they are in horribly abusive marriages, or have remarried but are forbidden from receiving communion. Or they come sobbing because they are pregnant again by a man they do not love."

"I know," Carter said. "And I doubt if it gives them much consolation to hear the Mass in English instead of Latin."

"Together, though, we can teach people more about what Jesus did, the way he treated people, the lepers and the women and the Samaritans."

"We can encourage them to think and make decisions for themselves."

"We'll bring a Gospel of peace, not fear."

We began finishing one another's sentences, and our faces were flushed. It was so exciting to imagine the work Carter and I could do together. We waved our arms in excitement as we spoke, occasionally colliding with one another.

Sitting on the bus carrying me back to the convent, the world looked different. Everything that was so real when I was with Carter now seemed like an empty dream.

How could we do all these wonderful things together if I remain in the order? I don't feel guilty about loving him. But I can't go on vowing celibacy and living like this. Why doesn't Carter see his priesthood as a problem?

It was so complicated and confusing. We had choices to make. And my time for choosing was running out. Our relationship was moving forward quickly.

In less than three months, I have to decide whether to make final vows, vows for life. No one else will question this final step. I am the only one who can stop the inevitable, and there is only one way out. I will have to leave the order, leave the people I knew, the chanting I loved, the daily communion, the retreatants, the community...and if I leave all that...will I be alone?

At the convent, I climbed the stairs to my room again. I took my veil and cap off and paced up and down. There was no longer a thesis to work on, to struggle with, to consume my energy. It wasn't really as though I had nothing to do. But my home was lonely. Carter could not come with me. I missed him terribly and hoped he missed me, although he hadn't said so

I should prepare the sacristy for the next event, and I could definitely make sure the library is in order and ready for the new retreatants arriving tomorrow. And I haven't written that condolence note...

I did none of these things. Such tasks couldn't quiet my heart or my mind or even my restless feet. They could not tell me what path I was on, which turn to take, where it would lead. And so I simply paced.

Where am I headed? Where will I be a month from now?

I found it impossible to settle down, took my long sleeves off only to put them on again. A pen lay on my desk, and I picked it up, took off the cap, reached for a pad of paper as though to write something. But I had no words, or rather I had too many words and they would not fall into any order. I tossed the pen and paper onto my bed, walked across the room and back, picked them up again, returned them to the desk. I braided my long hair and twisted it with my restless hands.

Silence was all around me. I didn't even have my Beethoven record playing. But that day silence could not soothe my soul or apply healing balm to my heart. The silence only left more space for the clamor in my soul. And the clamor grew louder and louder.

How can I stay and be with Carter? I'm living a secret, a lie in fact. I can't make a permanent vow of chastity and press my body against the body of a priest!

What will happen if I leave? Were my parents right all along that entering the convent was a betrayal of all the family stood for?

I squeezed my eyes shut, as though that would make me blind to images of the pain I had caused them, perhaps pointless pain.

I need to be on the street, with the people, but I love the liturgy, the recitation of the psalms, and I love the silence that pulls me deep down inside to the God alive within me.

I picked up my long sleeves again, staring at them as though they might speak to me, provide some answer, some resolution to my discord.

Carter and I need to work together, but we are not just a team, we love each other. If I leave my order and he leaves the priesthood, what happens to our work? If we don't, what happens to us? Is there an 'us?'

I looked over at my cap and veil thrown aside. But this time it was I, not Carter, who had removed them. And they lay not on the floor of his office, but flung on my bed. They gave me no answers.

I jumped when the bell rang for Vespers.

Put them back on.

Folding the stiff strip of linen over my forehead, winding the string round my head that would hold my cap in place, I snapped on the long veil.

Put them back on, and go downstairs. Be part of the group. You'll feel better.

Descending two flights of stairs, crossing over to the main building, entering the choir with my sisters, I did feel part of it all. Here was a community. Together we would create the slow, gentle, familiar rhythm of the chant, a verse from the row where I sat, then a verse from the nuns facing us across the choir. Back and forth. Call and response. There was peace there.

But the other part of me hovered nearby. I knew I might still be part of the group but was very close to the edge. I just didn't know where I was or, in truth, who I was. And there was no library book drop to throw everything down and declare triumphant closure. I just chanted on, not sure why.

The following morning brought new information. After lunch the news broadcast showed a protest march downtown, led by Father Groppi. He and three young African American men were carrying a coffin down busy Wisconsin Avenue. Some passersby stopped to gape or curse or even throw something. But behind the little priest came a throng of people. Black and white, young and old, rich and poor. They followed the coffin, and I so wanted to follow with them. So many deaths. So many deaths of young African Americans. So many senseless deaths in our own country. So many in Vietnam.

Mother Walker's words rang unceasingly in my mind like a melody gone flat: "It is important work, but not our work." I so desperately wanted it to be my work. I knew she didn't intend to be cold or unkind. Mother Walker was simply a woman who kept her feelings very tightly regulated. She was simply stating a fact.

I couldn't be where the music was. I couldn't be on the street marching. I could only watch the protestors on television. I could not be with them, could not be part of them.

Ten minutes later, our new Provincial, Mother Robertson, head of the Midwest region, asked to speak with me. She had a warm smile, and her hazel eyes sparkled as she spoke.

"Sister Temkin. You will be making your 30-day retreat in Rome and your final vows in just a couple of months. When you return, I want you to be an Assistant Superior."

I knew she couldn't hear it, but I did, and I knew it was real: the lid of a coffin slammed down on my soul, burying me alive. A scream rose up from my heart. But all that came out through my lips was a quick, muted response, the rules of silence giving me protection from any real conversation, any expression of emotion.

Then, racing on the inside but maintaining decorum on the outside, my feet moved as fast as they were allowed, straight toward my room. Reaching the stairway, I flew up the two flights, threw open my door, and turned on Beethoven as high as I dared.

I know what this is about. 'Take the ones who rock the boat and put them in charge.'

That's the maxim. Leadership responsibilities weigh heavily, paralyzing the adventurous, silencing the prophets, killing the dreamers. Yes, rocking the boat while steering it through rough waters and narrow passages is too much for one human being. I would die.

No. This will not work for me. I won't do it.

I was pacing up and down and had circled round my room four times already.

Some people are born to follow the wind. There are other people who make sure the ship doesn't get dashed against the rocks. I am born to join the marchers, to work for a new world, a new church, following the wind of the Spirit of God. I am a prophet, a small one, but a prophet. And I won't be made into an administrator. I can't be.

And Carter? I certainly couldn't continue the journey with Carter if I were Assistant Superior. I don't see how I can keep living like this now....

I pulled off my purple cape and flung it across the room onto the bed without breaking my stride. I pivoted and began pacing in the other direction, then down one flight of stairs, the music rushing into the staircase.

I can't do it now.

And neither can he.

I stopped, turned, and ran up the stairs again and closed the door.

We both need to get out. Surely he must see that too?

I have to talk to Carter.

I started down the stairs again, turning the music off definitively this time. Down one flight, halfway down the next, the thought of simply running, running with no cape, no veil, running out the door and all the way to Carter's office, running to him.

Stop! What am I doing? I can't go down the street like this. I can't just disappear from the convent. And what would Carter say anyway?

Slowly I dragged myself up to my room, opening and closing the door which, at that moment, weighed a thousand pounds.

I don't know what Carter would say. I don't know what life would be like if I leave. I don't even know how I would survive.

I threw myself on my bed face down on top of the crucifix, pulling the pillow toward me, burying my face in it, twisting and turning, throwing the pillow on the floor, and held my head in my hands, tears running down on the bedspread. And then I sat up and picked up the crucifix, gripping it tightly with both hands.

But there is one thing I'm certain of: if I stay here, I shall die.

This time it was my whole self, very life itself, not just my cape or my veil, that I had flung onto the bed. I lay there, exhausted, tangled up in a heap of clothes, shaking as my tears flowed.

I felt so very alone.

In my mind I returned to my last visit to Carter's office. "I've been thinking of leaving the order," I had said, sitting on his lap with my hand against his chest. "I can't just live a lie, pretending to be celibate, chaste, and all that *and* being with you. And I can't think of it as anything but a lie."

"I understand," he murmured, lifting my chin and stroking my face. "And I wouldn't want you to do anything that doesn't seem right to you. But I can't imagine leaving the priesthood."

He looked away.

"There wouldn't be much left of me for you to want."

It was not the first time we had spoken of this. I had moved further and further in the direction of leaving, and he remained stationary.

"I need you precisely because I'm a priest, not just because I'm a man," he always said. "A priest is what I am, but I cannot be whole alone. I need you to help me be fully human, fully priest. That's what the Third Way is all about for us. Together we will make a whole priest that God wants!"

So this is how it will be. At least for now. I will leave. He will stay. I will not be a hypocrite in a habit. I will be a woman committed to a man who is a priest. We will be priests together. Maybe one day that may change. But he must be who he is. For now, I can be true to myself and still be with him. It will be hard, but it will be worth it. Can I do it? Yes, I can. I can love that much. I want to!

And I clung to the desire for a large love the following day. All the women heroes I had read about and loved somehow rose up in my heart. The little girl in *The Secret Garden* who rescued the lame little boy; Gladys May Aylward, the missionary who led over a hundred Chinese children escaping from the Japanese over the mountains; Madame Curie in her laboratory bringing healing; Susan B. Anthony, Eleanor Roosevelt, and on and on, forming a long line, a lineage in my heart and in my very bones. I, too, would be a strong woman. A pioneer. I would put myself in harm's way, like my mother who married a German Jew in 1932.

It wasn't just that Carter was terribly smart and mightily credentialed. It wasn't only that he invoked God to support his position. It wasn't just about being the good, loyal woman I was trained to be. These things were part of my determination to remain with Carter, regardless of his choice. But they were not the biggest motivating factor.

This would be about a big love. It would be about an adventure, a big and important and tremendously meaningful adventure. An adventure that would pave the way for others. It was a "We Shall Overcome" kind of adventure with God, with many people, and with a man.

I wanted that. I was not afraid. Perhaps because I was strong. Perhaps I wanted to be a hero. Perhaps because hope still stirred in my heart that Carter's love for me would lead him to a bold, creative new path too. Maybe he would come to see that he could be fully priest with me, free, no longer chained by clerical collar or defined by title. Perhaps he might realize that his ability to influence the future was not limited to one position. The hope still stirred that he would choose a priesthood embodied simply by love.

And until that time comes, if it does, I will love him as he is. And if he never leaves…I will still find a way to love him. Maybe that Third Way he talks about…maybe it's possible for us…

On that path, God's love would fill us and spill over to heal many we would touch.

All this filled my heart and soul as I lay in bed that night. I was exhausted, and sleep was forcing its way into body and mind. Even as my thoughts became less distinct, more distant, they kept flashing back to Carter.

Leaving the kind of priesthood he knows would mean stepping into harm's way. He would have to face his fellow priests and his superiors. They have such hopes for him.

The darkness of sleep consumed me for a moment, just a moment. Then I returned to this world and saw a terrible truth: he would have to break his mother's heart.

Be Still

The wind came at Flying Bird so hard that night she struggled to remain on her feet. Surely any moment she would be lifted into the air and carried off, only to be dashed against a rocky cliff. The sand beat at her face, her hands, her legs like needles and seemed to enter every orifice, every pore. Roaring sounds howled about her like a pack of wolves, and she was rendered nearly blind.

She had to find Deep River. Her life depended on it.

Frantic, she ran to the left and then to the right. Up dunes, down to the water, and then up to the tree line where the houses began. Her cries were swallowed by the wind, and she could barely breathe.

Until, in one holy moment, she felt the arms of Deep River envelop her, shelter her, pull her to safety.

And a voice was heard and the storm subsided.

"Be still and know that I am God." (Psalm 46)

The Blessing

Two days later, I had to speak. We were in the sacristy after Mass.

"Carter, I have to leave."

"You know *I can't*," he whispered, unconsciously touching his collar.

I was washing the chalice and other dishes from the Mass, and he was putting away the vestments he had worn a moment before. His hand grazed my back as he passed behind me.

"Well, we have to talk about this," I insisted, reaching to touch his hand for just a moment before setting the gold chalice firmly back in its place in the cupboard. "And not here."

"I have an important meeting Thursday. How about Wednesday at my office?" He was putting on his jacket, checking his pockets for all his stuff, seeming distracted.

"Two o'clock?" I asked, and he nodded.

Footsteps padded softly in the corridor. I turned abruptly and busied myself putting away freshly laundered altar linens as the door opened.

"Hello, Father DeLuca. I just wanted to say how much the community has enjoyed having you with us."

It was Mother Walker. She stood smiling graciously, her eyes fixed solely and respectfully on Father DeLuca. I stepped behind her and left the two of them to exchange empty pleasantries. Again I was grateful for our customs; custody of the eyes allowed me to look down at the floor and glide out as though invisible, as she preferred to view me and as I hoped I was.

Time dragged from that Sunday until the following Wednesday. Fortunately a woman I knew arrived to make a private retreat with me as her spiritual director. She was going through a divorce and seemed quite lost. I listened and mapped out some meditations that I prayed would give her hope and perhaps return her to some sense of belonging. Time passed as I busied myself with these responsibilities, our usual prayer times, and the other more mundane duties.

Wednesday morning my thoughts were very scattered during meditation. I was growing more and more anxious. Because I was the one appointed as reader for the community noon meal, I ate early and was left to my own thoughts.

This is so final. Should I really do this? There won't be any going back...

Although I was generally an expressive reader, I performed refectory duty mechanically and left for the community room with the other nuns at the meal's end. Excusing myself from recreation a bit early, I climbed the stairs to the retreatants' area and out the front door.

The bus was noisy that day, and I needed quiet. A group of German-speaking women were talking about their boyfriends and their sex lives in loud voices, probably convinced no one could understand them. I could, and I really didn't want to, so I got off the bus early and walked the last couple of miles. I was early anyway. The exercise was good; it got out some of the adrenaline racing through my system since Sunday.

"Hello, Mrs. Washington. How are you today?" I had reached my destination and greeted the smiling housekeeper who had opened the door.

She told me her arthritis was better, and I tried to look calm and relaxed as I acknowledged this good news. She was quite used to seeing me by now, and I wanted today to look like any other day. Only I knew that this was the day I would announce my decision, making it real. And so Mrs. Washington and I smiled and nodded in our usual, quiet way, and then she stepped aside and I mounted the staircase.

That day Carter was not standing at the top of the stairs, but his office door stood wide open until I crossed the threshold and closed it firmly behind me.

Carter got up and quickly moved toward me. He pulled me to him and held me for a long time. Then he kissed me, moving me back so he could look into my eyes and said, "You know this is who I am. And I cannot change who I am. And if I tried...I am afraid there would be nothing left."

"And to you it wouldn't be living a lie? Not just being a hypocrite? Hiding?"

"No, for me it wouldn't," he replied, and we stood still for a long while, close but not touching, each of us looking deep into the soul of the other. "I believe in the Third Way, believe it is what God wants for some priests. I can make a difference. My position, the time in history, the authority I carry...I can't walk away from the church. I have to be part of moving it forward. And I also can't walk away from being fully human, and that includes loving you. "

"You can't walk away from the church. You were born to move things forward," I broke in, laying my hand on his arm. "I understand that. But is there only one way you can do that? Only one role, one place that makes that possible? Aren't men who leave the official priesthood and serve in other ways moving the church forward too?" I took my hand away. "I want to support you. I just don't know about this Third Way."

"I've been talking about it for a while with some other priests. For you, it's new and must sound strange. For us, it's simple. Basically, God is love. Jesus came to free captives. How can I follow him if I'm enslaved? If I'm afraid of love and freedom?"

"Love and freedom can mean a lot of things." I pulled away just a little. I still wasn't sure what this Third Way kind of love was all about.

Carter walked across the room with his back to me. He was waving his arms around as he spoke, his voice rising too. "We say God became flesh and then we hate our own flesh? That's exactly what the church has done for centuries."

Coming back toward me and placing his hands on my shoulders, he lowered his voice. "No, I really believe I must be a priest who makes a difference, and that to be that kind of priest I need to live as other men do, with the love of another. And for that, I need you."

Carter bent and kissed me deeply, and then we stepped a few inches apart and again stood looking into one another's eyes. Neither of us reached out to touch the other.

I broke the silence. "Do you understand that *I have* to leave the order? And it's not just because I would feel like a hypocrite hiding our relationship. I've been thinking about it for a long time. I belong outside, with the people, on the streets. That's where I can breathe. And if I stay inside, I shall die."

I took a deep breath and moved back a step, trying to read his face, discover his reaction. I thought he might say we could not go on. I couldn't uncover his response, took one more very deep breath and continued.

"I have made my decision."

I had done it. There was no going back now, no matter what he said.

"I know," Carter responded finally, pulling me toward him again. "And I believe you are right. That is where God is calling you. And after you leave, we will work together. We will be partners. For life." He was pulling me closer now. "You will be so much freer to do things with me. In fact, some people talked to me today about having Mass in their home once a month with a small group of people they know. They want something more intimate, more meaningful than what they have in church. We could do that! And it would be just the beginning."

I let him remove my cap and veil and run his hands through my hair.

"So," he asked, grinning a bit like a kid heading out on an adventure, "what comes next? When will you start your new journey?"

"I have to have a lot of conversations." My brow wrinkled at the prospect. I stepped away from Carter and walked over to the window. "I have to talk with Mother Walker, and we don't have such a great relationship. I need to speak with the new Provincial, Mother Robertson. She's wonderful. But she told me the other day about her plans to make me an Assistant Superior after my final vows. Now I have to tell her I'm leaving and right after getting my Master's, which they paid for. I dread all of this."

I paused, and although it was hot in Carter's office, I wrapped my arms around myself as though to keep warm, staring out at the street below.

"And I guess I have to talk with Mother Shelley. She used to be the Provincial but now she is old and ill. That's going to be really hard. We have a special bond. Her parents opposed her entering the convent just as much as mine did. She is a great woman. I hate to disappoint her. She is the one who made the decision to integrate the retreat house in New Orleans even though some people tried to bribe us not to and others threatened. She's brave and has a huge heart."

Carter listened patiently as my words came more and more rapidly.

"The changes that came after Vatican II have been hard for her — giving up the beautiful Latin, hearing the Mass and the psalms recited in English, knowing that some nuns were moving into apartments, giving up their traditional habits. We haven't done that yet, but she surely knows it will be coming. And with riots in the cities, anti-war demonstrations, the ecumenical movement, she must wonder where her world has gone..."

I stood there silent for a long time, watching the people below, the cars passing, the traffic light changing colors while Carter quietly waited.

"I know she loves me and sees me as a daughter in a special way, although, of course, she never said that. It will hurt her when I say I'm leaving."

I stopped, biting my lip. Finally I turned back to look at him.

"But I have to face her."

"Yes, you do."

"I want to start right away. It's been a long time of going back and forth, up and down. Time to move forward."

I was ready to act. Carter and I kissed briefly. I turned to leave. He didn't try to stop me. I took the steps one at a time, slowly but steadily as though in a trance, and left without thinking to say goodbye to Mrs. Washington.

That evening I approached my Superior after supper. "May I speak with you for a moment, Mother?"

We moved into the library and stood, since she made no move to sit down. I felt awkward and tongue tied while she looked at me as though to say, "Well, what do you need?"

After what seemed like a very long time, but was probably only a few seconds, I blurted it out. "I have to leave, Mother. I have been praying about this for a long time. I think my vocation is to be out among the people."

Her response came quickly. It cut me like a sudden gust of frozen air.

"Well, Sister, I am not surprised. I suppose it would take a lot of grace for someone from your background to remain faithful."

I winced but said nothing. I was hurt, but the truth was I had never felt close to her and was only telling her my decision because I had to. Her reaction was more or less what I would have expected. At last, it was over.

"We will discuss details later, Sister," she continued, her tone softening. "Now it is late." And then she was gone.

The next morning, right after Mass and breakfast, I knocked on the door of Mother Robertson, our Provincial.

"Come in, my child," she invited warmly. "Sister Temkin. How are you dear? Come, sit down."

I swallowed, then looked at her and just began opening my heart, revealing what had been going on with me. Of course I omitted any mention of Carter. I certainly didn't want to get him in any trouble.

"And so I must leave the order and go out into the world. There are so many people in so much pain who won't come here to us."

Mother Robertson smiled a warm smile and took both my hands. "You have a great deal to give to people, Sister. Go. Fly with the wind. We will miss you, but you must follow God's call for you. And I believe you are."

"I feel guilty about the order paying for me to get a Master's degree and then leaving. I didn't know a year ago that this would happen..."

"I know you didn't, my dear, and I don't want you to worry about it. God knew, and you followed God then and are following God now."

I took a deep breath and relaxed a little.

"We will talk later about more practical things," she continued, "but now you must speak with Mother Shelley. I am happy for you both that she is here these days, so the two of you can speak."

"I know I must, but I think she will be disappointed, and I hate to do that to her. She told me about how upset her family was when she entered the convent. She understood what I was going through. We have had a special bond because of that. And now I'm leaving..."

"I know she has always been very fond of you, Sister. You have been kindred souls in many ways. Yes, this will be hard for her, but she is a holy woman of courage and wisdom. Put your trust in God."

We both rose, and she took me in her arms and hugged me, our caps almost colliding, and made a little sign of the cross on my forehead. A blessing.

"Go. Go and speak with Mother Shelley. She hears the voice of God. She will accept your decision."

I found the bedridden Mother Shelley propped up on pillows, looking very tired when I entered her room, but she smiled seeing it was me and reached out her hand to take mine.

"Pull that chair over and sit close to me, my dear. It is not often I get to see you. Tell me what is on your heart."

I had rehearsed what I would say about God's call and my need to answer it and do the work God had for me to do. I was very anxious despite all my rehearsing and almost tripped over my skirt pulling the chair over. I didn't want to hurt her, and I didn't want to lose her affection.

When I finished, her face was full of light.

"God bless you, Sister," she said. "There are many changes in the church and in religious life today. I can see that it would seem there are more opportunities to serve God outside the order than within. It is different now than in my time. You must live your call for today."

I was so grateful, and thanked her for understanding, clasping her hand.

"Come, let me bless you and your new journey."

So I knelt by the side of her bed. She laid her hands on my head and prayed for me.

"Turn your face toward your daughter, Father. She has suffered and desires only to do your will. Bring an end to her turmoil; give her the Peace only you can bestow. Take away any doubts. And above all, may she feel your presence and your arms around her each day as she walks out to bring your love to those in need."

She pressed the sign of the cross onto my forehead with her thumb and finally took my face in her hands and kissed me on the forehead.

I held back my tears as I left this beautiful woman. Just before I closed her door, I looked back; she was smiling at me. I would never forget her.

Mother Robertson told me I could stay as long as I needed, buy clothes, make various arrangements. But despite what she had said, I felt guilty about the money the order had spent for my Master's degree, and I didn't want to cause them unnecessary expense. Besides I was impatient to begin my new life. And I alone knew that Carter would be there for me, so I wouldn't be out in the world by myself. In the end, I did accept the $500 the Provincial urged me to take to get started. I would need it.

The next night I approached one of the Filipino nuns. I had helped her a little when she was assigned to the depense. She had never baked anything in her life—Filipinos all had servants unless they were poor—so she knew even less than I did when I got that onerous duty in New Orleans. She didn't even know about recipes, and the desserts she produced were, well, very unusual. When I showed her a recipe book, she broke out in a smile and exclaimed, "Oh! Eet is joost like my class in chemeestry."

I told her I was leaving. She grinned and hugged me and said she wasn't too surprised.

"Do you think you could cut my hair?" I asked, sitting down on the edge of her bed.

She giggled and went straight to the nearby community room, returning with some scissors.

"Take off your veil and cap."

I did and my dark hair fell down to my waist.

"Wow," she said. "You have some hair! How much do you want me to take off?"

"How about right about here?" I said, pointing to my shoulders.

"That's good," Sister agreed, pulling over a waste paper basket. "Better take off your cape too, or it will be full of hair."

So I sat there while my sister deftly wielded the big pair of scissors. Long bunches of hair fell into the wastepaper basket, which I held and moved around to catch the lost locks. I wouldn't see them again, or braid them or toss them in the air. Still, I felt lighter.

When it was over, we laughed and hugged. I thanked her, said I would return the scissors, and left her room.

The next morning I put on the modified habit instead of my long skirt, blouse, and cape. It had been hanging in my room for about a month, awaiting the day we would all change into something more modern. I was just ahead of schedule. The dress hung just below my knees, had three-quarter sleeves, and was made of winter wool. I hadn't gotten any new shoes. The suitcase with which I entered had been put in my room. My purse, clothes, and a few other belongings were inside. I pulled a pair of shoes and some stockings, so I wore those and a bra. The bra felt a little tight. The three-inch silver cross I had been given when I made first vows had to be left behind. The order would keep it and give it to someone else.

Just before Mass, Mother Robertson appeared in my room smiling. "Sister, I have a little surprise for you," she said, handing me a small envelope. I opened it, expecting a greeting card with well wishes, maybe even signed by the whole community.

I couldn't believe my eyes. It was the photo of my father when he was four years old.

"I thought it had been destroyed when I entered, Mother," I said beaming, tears coming to my eyes.

"No, my child. You were asked to surrender it, but we kept it safe for you. And now it is yours again. Take my hand, and we shall walk to the chapel together."

It was a hot and wonderful August 28, 1968 when I attended Mass for the last time in the convent. My attire wasn't very well suited to the weather or anything else, but I planned to use some of the $500 right away to buy a few new things. Mother Walker instructed me to sit in the retreatants' chapel rather than with the community, so I could hear them and see some of them but was no longer part of them. I heard Mother Walker explain, with the usual brevity, that I was leaving to serve out in the world. Father Haverty, the priest that day, had me come kneel at the communion rail and prayed for me, blessing me and my new journey, and the community all said, "Amen."

When Mass was over, the nuns came out of their chapel, and I came out of mine. We met by the front door. Some prayed for me, and I hugged everyone. Then it was time to leave.

A cab had been called. Smiling, I picked up my small suitcase, opened the oak door, which felt light that day, and stepped out into the open air. There I took a deep breath, closed the door firmly behind me, and walked down the three steps to the waiting taxi.

"Take me down Prospect to Wisconsin Avenue, and drop me at the first bus stop, please," I told the driver.

"Any special address, Miss?"

"Just take me to the first bus stop on Wisconsin Avenue, please."

My right hand reached into my pocket for the latest pack of cigarettes Carter had given me. I could feel there was one left. In a few minutes I could buy myself a pack with my own money.

Settling back in the seat, I took out the cigarette, crumpled the pack, lit up, and drew the smoke in deeply. Exhaling, I smiled as the smoke curled upward.

Consummatum est. It is finished.

My heart sang.

Strollin' Down the Avenue

The door opened, and I leaped aboard. My money jangled in the conductor's box.

It's my money now, and I can buy bus passes without asking anybody.

Dropping into a seat near the front, holding onto the pole as the bus jerked forward, I smiled at the woman across from me. She was solid in a Wisconsin kind of way and smiled back, then turned away without another glance. If she noticed I looked odd, she didn't show it.

I'm so relieved.

I knew exactly where I was going. The Boston Store was on Wisconsin Avenue. It was a department store and would have whatever I needed. There was a beauty shop where my hair could be cut with some skill so it didn't just stick out all over the place. There were dresses, shoes, underwear, and others things I might not have thought of. I definitely needed a couple of dresses and some normal looking shoes. I had a bra but having two new ones seemed like a good idea. Other things would make themselves known to me when I saw them.

Sitting in the bus, I opened the purse which the nuns had kept for me since I entered the postulancy. I pulled out my father's photo, the one I thought had been destroyed, and looked at it again for a long time.

He was just a little boy, a four-year-old, standing straight and stiff in his uncomfortable good clothes.

That photo had been taken in 1906. My father was a Russian immigrant then, and would remain a Russian citizen and an alien in Germany until adulthood. That alien status doomed him, a brilliant student, to being put out of public school during World War I and forced to attend Herr Schiller's brutal school for problem boys. When he was able to apply for citizenship, it was this very photo of the boy dressed in an unmistakably German suit that allowed him to succeed. It was his only proof that he had lived on German soil from that young age. I treasured that photo and could hardly believe I held it in my hand once more.

Then I discovered two more pictures in a compartment of my old purse. There were several family pictures and one of Joyce Megay, my music teacher and close friend who asked me for a ride to church when I was nineteen. I had forgotten I had brought them with me when I entered seven years before.

Until now I hadn't been able to think about how to tell my family or Joyce that I had left the convent.

Joyce will be disappointed, and that will make me feel terrible. But my parents. I have to think about what to say to them...

I hadn't seen my parents for years, not since that really terrible day when I was a novice and they came to visit. At least Mother Lowell had allowed us to visit in private, not with lots of other nuns and their parents around. Still, it was...so hard. Mother did her best to keep a stiff upper lip, until she, who never wore make up, blurted out, "I'll buy you a whole tray of lipsticks if you come home."

I must have sounded so cold when I said I couldn't go home. At the time, I was just trying to hold myself together...

I shuddered remembering that day, and looked at the pictures again, tears running slowly down my face. I knew I had broken their hearts... Every bone in their bodies rebelled against the oppressive history of the Catholic Church, and as academics they could not understand that a daughter of theirs would give her mind over to some person or institution. I had taken a step that seemed opposed to all they had taught me. They must have thought I just didn't care...

'Ihe bus lurched as it turned the corner, and I grabbed onto the edge of my seat. The photo of Joyce fell on the floor, and as I picked it up and put everything back in my purse, my thoughts returned to the present moment, to the bus, to my new freedom. We were starting down Wisconsin Avenue. We started to pass Marquette where I had gone to graduate school and marched for civil rights. This was a perfect place to get off. Boston Store was about a mile away, I guessed, but I had to take this long anticipated walk. The cord over my head made a happy "ding" when I pulled it, the bus slowed to a halt, doors opened, and I got out.

The street was filled with students, shoppers, and busy working people, and I became part of the throng. No one noticed me despite my wool dress in August.

How wonderful! Nobody is staring and deciding they know all about the modern nun because they see me here downtown, because of what I'm wearing, because of the grin on my face. Happiness is invisibility.

Oh, there's a drug store.

I hurried inside and headed straight for the cigarette counter. "Pack of Winston Longs, please," and then I quickly added, "and some matches."

The young blond woman behind the counter handed them to me and took my $20 bill, all the while trying to make eye contact with a good looking manager walking by. She handed me change, barely looking down to count it out, and then, seeming to remember I wanted matches, she reached under the counter and handed me those too. Apparently matches didn't cost anything. I had lots of change from my $20, figuring the pack must have cost about 50 cents.

Outside, I stepped close to the drugstore, putting my back to the wind that always swept down the avenue without getting hit in the face. I opened the pack very carefully without tearing any of the cellophane off, tapped it on my left hand to get out that first cigarette. Putting the cigarette between my lips, I struck a match and held it to the cigarette long enough to see the end glow red. Then I took that first exhilarating draw, holding the smoke in my lungs for a long moment before finally exhaling. Ahhhh, wonderful.

I put the pack and the matches into my purse and began to stroll, puffing on my cigarette, flicking ashes on the sidewalk, looking at the faces of all the people passing by. I didn't feel the heat of that August day. My dress was black and wool, the temperature was in the 90's and the Milwaukee air was filled with dampness from the humidity rising off the great lake. But I was not bothered. My shoes were heavy and awkward, but their heaviness and that in the air could not weigh me down. My feet were light. My head was high. My hair was loose and moving with the wind. My emotions soared.

And there is was: Boston Store. I had never been inside, even though I had lived in Milwaukee for about two years. The glass door looked heavy, but it seemed to open almost by itself when I pushed the handle. Three tiers of lockers were just inside, and I shoved my suitcase into one, put in a quarter, and locked it.

Lots of people milled around inside, more women than men, all looking very purposeful

Hmm. Where do I go? This place is huge. So much stuff!

A woman bumped into me, and I apologized.

Careful. This isn't the convent with everyone gliding along surrounded by lots of silent space.

Rounding a whole set of counters selling cosmetics, I was about to head toward the escalators but stopped and turned around. Perusing the multitude of lotions, powders, and things to make your eyes bigger and your eyebrows thinner, I stopped at the lipsticks. A saleswoman sauntered over, enthusiasm plastered like too much makeup on her worn face.

"May I help you, Miss?"

"Yes, please. I would like that lipstick," and I pointed to a bright red one.

"That'll be $8.68 with tax," the woman said, and I handed her a ten dollar bill.

Walking away with my change and the little bag with my purchase, I took out the lipstick and stopped right in the middle of the store in front of a mirrored column to put some on, pressing together my newly anointed lips.

Decorum be damned.

Now for some clothes. Think I'll start from inside out.

Heading toward a sign which read "Lingerie," I soon found myself overwhelmed by bras and panties.

So many kinds and different colors. Oh, there're Playtex ones.

I tried on some just a little larger than the one I was wearing, and soon had two new bras in beige, not white. Then added some panties—blue and pink—no more plain white!

Soon I had purchased two dresses, both shirtwaists which I thought would be versatile and good for job interviews.

I have to find a job...

I walked away wearing the purple one, crossing the floor to the hair salon.

"What wonderfully thick hair you have," the stylist cooed.

"I'd like a simple cut, just above shoulder length and something that will stay neat please."

I settled in the chair and found myself staring at my own face, confronting it in a mirror for the first time in seven years. Was that really me? I had been looking inward for years. Of course I had caught glimpses of my face, but here it was, staring back at me. Stuck in my chair, I couldn't escape it, this view of the outside of me, red lips and all.

Fascinated, I watched myself and the stylist in the mirror as she put a purple cape round my shoulders and ran her fingers through my hair, getting a sense of its fullness and natural flow. Then she began to quickly snip, shaping on one side and then the other. She soon ran her fingers through my dark hair again, bent down to check the symmetry, made a few more carefully calculated snips, and stood back admiring her work. I admired it too.

"Well, what do you think?" she asked, removing the cape which was full of hair now.

"It looks great," I said, smiling. Then I just grinned at the mirror, thanked the woman, and jumped out of the chair. "How much do I owe you?" It felt good to have money in my purse to pay people with.

My hair felt wonderful. It swung around my head freely while keeping its shape, and I moved my head back and forth a little just to make it swing further.

As I searched for the shoe department, I kept coming across mirrors. Every time I stopped and took a look at myself in my new dress, I saw my figure which I hadn't seen in a while. I decided it looked pretty good, especially with the bra.

Passing a lunch counter, I stopped and bought a chicken sandwich and a Coke.

Been seven years since I've had a Coke. It's more fizzy and tickly than I remember.

And then there it was, the shoe department, right in front of me. Shoes were a little tricky. They were expensive, and the styles had changed a lot in the last seven years. They looked more comfortable. Soon I had a pair of sturdy sandals and some black pumps with very slight heels, perfect for job interviews.

It's four-thirty! I'm tired. So many people and stuff and noise with Muzak gliding out of speakers from every direction. Time to get out of here.

I moved toward the exit labeled "Wisconsin Avenue," moving past more mirrors and looking in each one. I soon saw the lockers, retrieved my suitcase, loaded it with my purchases, and easily opened the imposing glass door. Outside there was a strong wind coming off the lake. I looked up at the sky. There were clouds gathering, but it didn't look like rain.

Stationed at the bus stop along with others wearied by their day's activities, I exchanged smiles with some. Quite a few were smoking, and I lit another cigarette and smoked along with them.

I loved being nobody, one of an anonymous crowd getting on the bus. Tired like everybody else. Just one of God's children.

Excited and smiling, I dropped into my seat near the front and watched buildings go by the window as we neared the hotel.

I have a reservation, so they expect me. I'll go upstairs, put my new clothes away, maybe take a shower. And then at 5:30, Carter will arrive.

The Good

The sun was bright and the sky the purest blue.

Flying Bird ran round and round in circles in the park, feet strong and sure against the Earth, arms held high and open to the wind, fingers spread to miss no touch of air. Flying Bird's face was bright with the wonders of life.

Nearby, Deep River sat on the grassy hill in the shade of the tallest oak, her back against the sturdy trunk with its bark that tickled just a bit. Legs stretched out, feet lolling to the side. Clasped hands raised, cradling her head. Deep River's eyes twinkled as she watched Flying Bird run.

Then she closed her eyes and smiled with the Divine. "This is good," she whispered. "This is very good."

Our First Evening Out

Carter stood there wearing a shirt and tie—no collar—carrying a leather briefcase and grinning at me as I opened my door. He looked at me, with my new haircut, dress, and shoes and bent down to kiss me deeply.

Passing a mirror in the lobby, I automatically looked at our reflection. It was amazing, a shock even. We looked like everybody else. We just looked like a couple in their 30's heading toward the dining room. There was nothing special or strange about us. In fact, we look quite ordinary. Anyone who cared to look our way could see us. We were out in the open in the big wide world, not in his office with the door closed. For the first time, we were visible as a couple.

And we were invisible too because we were *not* just one more couple in a restaurant. It wasn't just that we had a secret. Lots of people have secrets whispered to one another leaning across the table, or with their heads close together at the bar, or hinted at with coded words or a raised eyebrow. Other people can see those secrets; they just can't hear them. It was different for Carter and me. We *were* a secret.

Carter seemed perfectly at ease being visible and invisible. He gave the hostess his first name and walked casually through the dimly lit room, passing mahogany tables and tall windows with heavy drapes across to the comfortable corner booth in the back he requested. Not once did he look around the restaurant to see if someone recognized him. This helped me set aside worries that someone might see him with a woman, and I did not look either, but I was glad to be at a table that was private.

He's not worried about being seen. Why should I?

Carter ordered a bottle of wine, which the waiter brought promptly, hardly glancing at us as he uncorked it and poured a bit for Carter to taste. Carter approved, and the waiter poured glasses for us both then walked away.

The waiter just sees one more table to serve.

I leaned back and lifted my glass, enjoying the deep, beautiful red color of the wine and the way the light played on it. Carter smiled as he lifted his glass to make a little toast to the occasion, looking into my eyes.

"Here's to you, Ann, with your splendid new haircut, dress, and pumps. You look great! Here's to the beginning of your new journey. And here's to us. To a long future."

"To us," I added as we clinked our glasses together, making the musical sound of real crystal.

I knew I was sitting across the table from a man who had not yet made a choice. Oh, he said he could not leave, but I hoped he would change his mind. I was sure we had not finished those discussions, but tonight was not the night.

Tonight I will just enjoy the wine and the meal and being with him.

Carter took a pack of cigarettes out of his pocket, offered me one, and held his lighter out toward me, looking into my eyes. He quickly lit mine and then his own, snapping the lighter shut as we drew in unison on our first cigarettes together in our new life.

I told Carter about my day at Boston Store. "I kept a perfectly straight face when I bought the bras. I don't think she knew I wasn't expecting so many colors and different kinds."

Carter laughed with me over each of my delicious memories. He told me about the boring meeting he sat through, and I commiserated. We talked about where I would live and what I would do. Carter had thought about my staying with his mother until I found work, but he didn't like that idea much. I hated it but didn't say it sounded like another convent. I just politely thanked him for the offer. I hadn't even met her. And who on earth would she think I was?

"May I take your order, Sir," the waiter asked. We had hardly looked at the menu, but I knew exactly what I wanted.

"The soft shell crab please," I said, ignoring the hefty price.

"Good choice, Madam," the waiter remarked.

Carter ordered a steak, medium rare. The waiter brought us both salads and spread my napkin across my lap.

"No, a couple of days ago, I talked with one of the women who makes retreats. She has a studio apartment on the East Side and is moving to Chicago this weekend. She's already told the manager about me. He hadn't sublet it yet and agreed I can take over her lease and move right in Saturday. It's on Cass Street, so it's not too far from your place. The rent's $140 a month though, so I definitely have to get a job."

Not wanting to worry about money, I turned to see the source of the violin music that had just begun to waft across the room.

"Some parishes are starting to have lay people on staff called 'religious educators,'" Carter said, stubbing out his cigarette, "and with your Master's in Theology, you would be perfect."

"I don't have my degree yet. And I can't get hold of the head of my thesis committee. Those three guys have to approve it soon for me to graduate by December."

The waiter arrived with the entrees, and the aroma of the crab rose with all the glory I remembered.

"Yeah. I know. Bernie Cooke's been away a lot. I've heard he has some personal business in Canada. Still, parishes will probably be okay with your word that you will have your Master's by December, and Bernie will have to get this task finished. You're not the only one with a thesis waiting for him to move, and the university won't let him keep all of you waiting forever."

I frowned, not being so sure of that. There were rumors about Bernie. What if he just stayed in Canada? I heard someone lived there named… Florence? Pamela? I didn't remember. Never met her even though she had been at Marquette early in my time there.

"What if he doesn't come back here?"

"If you don't hear from him soon, you probably should go to the Dean," Carter responded, frowning. The rumors had no doubt reached him too.

I smiled at that good idea, and we raised our glasses to getting the thesis over with.

"Anyway," Carter went on, "I brought along something I found in the paper. It's an ad for a Director of Religious Education out on the West Side." He pulled a carefully folded page from the Milwaukee Journal out of his pocket and passed it over to me.

I read the small ad he had circled: "Suburban parish looking for Director to coordinate all levels of religious education for children attending public schools and adults of the parish. Master's degree in relevant field required. For more information, call 414…"

"Oh my gosh, I can't believe it. Right in today's paper. What perfect timing! I'll call tomorrow."

"Good, and you can give me as a reference," Carter added, grinning.

We finished our entrees, ordered chocolate mousse for dessert, and just talked. Leaning my elbow on the table, I hadn't been so relaxed in a long time. I wasn't thinking about anyone else in the room, and the waiter kept a discreet distance. So much to share, and no bells ringing to pull me away or people coming in to interrupt us. No anxious watching the door and keeping our faces looking ordinary and colorless. No ears cocked for footsteps. Just us.

Eventually Carter looked at his watch.

"Time for me to go," he said, folding his napkin. "Early Mass in the morning. Let me walk you back to your room, Ann."

He paid the bill with cash, thanked the waiter, and we both slid out of the booth. The walk to the elevators was leisurely, but I did see Carter look around before stepping in and pushing the button for my floor.

Back in my room, he kissed me first on the forehead and then on the lips, one arm around my waist drawing me toward him, the other hand supporting my head. Then he released me just enough so we could look into one another's eyes. We stood there for a long moment. Then he gently kissed me once more and pulled away, picking up his briefcase and putting his hand on the doorknob.

"I'll call you tomorrow," he said. "Maybe we can have dinner again."

I watched him walking down the corridor and saw him take his handkerchief out of his pocket and run it across his mouth. Then he was gone. I closed the door quietly and looked around the room. It was time to prepare for my first night alone.

Building a New Life

I can do this. I know I can.

I was clear. Spirited forward by the exhilaration of my first day and night of anonymous participation in humanity's throng, I set about building my new life. Carter was there cheering me on, but since he was still committed to staying in the priesthood, he could not risk being associated with me too much and wouldn't be able to be of much practical help.

Okay, so the priorities are a place to live—I almost have that—and a job. I'll call Our Lady of Cana, the parish with the ad Carter showed me last night. God knows, I don't know anything about educating people about anything, but I'll find a way. Right now I need an interview! Second priority is securing the apartment.

I walked over to the mirror in the hotel room and sized myself up. It was still a new experience to see myself in a real mirror, not just an indistinct reflection in a window.

I really love my new haircut, and if I were interviewing me, my first impression would be 'she looks smart and energetic.' I know I can talk well, and even though I don't have my Master's yet, I can show I'll have it by December. Marquette's a good school too. The dresses I bought are fine, simple, but that's good for a church, I guess. Yes, I can do this.

Carter had given me the phone number of the rectory where the priests lived. The parish was on the west side of town, an area I didn't know much about, but it was in the city and would be accessible by bus.

Picking up the phone, I dialed the number, walking around as far as the cord would let me to dissipate my stress. A man answered quickly.

"Hello?"

"Hello? May I speak with Father Blakely, please?"

"I am Father Blakely. How can I help you? "

"My name is Ann Temkin. I am aware that you are looking for a Director of Religious Education, and I would like to apply." Holding the receiver to my ear, I picked up the solid black telephone with my free hand and started pacing again.

"Well, thank you for calling. Can you tell me something about your background...ah, I'm sorry, I didn't quite get your name."

"It's Ann T-e-m-k-i-n, Father. But please, just call me Ann. Well, I've just completed my Master's in Theology at Marquette..."

"Very good. Great school. My nephew went there for undergraduate. Great basketball team too."

"Yes, it is a really good school, and Al McGuire is a terrific coach!" I could hear Father Blakely's voice brighten at the thought of Marquette's basketball fame. Not that I'd watched any basketball games in the convent, but McGuire's name was in the news, on campus, and connected with the championship celebration we protested. In any case, it just popped out of my mouth. Lucky thing.

"Father Blakely, I should tell you I have not actually graduated yet. All my course work and exams have been completed. As soon as Father Cooke returns to town and convenes the academic committee, my thesis should be approved. It's so exciting that churches are hiring lay people now in these new positions, and I would love the opportunity to apply."

Now I was holding my breath.

"Well, I would like to review your resume and meet you. Actually, I'd like to do that as soon as possible. It's already the end of August, classes start in just two weeks, and we need someone in place. Would you be able to start then?"

"Yes." I inhaled. "Since I've just finished school, I am available now."

"Excellent. Can you bring your resume out tomorrow afternoon? Today is the Associate's day off, and I definitely want him to meet you as well."

I gulped a little.

Resume? What should I put on it, and how would I get it typed by tomorrow? I'll find a way.

"Yes," I replied, without missing a beat. "I can come out tomorrow. What time would be convenient?"

"How about 2:30? Summer School lets out at 3, and our principal might like to meet you too. Just come around to the rectory. It's behind the church, and the housekeeper will show you to Father McMalley's office. He is our Associate, and the priest who will work most closely with the Religious Ed Director."

"Thank you very much, Father. I will see you tomorrow."

"Well, I'm looking forward to it, Ann. Goodbye, and thank you for calling."

"Goodbye, Father. Thank you again."

I threw myself on the bed, telephone in hand.

I did it! I have to tell Carter!

My finger started turning the dial, 414-93...and then, stopped.

Maybe I shouldn't call him, should wait till I see him tonight. He might have someone in his office. It might put him in an awkward position...

I replaced the receiver and returned the whole phone to its place on the nightstand. For a while I just lay on the bed, staring at the ceiling, focusing on the little dots in the ceiling tiles and the way the sun lit up one side of the room more than the other, resting in the stillness.

Then I bounced up.

Got to get moving. Better call Debbie about the apartment. I can't stay long at this hotel. Must be costing Carter a lot. He doesn't get much money, just room and board and a very small salary. And I have to write a resume...maybe Debbie can help me.

I paced back and forth across the small room a couple of times and then paused by the nightstand. I grabbed the phone and started dialing Debbie as my feet continued to move.

She answered her office phone right away, and we agreed to meet at her apartment that evening after work. She told me she had a typewriter at her place too, and I could put my resume together.

I'd better start working on it now, but I don't have any paper or even a pen.

There was a small desk in my hotel room so I opened the drawer hopefully; nothing but a Gideon Bible. No community room stocked with supplies like in the convent. Realizing I also needed more clothes—I couldn't wear the same two dresses day after day—and that I hadn't had anything to eat that morning, I decided to go out.

The hotel lobby had a coffee pot and some apples. I took a big red one, which I consumed quickly, put a second one in my pocket, and then walked out into the heat. Heading in the direction of Boston Store, I saw a Woolworths and went in to explore. Standing in line at the cashier's with paper and pens, unhealthy snack food, a pair of jeans—prefaded since that was what everyone was wearing—and a couple of t-shirts, my eyes went to some paperbacks. I grabbed "Writing a Successful Resume."

That afternoon I read and wrote, and re-wrote and re-arranged, and by the time I arrived at Debbie's, I finally I had something I hoped looked like a resume. Her Cass Street apartment was on the East Side not too far from the lake, just up Wisconsin Avenue from the hotel. The building looked nice on the outside: brick, two stories, solid.

I hit the button next to Debbie's name on the directory and heard the door click open immediately. Entering, I found myself in a small foyer with double doors leading directly ahead to a courtyard outside. The building, I could see now, was U-shaped with the outdoor space in the middle. I found Debbie's apartment on the first floor on the courtyard side of the corridor, so when she opened the door, I could see that her window looked out on the little garden.

"Oh, you look wonderful," Debbie exclaimed, clapping her hands. "I didn't know you had hair! Thought maybe they made you cut it all off."

"No, this is actually shorter than it was," I replied, laughing. "Two days ago, it hung down to my waist."

We hugged for the first time, because nuns and retreatants didn't hug in the convent.

"Come in, come in."

She held the door wide, and I entered, maneuvering around piles of boxes almost covering the small floor space.

"Oh, excuse the mess," Debbie cried. "I've packed up most of my things. Plan on moving to Chicago this Saturday. I'm so excited."

It didn't take long to look around her place, which was a utility apartment of one room with a couch, table and chairs, and a kitchen, including a small fridge, stove, and sink along one wall. The only other room was the bathroom; looking in, I saw it was small, equipped with everything necessary, and a thin person could squeeze past the sink and toilet to use the tub. This small space was not at all like the convents with large rooms, bathrooms with several showers and stalls, big community rooms and dining rooms. It was, in fact, tiny, but it would all be mine.

"It's furnished, like I told you," Debbie said. "So the bed, table, chairs, and bureau all stay here. The bed's pretty comfortable."

She pressed down on the mattress to show me it was solid but not a rock. I did likewise, nodding and looking pleased.

Never did that in the convent. We just took what we got, and if it wasn't too comfortable, we thought that made us holier.

"Oh, and here's the closet," she went on proudly, opening the door of a small closet packed with clothes, the shelf lined with books, bags, and assorted stuff. The closet was so full that Debbie could hardly close the door; shoes kept wanting to tumble down, and coats and dresses kept bulging out.

If the closet is full of clothes still, where on earth had everything inside all those boxes come from? There must hardly have been room to move around. There's hardly room now.

"I'll get this all cleared out this weekend," Debbie assured me as though she could read my thoughts. "You'll have to buy some dishes, pots, and pans, and I guess you don't have sheets or towels either. Do you have any money?"

"Oh, yes, they gave me $500 when I left. And I've already been to Boston Store, and they have those things there in the basement, but they might be cheaper at Woolworths. That's where I got the jeans." I put my hands in the pockets like a cowgirl and grinned. "I just haven't gotten anything for the apartment yet, wanted to see it first. It's perfect. I love it. Can I move in this weekend?"

"Yep. It's all yours. Chicago, here I come!" Debbie exclaimed enthusiastically, punctuating her declaration with a little hope. "Well, heavens, sit down." She pulled one of the chairs away from the small wooden table, waving me to sit down, and put a kettle on the stove. "Want some tea?"

I accepted both the chair and offer of tea gratefully and continued to look around. "The pictures are mine of course," Debbie went on, seeing me notice some prints still hanging on the wall. "I don't imagine you have anything to put up yet."

"No, but that won't take long. I told you on the phone about my job interview tomorrow."

"Yes, I'm so excited for you! Oh, I'm sure you'll get it. I mean, you're so smart and caring, they would be fools not to hire you on the spot."

I thanked her. Her enthusiasm and certitude were definitely excessive—my mother would not have approved of such high emotion—but they were comforting and reassuring nevertheless. My British mother wouldn't have approved of the way she made tea either: a tea bag in each cup with no-longer-quite-boiling water poured over it. She would have called it "beverage," not deserving of the word "tea." I didn't care; it felt so good sitting with a friend in the apartment that would be mine in just a few days.

Once we had our tea, I asked Debbie about the typewriter. She unearthed one from under blankets spilling over the sides of one of the boxes and put it on the table before me.

"Oh, I forgot to get some paper for typing, Debbie. I just bought a pad with lines on it."

"Don't worry, I'll find some." She rummaged around, looking at the writing on her boxes, found one saying "office," pulled it out from under two other boxes, and triumphantly handed me a ream of paper.

"Do you think this resume looks okay? I didn't have to write one for my last job before the convent."

"What kind of job was that?" Debbie asked, taking the handwritten draft I had spent the afternoon composing.

"Oh, I worked in a college library, acquisitions desk and then the research department," I told her, opening the pack of paper.

"I think it's fine. You have a question mark here by the convent years. I would definitely include them. Otherwise they might think you were in jail or just lounging around or something. And make a little indented paragraph summing up what you did there, especially whatever would be like the Religious Ed job they have."

It didn't take long to type out my resume. I did sum up some of the interesting parts from the convent years, like the time in the New Orleans shelter, the interdenominational and interracial work. Still, it didn't take up much room. Fortunately there was a long list of things under "Education" which filled up most of the page.

I showed the finished product to Debbie, who had been packing up some odds and ends. "Looks great. You're a good typist too. When you get to the hotel, go to the business office, and ask to make a copy of this. Might as well keep it. You might apply somewhere else too."

"Good idea," I agreed.

She handed me a folder, and I put the resume carefully inside.

We talked for about an hour, with Debbie telling me excitedly about her new job at a newspaper and how great Chicago would be. So much happening.

"Now here's a key," Debbie said, handing it to me as I was leaving. "You're coming Sunday you said. I won't be here, and I'm not sure when I'll see you again. But probably I'll come visit some friends in Milwaukee. Chicago's only an hour and a half away. And you could come visit me," she brightly chirped. "I put my new address on the outside of the envelope with the key. See? And the name of the manager and his apartment number is there too. I don't know my new phone number yet, but I'll let you know when I do."

"Thank you so much for everything, Debbie. I don't know how I would have found a place to live without your offer to sublet."

"I hope you love the place as much as I have," she said as we hugged and said our goodbyes.

I was relieved to get away from all her exuberance, but I was grateful to Debbie too. Then realizing I wouldn't see her again for a long time, I felt rather sad.

And I was eager to get back to the hotel. It was after 9 o'clock, and Carter had promised to call around 10. My new shoes beat a steady rhythm on the sidewalk as I hurried along the windblown street, holding the folder with my resume carefully so it wouldn't get bent. I started imagining how I would tell Carter all the news of the day, especially about Father Blakely and my upcoming job interview. He would be so pleased. I smiled thinking about it, and walked into the hotel lobby.

Pots, Pans, and Police

I got the job at Our Lady of Cana, and my life was taking shape fast. I bought pots, pans, sheets, and more clothes. The Olsons, members of the new parish, gave me a whole set of dishes retrieved from their attic, and Mr. Paulson, another parishioner, sold me a rattletrap but very serviceable used Chevy for practically nothing. Every other Friday I brought home a check for a little over $300 and thought that was wonderful. Life was moving forward; I felt so grateful.

But during these first six weeks of my new life I found Debbie back in town from Chicago and sitting in my apartment every Friday, making me walk around her and all her boxes every weekend and listen to endless excuses.

"So sorry, my brother couldn't come. He'll help me move all these things next week though."

I really wanted the apartment to be mine — my clothes in the closet, my place to sleep, my floor space to walk on, small as it was. I wanted to be able to invite Carter to come over to my apartment and to have privacy when he called. Every weekend my anger grew; I wanted her out!

Finally I had enough. "Debbie, if you are not gone by Sunday morning I am loading your things in my car, driving them to Chicago, and dumping them on the sidewalk outside your building!"

Returning from church that Sunday I found her gone, along with all her boxes and all the clothes that had consumed the sole closet. I started putting my clothes away and unpacking my meager boxes.

And I've learned a big lesson. When I first met Debbie, she told me about her hard life. I learned about her many experiences of being cheated, rejected, abandoned. But I learned that when someone has a long, long list of people who have treated her badly, you will often end up becoming the next on the list, no matter what you do.

But the main thing was that the place was now mine. Mine to decorate as I wished, to live in as I wished. I loved it.

And I loved my new job, which was going pretty well. I didn't know the first thing about teaching children's religion classes. Graduate school didn't include one lecture on anything practical, and I didn't even have any church experience from my own childhood to draw on. What I did know how to do, however, was work with volunteers, and those at Cana had lots of experience with kids. And I knew how to broaden their religious perspectives.

Mrs. Emerson, Ellen, was round and smiling and ready to help me and everyone else of whatever age. She had been a warm, nurturing Sunday School teacher for ten years; everyone loved her, and she was also smart. My second week on the job we were sitting in my office looking at Sunday School books.

"Ellen, you have so much experience teaching, and everybody I've met here obviously loves and respects you. Would you be willing to be a kind of Sunday School principal? You know, help me make sure we have enough teachers, that the curriculum is a good one, give new teachers some guidelines for working with the kids? Then I could hold some theological workshops for the teachers, design some special projects and programs for parents, and make sure all the admin tasks get taken care of. What do you think?"

"Love to," she replied enthusiastically. "And I am so happy you are going to work with the teachers and the parents too because the church is changing so much. Everyone has questions and concerns. It's a confusing time...but a really good time too."

"Wonderful. We'll have so much fun working together. And it really is a great time to be in the church," I agreed. "Vatican II has encouraged, in fact, urged us to come up with new ideas and ways of doing things, making the church more relevant."

I got up, opening a desk drawer and pulling my brand new copy of the published Vatican II documents out of my purse.

"Have you seen the published papers that are out now?"

She shook her head.

"No? I'll get you a copy, Ellen. There are papers on everything: how the church should relate to the world, about how to approach the Bible to people of other denominations, relating in a positive way to people who aren't Christians...it's really exciting. People have a lot to get used to. But some traditions will be hard for people to give up, like seeing the class of seven-year-olds walking up the aisle together for First Communion dressed as little brides and bridegrooms. We can work together, Ellen, to help them make the adjustments and see how wonderful it can be. I'm excited, and we have a lot of work to do."

I had been rattling on, and Ellen was grinning at my enthusiasm.

"Let's do it," she said, getting up to give me a big hug. It felt so good to be working with this woman who was not just bright, but open and warm.

Ellen and I were a really good team, and we soon had a great group of teachers ready to work with the kids of all ages. I had the first workshop to help the teachers understand what Vatican II was saying about the role of the church in the world, about the sacraments, and about the Bible. They had lots of questions, which was wonderful. At my parish, both the priests and most of the people were very receptive to the changes happening in the church. We were fortunate. Not all parishes were so willing to try new things.

The Welbys were among the best teachers at Our Lady of Cana. They had worked for years with children of various ages and knew a lot about kids, being parents of seven themselves. Chuck worked with his hands; he was a plumber. Betsy got a secretarial job when her youngest was no longer a baby. Kind, warm, and loving people, they welcomed me as a member of their family. I went to their home and shared their dinner table every week on the evening I had to be at the church for the children's religious education classes. But to be a real family member I needed to contribute, not just receive. So I got to babysit when the parents took their annual weekend away, a tradition they had held from the time their first born was an infant. It was the easiest babysitting I had ever done because the older children took wonderful care of the little ones.

The Welbys were no cookie-cutter Norman Rockwell family; they were simply the most loving, genuine, and near idyll family I had ever known. When Chuck was unable to work for almost a year because of an injury, they were very poor materially, but certainly not spiritually. One Christmas, the children had no money for presents. The gift they gave their father was the most valuable in the world though; they made a tape recording—all seven of them—of the things they loved so much about him. They wrapped it carefully in newspaper, the baby putting on the final piece of scotch tape.

The Welbys not only took me in, they also shared my passion for social justice. They lived the Gospel and took Jesus' words seriously about feeding the hungry and serving the marginalized.

I knew from my days at Marquette how divided Milwaukee was. Now, living outside the convent and working in a parish, I saw this fact even more clearly. Sunday morning at 11 a.m. was indeed, as Dr. Martin Luther King, Jr. said, the most segregated hour of the week. While southern blacks and whites were segregated by law, the races lived far apart in Milwaukee. Just as in the south, they did not attend the same schools, eat at the same restaurants, shop in the same stores, or go to the same churches.

Blacks knew whites, of course, and knew how white culture operated because they largely worked for white people. The reverse was not true. Whites simply did not know blacks. That is, they might know "Mary" who cleaned their house or "Sam" who worked on their car. But they did not know them at all as people and had virtually no familiarity with their culture. Simply put, most whites had never sat at table or attended church with a black person, had never been to a black neighborhood, had never seen a black doctor or other professional.

And in addition, in Milwaukee, almost all blacks were poor.

So I began bringing people together in simple ways. It was important in those days and in that place for whites to be in the same room with blacks, to talk about children, share activities like mending clothes, or having coffee and a snack at the same table. So we did that, forming relationships of a very basic nature with some black neighborhood organizations. We always met in the inner city where blacks lived, not in white suburbs. We had a sewing group, activities for pre-school children, and some family gatherings.

Almost immediately I had my first personal experience with the Milwaukee police practices in African American communities. It happened when I drove a group of white suburban middle school children to an inner city organization about a month after school started that fall. It was already dark, around 7 p.m. We had just gotten off the expressway and were driving down streets where pedestrians were all black, where the streets themselves were narrower and less well lit, and there were no spacious lawns. There were four children in my old, battered car. This was the first time these kids had been to the inner city, their first interracial activity. The kids were excited; their parents, on the other hand, were fearful and had given permission quite reluctantly.

My attention was pulled away from the children's easy chatter by the whining of a police siren, and one glance in the rear view mirror made my heart rate go up. The cop was right behind me, light whirling, siren blaring. He wasn't trying to go around me either. He wanted me!

Pulling over, lowering my window, I waiting until the overweight, white officer lumbered clumsily out of his car. "Keep it down, kids," I said to the children, who seemed to be excited by this adventure.

"Where are you coming from?" the officer asked in a loud voice, leaning into the car and shining his huge flashlight around. He seemed to stare at the kids as though surprised that we were white. Then he blinded me, aiming the flashlight right at my eyes for a long time. Still unable to see, I kept my hands on the steering wheel and answered his questions about where we were coming from, the name of the church, and the suburb. Then, in a respectful tone I didn't feel, I added, "Is there a problem Officer?"

"Where are you going?" His voice was rough, bullying, and rising in decibels.

As I told him the organization, wishing I could say "none of your business," I was aware that the kids had become silent and motionless.

"What year car is this anyway?" He finally lowered his flashlight, running the beam instead over my little vehicle which, I gathered, he disdained.

Now I was angry, but of course I didn't dare show it and told him, as calmly as I could, the year of the car.

"License and registration!"

"What is the problem, Officer?"

"You made an illegal left turn back there," he snapped, leaning further into the car causing the kids to shrink into their winter coats and hoods, pressing their bodies into the back of their seats.

I produced my license and registration as demanded, and the policeman disappeared into his patrol car. The children were now shaking, partly from cold but mostly from fear. I was probably more frightened than they because I knew I had not made an illegal left turn and I knew about the Chief Breier's reputation. I knew this officer had stopped me without cause, that he had probably assumed I was African American, and that this would not have happened in a white neighborhood.

A nightmare of being taken to the police station played like a full-length feature film in my head, fantasies of calling parents and saying, "Mrs.

Smith, I am really sorry to tell you this. Your daughter is with me at the 3rd precinct. Can you come down and get her please?"

"This is what comes of these new ideas of mixing," Mrs. Smith would probably say.

This would, of course, be followed by outrage, the cessation of all my social justice programs, and would probably cost me my job. That was how the mental movie went anyway.

As the minutes dragged on without the cop returning, we all grew more and more cold and frightened. I sat silent and petrified, still keeping my hands resolutely on the steering wheel.

Where is the guy? Why isn't he coming back?

"What's he doing, Miss Temkin?" Sally ventured, her nervousness betrayed in the dark by her small, quavering voice.

"I guess he's checking to see if I'm a big criminal," I replied in an attempt to ease the tension. I turned around to look at the kids. "We'll just have to wait. And let's say a prayer."

One of the girls pulled a rosary out of her pocket.

"Hail Mary, full of grace..."

The others joined in. And so we waited and prayed a very long, cold ten minutes.

Finally the door of the police car opened, and the cop stuck one leg out. I could see he was bending over his leg starting to write a ticket, then pausing, perhaps to contemplate the presumed violation and resultant fine. None of the children said anymore. Neither did I.

At least maybe it's just a ticket. He's not going to take us to the precinct. I hope.

The officer's body followed his leg out of the squad car.

I held my breath as he returned to my car.

He ended up only giving me a warning ticket.

I believed I would have been given a ticket if my skin color had been as dark as the officer expected.

He shoved it at me without comment. Then, turning and taking a step toward his cruiser, he kicked my car.

What the children told their parents, I shall never know. Perhaps they kept wise silence.

The First Thanksgiving

The glorious red and yellow leaves of fall drifted slowly to the ground, and suddenly it was almost Thanksgiving. It would be my first long weekend. And I was thankful for so much. That day in August when I stepped out of the convent into the streets teeming with people seemed so long ago. Actually it was less than three months, but so much had happened, so many changes in my life.

My relationship with Carter continued to grow, enriched by our avid interest in each other's work and all the stories I now had to tell about my new activities. There was still no intercourse. He told me how terrified he was of my getting pregnant, how he had to work with other priests whose women friends had babies and how traumatic that was.

I was disappointed, even though it was not so strange in 1968 for Catholics to wait for marriage to have sex. Still, I missed the physical intimacy, and I missed the opportunity to give myself to Carter in that total way. I missed the proof of desire on his part. I was on the pill. Why didn't he want me enough to stop worrying that I would get pregnant? We were living in the '60s; the sexual revolution was in full swing. Experimentation was not only allowed, it was expected. Why weren't *we* having sex?

I told myself that he wasn't ready, that he just needed more time. And I still fanned the hope that Carter would one day leave the priesthood.

So many others did—eventually—after a long struggle. Maybe he was still struggling.

Thanksgiving would be a milestone: our first holiday. I didn't count Easter and July 4th when I was still in the convent. How would we celebrate it? Images of former Thanksgivings floated through my head.

As a child I always looked forward to Thanksgiving. We didn't have a big extended family. There were actually only the four of us, but it was still a magical day. As a young child, I didn't even realize this holiday was new for both my immigrant parents. There were no prayers of gratitude because there were no religious observances. But my parents were thankful people. My father was always tremendously grateful to be living in America.

Not that this country was perfect. There was active anti-Semitism in this country. In the 1947 film *Gentleman's Agreement,* Gregory Peck plays a journalist who poses as a Jew to do research for a story. His life changes in many ways, although all his credentials remained the same. There were plenty of stereotypes and anti-Semitic jokes, even church people who called Jews "Christ killers." I myself was chased home from school by a group of kids throwing stones at my head, calling me "dirty Jew."

Jews might not get promoted, were not admitted to many educational institutions, could only live in certain parts of town, and were barred from clubs and recreational places like swimming pools. But houses in Jewish neighborhoods were not burned down, attacks on synagogues were rare, and Jews in America were not rounded up and shipped off to camps. My father had escaped the pogroms in Russia and the Holocaust in Germany, and he loved the United States.

My mother was grateful as well. Since she came to the US from England, the adjustment wasn't great, and America made it possible for my father to leave Germany and for them to marry. Just like other American women, Mother made turkey for Thanksgiving with salad, sweet potatoes, and cranberry sauce. Dessert always consisted of homemade pie, not pumpkin which she wasn't fond of, but apple or mincemeat. Sometimes she made real strudel, and I remember her rolling the dough out until it stretched over the whole kitchen table, creating an amazingly thin crust which was rolled up with all kinds of fruit and nuts. And there was always wine at Thanksgiving dinner to make the meal more festive. My parents even gave me a thimble full.

Our Thanksgivings were not extravagant because nothing in our home was extravagant. But it was warm and special, and the food was excellent and plentiful enough to require a break between the main course and dessert. I routinely spent this break lying on the carpet in the living room, allowing my stomach to do its work in peace.

Thanksgiving in the convent was a special day as well. There was more by way of prayers of gratitude. We too had turkey and potatoes, cranberry sauce, and pie, even wine. And there were more additions to the meal, like nuts and olives. And that afternoon, there would be chocolates during recreation. But the best part of the convent Thanksgiving was that it was one of those rare occasions when we could talk during the meal.

What would I make this Thanksgiving? I wasn't much of a cook; my sisters in the convent could vouch for my inadequacies in that department. But I was determined to rise to the occasion.

How hard can a turkey be? And sweet potatoes can just go in the oven, I suppose. A salad? I'm great at making salads. Pie? Hmm. That's a problem. Well, they sell them. I'll go to Sendik's. I usually don't shop there because it's so expensive, but Thanksgiving is different.

When Carter came over one evening about ten days before the big day, we were sitting in the apartment on the couch talking about our day and smoking cigarettes.

"I've been thinking about Thanksgiving. Do you like apple pie?" I asked. "Or maybe you would rather go out to eat?"

"I didn't know you were thinking about Thanksgiving."

"Well you know I like to plan ahead, Carter."

"Oh, I know. I guess I don't. Anyway, I haven't thought about it yet."

"Well, it's hardly more than a week away, Carter."

"Uh, I guess I should have explained to you before. I have to have Thanksgiving with the other priests. I can't be here."

For a moment, I said nothing.

"Oh, well, that's okay."

I perked up, sounding cheerful, although I was terribly disappointed.

Well, at least I don't have to worry about all that food.

"I can go to the Welby's, the family I've been telling you about. Then we can get together later."

"No, Ann. I can't."

Carter didn't say more about his reasons. I didn't ask. I was too stunned to react. Too stunned to feel the weight of the loss. I just made myself brave.

The rest of our time that evening went by in a kind of haze.

I knew then that every holiday would be like that. I would never need to cook anything at all. Carter would never be with me. I would be left alone for Thanksgiving and for Christmas and for New Year's. That's how it would always be.

Am I stupid to expect anything different?

My lover left early.

Dimming

The colors were a bit less bright, the sun a shade paler, the sky no longer seamless. The air turned somewhat gray that day.

Deep River quickened her steps as she passed the store, careful to make room for mothers with children in tow, to dodge the young man moving dangerously fast in his wheelchair, a pie balanced on his motionless legs.

A grinning little girl proudly staggered under the weight of the family bird, determined to carry it to the car herself, her mother looking on amused. And a small boy in his stroller, rode majestically perched atop a pumpkin's orange bulge.

"Was that thunder in the distance?" Deep River faltered for a moment in her walk, listening. "Better hurry home," she murmured to herself, clasping books closer to her chest, "just in case."

The Man and the Mother

Will she like me? Will she think I'm good enough, smart enough, pretty enough, industrious enough?

I was petrified. Meeting your lover's family for the first time is frightening for the most stalwart among us. But when the lover is a Roman Catholic priest...my fear was sheer terror.

Carter had lost his father. His mother was still living, and he had one brother.

What on earth will his mother think of me?

This question made my whole body tremble. And this wasn't just about being good enough for her son. She knew about all the men leaving the priesthood to get married.

I'm a threat to her son's priesthood, his whole identity, and hers too.

For American Catholics, priesthood is the highest calling. Priests are close to God, presumably not mired in worldly concerns. Priests are interpreters of divine instructions and intentions, gatekeepers to marriage, communion, and even burial in holy ground.

Women are not allowed to be priests. Women can't be wives of priests since priests can't marry. But a woman *can* be the *mother* of a priest. At a son's ordination service, the mother receives the cloth which was wrapped around her son's anointed hands. She who has birthed this man is forever linked to him and to his holy station so intimately, she could almost be said to share it. She is a queen.

If Carter leaves the priesthood, she will no longer wear the crown belonging to mother of a priest.

I paced up and down, twisting a paper napkin in my hands.

And I'm the one who might humiliate and dethrone her. No matter that the decision would be his. It's always the woman's fault...my fault.

Shredded napkin bits littered the carpet.

Worse still, Carter's mother would be the mother of a defrocked priest, the mother of a man who betrayed God and honor for the sake of a woman, a daughter of Eve the temptress. And people would gossip. They would murmur, 'Better never to have been called to be God's priest. Better even to have been deaf to the call than to have fallen and foresworn this service to God and the Church.'

I felt sad, certain she would hate me. She would not only see me as becoming the most important woman in Carter's life, taking a place she had always held, she would be afraid he would leave the priesthood to marry me, leaving her the widowed mother of a fallen priest, worse than a nobody. Her place in society, her honor, all lost.

The intercom buzzed.

"Hi."

"I'm here, Ann."

"Okay. Coming right out."

Nothing was going to prevent this terrifying encounter. I walked down the corridor and out of the building. Carter stood by his car holding my door open. He kissed me hurriedly, his lips barely brushing mine.

Surely no one could see such a kiss.

I climbed in.

"My father was a hardworking man who supported his family though the work of his hands," Carter began, jumping into his family's story without preliminaries as he started the engine and pointed the car away from my apartment and toward the lake.

I sat petrified next to him.

He's taking the long way around so we can talk.

"What kind of work did he do?"

"Construction and carpentry." Carter's voice was subdued.

I knew his father was dead but waited for him to tell me more about that.

Carter let silence hang in the air for a minute.

"He fell off scaffolding on my 10th birthday," he continued quietly. "I thought it was my fault. That morning as he leaving the house I called out, 'Don't be late for my party dad.' I thought maybe he went too fast and that made him fall."

"Oh, I am so sorry," was all I knew to say.

"I wasn't like him," Carter continued, pushing his voice as though he was determined to tell me things he didn't talk about and tried to forget. "Yeah...I loved books and did really well in school...but not so with hammer and nails..." Carter turned and looked at me briefly. "He told me once he didn't think I would amount to much."

"That must have felt awful...and he was so wrong."

"Yeah, he said that when I got a scholarship to a private school. He said I could go but that you can't eat books, and then he said that about not amounting to much...he never even saw me graduate from high school."

We were driving over the 27th Street bridge now to the South Side. I sat silent, my hands clutching my elbows, looking out the window down into the valley.

"Every time I won some honor in college or my doctoral program, I wondered, would he have smiled, shook my hand, been pleased? Or would he have said 'well, can you earn a living with that?'"

Carter turned toward me and took my hand, and I turned to look at him.

"Anyway, enough of that. You're going to see the house I was born and raised in. My mother and brother never moved."

"Tell me about your brother," I said brightly. "I know he's a couple of years older than you."

"Yes, George is three years older. He never married."

Another long silence followed, Carter staring intently at the road.

I had wondered about this mysterious brother for a while, and now a different sense of dread overtook me. What was Carter about to tell me?

"George was riding his big boy bike, and I had my first two wheeler. I guess he was eight and I was five. I wobbled along the sidewalk while George showed off, jumping curbs, darting into the street, riding one-handed. He looked back to see if I was okay and, suitably impressed, when all of a sudden a car came round the bend. George tried to get back on the sidewalk, but he missed the curb and fell off in the street. The car hit him. He had a lot of injuries, but the worst thing was a head injury. He was never the same. George can't hold a job. He gets really angry and out of control sometimes over small things. He couldn't finish school. I always looked up to him so much when I was little. He was showing off for me... So he lives with Mom and works in a sheltered workshop. What a family, right?"

"You've had a lot of tragedies. And your mother has had so many losses. That must put a lot on you. You make her proud. She gets to see you be so successful."

I pulled out my pack of cigarettes. It was almost new, and the cigarettes were packed tight, each one right against its neighbor. In my nervousness, I broke the first one pulling it out. I opened the window a crack and tossed out the crumbled cigarette with its torn paper and leaking tobacco. I tried again, more carefully this time, and I was successful. I took a long drag, inhaling deeply, feeling the nicotine calming me a little.

"Yep. What I do means a lot to her. And I'm glad I can bring her some happiness. When I was ordained and they wrapped my anointed hands in a cloth, and gave her that cloth, she just looked radiant. I had never seen her so happy, as though her whole hard life was worth that moment. "

I cringed. That was exactly what I had been thinking about.

"Carter?" I took a deep breath. "How is she going to feel about me? What have you told her?"

I could tell by the street signs that we were getting close to the house, and I needed to be prepared. I gazed at the trees, just beginning to bud, and the purple crocus, and breathed.

Spring is coming. Maybe that's a sign this will be okay.

I knew we couldn't put it off; we known each other for a year now.

"Don't worry. I told her you are a very special friend. She knows you were in the convent. She's not dumb, you know. She's figured it out. She'll be nice to you. She will want to please you because she wants to please me."

I wasn't so sure. The words "special friend" just made me even more anxious. But I said okay and hoped he was right.

We drove slowly through the South Side Polish neighborhood and soon reached the Italian sector. The lots seemed to all be the same postage-stamp size rimmed by a long continuous sidewalk. Walkways carved neat concrete ribbons through the precisely cut grass straight up to small neat box-like bungalows with white siding or stucco walls. Awnings shaded the front doors and some of the windows. The differing colors of the awnings were all that lent some individuality to the houses in this solid, working class ethnic neighborhood. Carter drove another six blocks, turned right, and stopped in front of a house with red awnings and cropped grass matching the precision cut of its neighbors. Only a potted yellow chrysanthemum by the door set it apart.

He had no need to knock or use his key. Before he turned off the ignition, his mother Elena ran out, apron flapping, to greet us. She took Carter's face in her hands and pulling it down to her rather diminutive level, kissed him on both cheeks. He responded with a bear hug that lifted her off her feet. As I stood watching, I noticed a thin man standing in the doorway: an observer, like myself. He looked at me briefly before fixing his eyes on Carter.

Carter put his hand on my shoulder now and smiled at his mother. "Mom, this is my friend Ann. She left her convent not long ago and is just finding her way around."

I extended my hand. "Very nice to meet you, Mrs. DeLuca."

"It's lovely to meet you too my dear. Welcome to our home. And please call me Elena. Come in, come in," and she strode energetically up the short walk to the house. "This is my other son George."

George shook my hand, his face expressionless, and stepped aside so we could all enter the living room. It was not large, and the small windows with their awnings didn't let in a lot of sunlight, but the walls were decorated with colorful prints depicting Italian villages and a photo of the Pope waving from his balcony. There were two armchairs with a table between them upon which stood a single framed photo of a dark haired, muscular man whom I assumed must be Carter's father. A card table covered with a bright red cloth and set for lunch filled up the remainder for the room.

"Please, have a seat you two," Elena said brightly, gesturing to the chairs around the table. "George, dear, help me carry in the food. I hope you like lasagna. Ann. I made it myself, of course."

She bustled into the kitchen, returning with a large, aromatic dish. George brought salad and bread, and I noticed he walked with a limp.

"Oh, I love lasagna, Elena. I hope you didn't go to too much trouble though."

Carter said grace, and Elena served us generous helpings. The conversation was easy and lively. Carter shared stories from his work, not the frustrating events, of course, just the successes. He asked George about how things were going at the sheltered workshop where George and others with disabilities worked under supervision. George replied that his boss was still a jerk but he had a new friend there. A girl, he said. Elena shot an anxious look at Carter, but he gripped his brother's shoulder, one man to another.

"Good for you, George. What's her name?"

They chatted for a few minutes, just the two of them, Carter getting all the details about the young woman.

As they talked, Elena directed her attention to me, asking how things were going. I told her about my work at the church and about my good fortune in getting an apartment right away. Elena nodded appreciatively as I spoke, only interrupting to ask everyone whether they wanted seconds. When we all declined while exclaiming how good it was, she got up to get dessert.

After the ice cream, Carter excused himself, asking George to show him his latest woodworking project. Elena took this opportunity to turn toward me, her face suddenly serious. She leaned forward slightly.

Here comes the confrontation.

I sat up straight and braced myself.

"You do know Carter has had other friends, don't you, dear?"

What?

Determined not to betray my astonishment, I kept my face expressionless and said nothing.

Elena had paused, watching me, but now she continued. "Women, I mean? It never lasts too long though." She paused again, waiting in vain for a reaction. Giving up, she leaned back. "His work means so much to him."

She might as well have thrown the remaining lasagna in my face. Everything inside my body pulled into a tight knot, but I was well practiced from convent years in not showing my feelings, and the outside of my body remained still.

Ignoring the comment about women, I replied, "Yes, he is so brilliant and such a great leader. The difference he is making for priests and people in the church is amazing. He cares so much about his work and the opportunities he has to help people."

When I mentioned one of his latest projects—instituting a course for priests on race relations and assumptions white priests make—Elena picked up my enthusiasm, and we had quite a long and amicable conversation.

About 20 minutes later, Carter reappeared with George and two carvings.

"You have to see the kind of work George does, Ann," Carter said, grinning. "Isn't it incredible?" He turned to George, who held up a lion and an elephant, both beautifully made with marvelous detail. "I couldn't carve like this in a million years." His arm was around George's shoulders, and George's face was one huge smile.

"Oh, that is amazing," I answered. "May I hold them George? I want to look at the detail."

George nodded enthusiastically, and I examined each animal slowly, commenting on every aspect of the truly wonderful craftsmanship.

After watching me for a minute and seeing George's relaxed demeanor, Carter walked into the kitchen, returning with cups and a coffee pot.

"Who wants coffee?"

We all did.

"George. Will you help me?"

George passed out cups and went to the kitchen for cream and sugar while Carter poured.

I turned to Elena. "You must be so proud of George's work, Elena. He's really talented." Then I returned the animals to their creator with a "thank you" for sharing them.

We stayed for another half hour, drinking our coffee until it was time to leave. There were hugs all around, and the door under the awning closed behind us. I knew Elena was watching us as we walked to the car, Carter opened the door for me and then went over to the driver's side, and we started off.

"Well, what do you think?" he asked.

"Your mother was really gracious and kind toward me, just as you said she would be. And George, he is so gifted. I wonder what he might have done if he hadn't had the head injury."

Carter was silent for a moment before speaking. "I always thought it was my fault when we were kids. Just like with my Dad. It wasn't, of course. But kids think like that... Life has been hard for George. Mom worries so much about what will happen after she dies."

He turned onto the expressway and seemed deep in thought for a moment.

"When I was ordained, they knew I would always need to take care of my brother. I wouldn't have gone ahead with it otherwise."

Carter was a brilliant and complicated man, more complicated than I had realized.

Who is he really?

After today I wasn't sure I knew. Lost in thought, I was quiet for most of the trip back to my apartment.

"*Ecce homo.* Behold the man," Pilate said, presenting Jesus, wearing a purple robe with a crown of thorns on his head. Pilate wondered who Jesus was.

"Who was this man Jesus?" so many ask to this day. The prophet Isaiah spoke of the "man of sorrows, and acquainted with grief." Who was he?

I thought about Carter losing his father at such a tender age. I was moved by the love he had for his injured brother, about Carter's gentleness and his quiet, sweet voice when he spoke with George, about the way he built his brother up, showcasing his abilities. I loved Carter so much more for that and reached over to stroke his leg.

I was devastated by the heavy burden of guilt Carter carried, feeling responsible for George's injuring, and then later for his father's death. I had not known these things before. And I was sure he bore these crushing thoughts all alone.

And now this man, who wears the collar of a servant of God, lives another secret. Does he bear a new burden of guilt because he loves me?

And then Elena's comment that there had been several other women in his life played over and over in my mind. I wondered if that were true and what he would say if I asked him about it. But that day I kept her words to myself and preferred to think Elena just wanted to push me away from Carter.

I know this man, know him better after today, seeing him with his mother and brother in the house where he grew up.

Ecce homo. Behold the man.

Yet, who is this man? `

When we arrived back at my apartment, Carter pulled up in front of the entrance, turning the engine off but leaving the key in the ignition.

"Thank you for coming with me today," he said, turning toward me and putting his arm around my shoulder. "I thought Mother liked you and things went well. Did you?"

"She was very kind," I answered, not really knowing what else to say.

Carter stepped out of the car and came around to my side to open the door. I squeezed his hand.

"I really can't stay. Have a meeting downtown," was all he said.

I wanted to kiss him—a deep, healing kiss—but didn't dare there on the street.

"I understand," I responded, and watched him get back into his car and turn on the ignition. He looked round at me one last time, his eyes fixed on mine for a long moment before he put the car in gear, waved goodbye, and drove away.

Alone on the sidewalk, I waved as he disappeared into the distance.

Down Low

"Duck down!" Carter's words broke through our easy chatter.

"What? What's going on?"

"Duck down! Quick! My boss is behind us." Carter gripped the wheel hard, his eyes fixed on the car's rearview mirror.

I shot down toward the floor of the car; no seat belt in 1969 to slow my dive. I was squeezed tight between the front seat and the dashboard, my knees bent up against my chest where my heart emitted an audible, rapid staccato rhythm. My feet were all twisted in different directions, having no real room of their own.

It was hot on the floor, and I was scared when the car swerved to the right, Carter yelling, "Damn truck."

My arms wrapped around my legs, but I managed to stick my right hand up into the tiny space between my head and the dash in an effort to protect my head. I was wearing a sleeveless blouse and shorts and had nothing to provide any cushioning.

"I saw my boss's car in the rearview mirror as we headed down the hill," Carter went on, having successfully avoided whatever the truck dropped onto the road. "He's just two cars behind now."

I could feel the tension radiating from his body. My own body began to hurt, all the way from my hand jammed against the dash to my feet, which were now starting to cramp. I stared down at an old dead cigarette butt and some gum wrappers strewn on the floor, which they had probably fallen out of the overstuffed ashtray weeks before.

We were returning from a weekend in Chicago, feeling safe and free until that moment. For months after the carefree freedom of our first real date, we had been chronically hyper-alert - scanning the crowd for a familiar face, wondering who might see us without our seeing them, closing blinds strategically. Carter had kissed me once outside my apartment building, but we both knew better than to risk such spontaneity again where we might be recognized.

But in Chicago we had been out of town and feeling liberated. We went to a movie, shared a hotel room, briefly held hands, and even kissed once walking down the street. But that sense of safety was now a distant memory.

"He's in the fast lane now. I'm going to let him pass us. Better to have him go ahead. Stay really low."

"I'm down as low as I can get," I tried to assure him, my voice muffled by my folded up body.

Carter slowed down just a bit, and for the next minute, I just waited. I had bent over as far as I could, but the bench seat left little room for even a small person like me. The floor was dirty; I was glad I had changed out of my good clothes for the drive. But I'm allergic to dust, and the sinus headache started across my forehead

"Oh, wow." Carter let out a sigh, his body loosened so that his leg grazed my arm. He laid his hand on my head gently. "You can get up. He just passed us. I'm pretty sure he didn't see you."

I began slowly uncurling myself. There was hardly any room to do it, and my foot had gone to sleep. I put both hands on the seat behind me and slid up till I was sitting on it again.

"That was scary. How do you know he didn't see me?"

"He waved as he flew by, speeding as he always does."

"Did you wave back?"

"No, I pretended not to see him. Didn't want him to figure out I'd been watching."

"We were been fools to believe ourselves safe," I said as Carter pulled off at the next exit to let his boss get far enough ahead so we didn't risk a second encounter.

"How can you be sure he didn't see me, Carter?" I persisted, stretching out my legs. "Or notice something funny? And driving west on the Dan Ryan, there was no doubt about the fact that you were returning from Chicago. Did you say anything about what you were doing this weekend?"

"Just something about some meetings. I didn't say what or where."

And it's only around noon. Who drives a hundred miles to a meeting or something and is on the way back by noon? If he suspects I'm in the car, he will know we were in Chicago overnight. I wouldn't have any reasons to be going to meetings with Carter. He will know...

I was definitely frightened, but was I also angry? My emotions were so shut down, so locked away with our secret, that I didn't let myself feel angry. And angry with whom? Carter?

"Stand By Your Man" was a hit song. I loved it, especially that line about loving him despite his hurtful behavior. I found it noble. And when we made love, which had finally happened in Chicago despite his terror of pregnancy, a lot of the pleasure came from the awareness of giving myself totally, even heroically, to Carter, in bed and out, belonging completely to him.

This Third Way is hard, but I love him that much.

And Carter? Did he love me that much, belong to me completely? Was he heroic?

Look at all the risks he takes to be with me. He could have a position in Rome one day, if he could find some way to take George with him. Everyone thinks so much of him they gave him all these responsibilities even though he's only a couple of years older than I am. He's so smart. And really creative and innovative. And it's time for more American leadership! But that will never happen if there is a scandal about us. He risks that...for me.

I had ducked down in the car instinctively, not questioning it as I hit the floor, not questioning it afterward. In addition to being partner, colleague, and inspiration, I was Carter's protector.

I was slowly giving up hope that Carter would leave the priesthood. Whenever we discussed the topic, he said the same thing: "It's my call. It's where God wants me." How could I argue with that? It was so believable that he belonged in the priesthood. He loved it and was so good at it, not just very capable, but innovative. And if God was behind that? Well, how could I dispute it?

It all seemed worth it as we worked together. The Molessons, the family that had asked him about doing services in their home, had followed through. They had a home church; three or four couples with grown children met once a month, shared at an intimate level about their spiritual lives, their struggles and questions, and had Mass. I always went with Carter. We were an acknowledged pair at the home church. That didn't seem strange to people, because we were ministering together. We were colleagues. I doubt that anything else occurred to them, but if it did, they didn't care. They were progressive post-Vatican II Catholics. Novelty was the norm for some Catholics in 1969.

Together we developed creative liturgies. Gathering in the Molesson's living room, Carter gave no sermon during those Masses. Instead we all talked about racial injustice and the Civil Rights Movement, about the war, the draft, the dying, about what we could do and should do. I played the guitar, and we sang folks songs, protest songs that cried out for peace and justice like "If I Had a Hammer" or "Where Have All the Flowers Gone?" Like many, we had a lot to protest.

We opposed the Vietnam War, horrified by the images of women and children fleeing burning villages, American bodies thrown in the air by landmines. We saw napalm, gasoline in jelly-like form, dropped by bombers, burning and stuck to human skin. For the first time, we participated in the horrors of war through the bombardment of sickening pictures brought by television into our living rooms on a daily basis.

We opposed the draft, which forced young American men into battles that destroyed their bodies and their souls.

"The rich buy their way out of the draft, going to college and getting student deferments," Vicky Molesson said angrily. "Yeah, it's mostly poor kids from small communities that get into this war. They're manipulated and pumped up to believe they'll be heroes."

"And they can't go to college or run to Canada," her husband, Walt, added.

"You're right," their neighbor, Jim Goodwin, joined in. "People with money and connections have lots of ways of getting out of the draft. I agree. It's mostly poor kids who go to Vietnam. And a lot of them come home in coffins."

"I've seen some who come home alive. They're a mess," said Goodwin's sister, Helen, a psychologist with the VA. "Nightmares. Sometimes they pull a gun on their wives in their sleep because they think they're getting attacked. It's horrible. We don't know much about how to help them either."

"I think it's disgusting the way some people treat them," the Molesson's teenage son, Pete, piped up. "Yelling at them, calling them names. They weren't the ones who started this war."

We nodded in agreement, and the group grew very quiet. I struck up another song. This time it was "Eve of Destruction," an angry song about the state of the world and the fate of young men old enough to slaughter but, at that time, not old enough to vote.

We supported the Civil Rights Movement, which was in full swing. Again, we desperately wanted answers, hope in the face of the seemingly endless struggle for racial justice. So many hopes had been dashed. Heroic leaders had been slain, giving rise to more anger and despair. We sang "Why Do the Good Die Young" and wept.

"We were always taught to pray, so I pray for everyone to be treated fairly, but I'm not sure anymore what prayer accomplishes. Does anyone else wonder about that? What about you, Carter?" someone asked.

"I wonder about that a lot," I chimed in.

"Still, prayer is important. It opens our hearts to God. And then we have to *act*," Carter urged. "The Kennedy boys are gone. Martin Luther King has been killed too. What they stood for matters! Every one of us has to do the job now. It's up to us. No leader to do it for us anymore, and God's not going to do it without us."

That night became an expression of our deep, shared grieving. We grieved over the war, the killing of our President, the brutalities of Bloody Sunday. We were bound together by the common experience of witnessing horrors just minutes after, or even at the very moment they occurred, by the immediacy of it all. What we shared was trauma.

We stood in a circle holding hands, a few candles burning around the room making the light soft. I asked the Molessons if they had some bells. They did and went to get them.

"Let's sing 'Why Do the Good Die Young' one more time," I requested. "Then I want to read the names."

Carter looked at me, nodding his agreement. With the bells at my feet and everyone in a circle, we sang, and then I lifted the first bell, ready to ring it each time I cried out a name, adding how death came to them.

The first bell was small, light, high pitched, like a vibrating school bell calling pupils to class. I rang the bell.

"Four little girls..."

Rrring...

"Addie Mae Collins,"

Rrring...

"Denise McNair,"

Rrring...

"Carole Robertson,"

Rrring...

"Cynthia Wesley. Killed by the bombing of their church, September 1963, Birmingham,

Alabama."

A much larger bell followed, sturdy and bold.

"Medgar Evers, shot in his home June 12, 1963, Jackson, Mississippi."

Two huge bells crescendoed to a roar.

"President John F. Kennedy, his blood on his wife's body in a limousine on a Dallas street. November 22, 1963. Three days later, Little John salutes his father's casket."

Several bells, like church bells, rang resonant, voluminous, rolling, interlocking deep and rich.

"Martin Luther King, the giant Dreamer, whose blood anointed a balcony in Memphis, April 1968."

A lone bell made a brave start. Abruptly silenced.

"Bobbie Kennedy, June 1968, California victory in hand, proclaiming an end to division to a cheering crowd in L.A."

I handed everyone a bell and nodded. They knew what to do, and all the bells began to ring at once: tiny bells, huge, glass, brass, singing high, singing low. Multiplicity of tones. On and on...

Then I cried out, "For all the others. They just keep killing them. And yet hope is not extinguished. The Spirit is not buried with the bodies."

I picked up the Bible, found the passage I wanted, and handed the book to Carter to read.

> I looked, and there was a great multitude that no one could count,
> from every nation, from all tribes and peoples and languages, standing before the throne...
> Then one of the elders...said to me,
> 'These are they who have come out of the great ordeal;
> ...and the one who is seated on the throne will shelter them.
> They will hunger no more, and thirst no more;
> the sun will not strike them, nor any scorching heat;
> for the Lamb at the center of the throne will be their shepherd,
> and he will guide them to springs of the water of life,

and God will wipe away every tear from their eyes.'
(Revelation 7:13-17)

We ended the service with Communion as we always did. Our regular final song became "Blowin' in the Wind," a mournful cry of longing for answers.

"We are not alone," I began. "There are millions of us. We want peace and justice and something better for everybody's children..."

Not being alone was what Communion was all about. After our passionate discussions, we always ended with this meal we shared with one another and with millions past and present, the meal celebrating our togetherness with the Prince of Peace.

Carter held up the loaf of bread, blessed it, broke it in two, repeating the words from Jesus' last meal with his friends. "This is my body which is broken for you."

I took one half, and he took the other, and we passed it round the circle, each person tearing off a piece of bread and holding it.

When we had all taken some, Carter said, "Take and eat, all of you. And remember me." And together we ate.

I lifted up a cup filled with red wine. I said the "Baruch" in Hebrew and then English, the Jewish blessing Jesus prayed. "Blessed art thou O God, maker of heaven and earth. You bring forth fruit from the vine." Then I continued with what Jesus added at the Last Supper with his friends. "This is the cup of the new covenant in my blood, pour out for the healing of all. Take and drink, all of you, and remember me." I passed the cup to the person next to me, who passed it to the next and to the next until we had all drunk from the one cup.

Carter and I were worshipping God and feeding the people together. We were priests together.

One by one, we sat down quietly, some in our chairs; others cross legged on the carpet. I lay down on the floor, looking up at the ceiling, at peace. Hope had in fact not died for us. It was truly a "best of times and a worst of times." The passionate belief that things could be better did not die with Kennedy or King. And so we stood, not only horrified and mourning, but also full of hope. The world was waking up. Together we could create something new! And the church would be part of it.

As I lay there, out of the corner of my eye I saw Walt Molesson get up and go to the bookcase. He pulled a thin paperback off the shelf. It was a letter to the church from popular and revolutionary Pope John XXIII, the Pontiff who convened Vatican II. Walt read the end of his message *Pacem in Terris* (Peace on Earth). It was a prayer, a plea, a cry of hope.

> Finally, may Christ inflame the desires of all men to break through the barriers which divide them, to strengthen the bonds of mutual love, to learn to understand one another, and to pardon those who have done them wrong. Through His power and inspiration may all peoples welcome each other to their hearts as brothers, and may the peace they long for ever flower and ever reign among them.

At that moment, I had peace. I knew I was called to say the words over the bread and wine, that same bread and wine about which I said, "I want that" when the Presence enveloped me back in 1956. I knew I was called to make room for people like Walt to step out, to speak out.

I could neither be ordained a priest in the '60s, nor a minister in virtually any denomination. I did not have the right body. I was a woman.

But here, with Carter, I could participate fully. I could share his priesthood. To the families present, it was simply one more creative and free thing we did during liturgy, right here in the Molesson's living room. To me it was everything, and it made the relationship Carter and I shared meaningful in so many different ways.

Still, my peace was disturbed by the secret that plagued me. Every time Carter and I went to the Molessons, we carried our secret with us. That secret belied the sense of openness, of community that was the very foundation of our times together. I felt like a fraud, keeping hidden the most important parts of who I was: priest and lover of a priest. And I kept Carter's secret as well. I felt we were deceiving the Molessons and the Goodwins and everyone else who came to the home church.

I openly expressed my love of oppressed people but not my forbidden love of a man. In the midst of all our spirit of community, I lived a lie. I broke bread with them and deceived them.

And my deceptive ways extended beyond the walls of that living room. I had friends like the Welby family whose table I shared every Tuesday evening. I was part of the family. I broke bread with them too, saw their children grow, heard their joy and worries, prayed with them. But they did not know Carter existed. They might possibly have seen him celebrating Mass somewhere, but they had no idea he was in my life, let alone in my bed.

The same was true for Jane and Cathy who taught school together and shared an apartment near my own. For more than a year, we had been good friends. We shared a momentous moment together. Sitting together on their huge broken-down couch, our eyes glued to their small black-and-white TV, we watched as history was made. We saw Apollo 11 land on the moon on July 20 that year of 1969. The following day, we saw Neil Armstrong open the hatch of the spaceship and climb down onto the moon's surface with the famous words "That's one small step for man, one giant leap for mankind."

But of course, they didn't know about my lover either. That secret made me a liar. And one lie leads to another and another. It becomes hard to keep them straight.

"What did you do last night?" someone would ask.

"Oh, I just stayed home and watched TV."

Actually I was with Carter.

"What about dating? Time to get back in the action, isn't it?"

"Yes, I guess. Actually there's a volunteer teacher at the parish who asked me out. I made an excuse the first time, but I think I'll say 'yes' the next time he asks."

But of course I wouldn't, since there was no such volunteer.

All the little lies lay like litter on my friendships. I kept my lie going day after day for years. It wasn't as simple as keeping quiet about telling a white lie or saying something really hurtful to a co-worker. This was about deceiving people I loved and who loved me, deceiving them day after day about something so important that I was not the person they thought they knew. We all loved each other; that's true. But there was a very large gulf between us, and they didn't know it.

The shameful truth is that I believed myself to be involved in a love affair that was very special, that the sacrifices were worth it, that I was being heroic. I was excited and exhilarated, but at what cost? My relationship with Carter turned me into a fraud.

I was flying all right, and it was heady. But I was flying down low, close to the ground, hidden, secret, a phony. My body was crushed and hurting, and the air I breathed was full of dust. I was perpetually that woman on the Dan Ryan Expressway, cramped and collapsed on the floorboard of the car. Afraid.

An Idea in the Shower

The inspiration came to me from out of nowhere one morning in the shower.

Carter and I had been together for almost two years now. We loved each other and did so many wonderful things. A tiny flame of hope that he would leave the priesthood still flickered off and on in my heart, but I was increasingly convinced he would never change his mind. And there was a part of me that didn't want him to. Who would he be if he left? Who would I be? What we had now was big. Our sacrifice was big; our love had to be big.

"You're part of everything I do. And I couldn't do it, couldn't *be who I am*, without you," he said over and over.

Did I really want to give that up? Not really.

The fact was I didn't have a choice. The truth was I didn't want to be ordinary. I had longed to be a hero, ever since I read that children's book *The Secret Garden* and saw Ingrid Bergman playing the British missionary Gladys May Aylward lead a hundred Chinese children to safety over mountainous enemy territory in *The Inn of the Sixth Happiness*. I didn't see myself as a hero, but this unconscious desire was part of my willingness to live a life of sacrifice, to love God and Carter enough for such a life.

My idea would seal such a love. And it would not be ordinary.

When Carter came over that night, I flung the door open excitedly. He jumped back a little in surprise, knowing something was up.

"Well, you look as if you're feeling good," he said.

"I am. Come in. I'll tell you all about it." I closed the door. "Oh! And how was your day?"

"Not so great," Carter replied, running his through his hair.

"What happened? Sorry, I was just thinking about this idea I had in the shower this morning. You know that's where I have my best ideas. But sit down. Let's have a drink."

Carter flopped down on the couch and took off one of his shoes with a grimace. I got out some glasses, wrestled with the ice cube tray, capturing rebellious icy chunks that flew across the room and corralling others into our glasses, which I carried into the living room along with a bottle of Scotch.

"So what happened?" I asked, pouring the amber liquid into the glasses and picking up my pack of cigarettes.

"You remember Joe?"

"Yes," I mumbled, cigarette clenched in my lips as I struck a match to light it. "I remember Joe."

"Remember how he wanted to teach in the public school in the city, not the Catholic school? Said the kids there needed him more?"

"Sure. And you gave him the okay to do that and then stood up for him when there was a lot of criticism from Catholic school parents. Sure, I remember." I handed him his glass, deeply inhaling the first cigarette of the evening. "What's the problem?"

"Well, there's a big problem," Carter responded. Instead of sipping his Scotch, he took a gulp. "Joe called me from jail this morning. Seems there was a fight at the school, and the police came. He was on top of a kid with his knee in the kid's back. The cops pulled him off and then they searched him. They found pot in his pocket."

"Why did they search him? He was trying to stop the fight, right?"

"I don't know. Doesn't matter. They did. And they found the pot. Now they think he was going to sell to kids. It's a mess. They arrested him, of course. I went over to see him. He looks terrible. Says he took the pot away from one of the kids. They were fighting over it, he says. I don't know. I don't even know whether to believe him."

Carter bent over his drink on the coffee table, clenching and unclenching his hands.

"That's awful," I said softly, starting to rub his back. "What are you going to do? How public is it?"

"I got him a lawyer, of course, a good one. Don't think it's hit the news, but it no doubt will. Then I'll catch hell, too, from other priests and from parents. They all want every good Catholic priest to live in a clean little bubble, safe from all harm, and especially not out where anyone will hear about it if they mess up. What a stupid fantasy!" Carter got up and walked into the kitchen, opening the refrigerator door and staring at its contents.

"There's some cheese and chicken if you want. And some salad."

"Thanks. And so, how was your day?"

"Wait," I said, getting up, taking a step toward the kitchen and looking at him, hands up for emphasis. "Didn't you sign up for this? Breaking the stupid bubble fantasy?"

Carter kept rummaging around in the refrigerator.

"Joe messed up. The priests and parents won't get it. Who knows what your boss will say...you didn't mention that. Sounds a lot like Jesus' experience to me, Carter. His closest friends like Peter didn't get it, messed up, said and did stupid things. The authorities were afraid of him. He was a threat to the status quo, the power of the Romans, and the jobs of the temple priests, and they were out to get him..." I reached up to open a cupboard door. "The cheese is in here if that's what you're looking for."

"You're right. I guess this is part of the picture. Of course, it wouldn't happen if I just played it safe, but I couldn't stomach that. Tomorrow I have to go to Joe's arraignment, take him home when he gets bailed out, deal with a bunch of phone calls,– all that stuff. I'm hungry. Didn't have any dinner before coming over."

He took out a loaf of bread and the hunk of cheese, stuck them on a plate, and flopped down to the couch again.

"But you're right, Ann. It's part of my call. I really wouldn't want a different one, so I'll do my best to be grateful to God for the whole picture and think about the guys who are doing well too…I don't know…"

He ran his hand through his hair again, and sat up straighter, leaning back against the cushion.

"So tell me about your day?"

I brought some crackers and fruit over from the kitchen. My day had been pretty boring, except for my idea, of course. Carter didn't seem in a good frame of mind to hear about that, but it just burst out without my permission.

"Well, I had an idea this morning." I looked at Carter, who sat slumped over, looking down at the floor.

"Oh? Will it cheer me up?" he asked, raising his eyes to meet mine.

"Maybe. I was thinking about how long we've been together. It's almost two years."

"Yes?" Carter said, drawing out the word and looking a bit apprehensive.

"Well, it's been so good and…well, I think it's time we made a commitment. I think we should get married."

As the words rushed out, Carter sat up straight, looking startled and not happy.

"But you know…I've told you…I told you from the beginning I cannot leave the priesthood. There would be nothing left of me." His voice was firm, and he sounded annoyed.

"I know, I know," I interrupted. "You wouldn't have to."

"I don't know what you are saying."

"Well, two people marry each other, right?"

"Right. That's how the sacrament works."

"And the priest, or judge or whoever is just the witness, right?"

"Yes, the witness for the community."

"So we can just marry each other. We don't need a priest or anyone else, just ourselves." I was looking right into his eyes to his very soul. "Will you do it?"

"Well...I don't know. I never thought about it." He pulled a cigarette out of the pack in his pocket and lit it. "When you have ideas," he laughed, "you're dangerous!"

"Well, think about it then."

We talked for a long time. Carter took my hand, and seemed to have forgotten about his wayward priest. I leaned my head on his shoulder, and we grew silent, cuddling there on the couch, kissing. Carter wanted to know if this was really important to me, and I said it was. Carter took two crackers and put a lot of cheese between them. He took some time eating, and then he bent over and slowly picked up cracker crumbs that had fallen on the rug. Then he walked over to the kitchen area and washed his hands.

"Okay," he said smiling, standing there drying his hands.

I jumped up from the couch, ran over, and kissed him. "Do you want to?" I asked, pulled away just enough to see his expression.

"Yes. It's a good thing. We already are committed. Let's make it official, for the two of us, of course. Want to splurge and get a room at the Pfister?"

The Pfister, the best hotel in Milwaukee, sounded like a great idea to me. We talked for about another hour, deciding to write our own vows. I offered to buy the rings. Carter said he would split the cost, and of course, he would have to wear his on a chain round his neck. Naturally I agreed. That made sense. It was something I hadn't considered, and I was disappointed. He couldn't go around wearing a wedding ring, but hiding our marriage felt sad. I didn't say anything though. We quickly agreed that the following Friday seemed like a good day.

"Let's do it," Carter said. And then, looking at his watch, he added, "It's after midnight. I've got a 6:30 Mass in the morning...and the Joe mess."

"And I have to go to work too," I said.

Carter kissed me, then put his shoe back on — he had been hobbling with one shoe off and one on all evening. Again he winced — "got a lousy blister," he explained. Then, with one more peck, he was out the door. I locked it and attached the chain.

I wasn't ready to sleep even though it was late and just putzed around cleaning up crumbs of crackers and bread, fruit, cheese. I washed the glasses and put the bottle of Scotch back in the cupboard. I opened the curtains and stood for a long time looking out at the garden, where patches of snow dotting the bushes and grass could be seen in the moonlight. A train whistled somewhere in the distance. Some people coming home from a late party walked past my door laughing, their voices fading up and out.

Finally I undressed, put on my pajamas, brushed my teeth, and washed my face, thanking God for how the evening had turned out. I checked my calendar for the next day—nothing until a meeting with the parish priests at 10—that was lucky, and I climbed into bed with a novel. It was at least a half hour before the adrenalin had left my body enough for me to turn out the light and dream dreams of Carter and years together.

Ring

Drums began; light, steady pulsings in the sun-drenched market place.

Flying Bird gathering friends and strangers, grandmothers, a tiny boy, a reluctant teenager.

Deep River joining, smiling, hand in Flying Bird's, who held grandmother's, who reached for tiny boy's, who drew in reluctant teenage sister.

Came then the flute, sounding a laughing melody, and Flying Bird began to lead them all in dance.

Men joined, fumbled, gained lighter feet as flute went fast, faster, faster.

Round and round in a circle dance, a ring dance.

Now everyone flying with many flutes and a violin and drum beat racing into one long, stretched sound.

Young man lifted tiny boy onto his shoulders.

Strong men put arms round grandmother's waist, lest her feet go amiss.

All flying with the Bird. All safe.

Finally the music slower, slower, men careful to keep grandmother standing, and she in turn loosed her long hair.

Circle coiling tight round itself 'til all together, one embrace...

Only then did the music stop.

Wedding the Priest

"Oh, you're getting married," the sales clerk giggled, taking the rings.

Boston Store had served me well before, and it did again. I was buying two gold rings and one gold chain.

"And I see you're letting him know it's a serious ball and chain thing." She pretended to wrap the chain round her wrist and pull on it.

Getting married. Just the two of us. No judge, other clergy, party, no leaving the priesthood. It would not be legal, according to the State of Wisconsin. But it was sacred. It was sacrament. It was what we needed.

"Did you see the lingerie we've got on sale over there?" She pointed across the store, adding, "It'll really turn him on."

She gave me a wink while I pretended to fumble for my purse.

The rings were similar to but not like other people's wedding rings. Gold, yes. But an abstract, geometric design rendered their significance ambiguous. And they were not too expensive. I would wear my ring on my right hand, of course, so *I* would know it was my *wedding* ring, but this meaning would be hidden from others. Carter would hide his on a chain round his neck.

The following Friday, we were at the Pfister in a room both extravagant and over-budget, but we splurged for the sake of festivity, luxury, and gourmet room service. It was a fairly large room with plenty of space to walk around the antique furniture. There were wide windows with heavy brocade drapes, two comfortable armchairs and a king-sized bed covered with a wedding pattern quilt.

We set a loaf of crusty bread, wine, a blue pottery communion plate and cup, and a vase with freshly cut red roses on the mahogany desk— our altar. I loved that it was not formal, not churchy, and definitely not stuffy. We had written our own vows, making them somewhat original but mainly sticking to the traditional ones to emphasize this was a real wedding. We laid the papers next to the bread and wine on our altar, alongside the rings.

A bottle of champagne sat in a bucket of ice on the night table with a fresh, unopened pack of cigarettes and bright red lighter. I searched the FM stations on the hotel radio until I found a classical station playing soft baroque string quartets.

Carter and I put on our best clothes. For him, this meant gray slacks, a nice sports jacket, and a blue dress shirt and tie instead of the open necked sports shirt he wore often or the collar he donned when so obligated. I wore an ankle length hippy-style dress in my favorite colors of purple, red, and blue. A new pair of red sandals with ankle straps and Navajo beading were on my feet. There was no veil on my head since I'd had enough of those.

We were ready. We faced each other, holding hands and grinning. It was time.

"I, Ann, take you Carter, to be my wedded husband. I make my promise to God and to you. I promise to love you, to cherish you, to honor you and be faithful to you. I commit to serving God and people with you, respecting the dignity of all persons, standing with those in pain, speaking for those whose voices go unheard, defending the weak. Carter, I give you this ring, a sign of my heart's pledge. It will remind you every day how much I love you."

I slipped the ring on his hand, and we stood for a solemn moment, gazing into one another's eyes.

"I, Carter, standing in the presence of God, take you Ann, to be my wedded wife. I promise to love you, to cherish you, to honor you and be faithful to you. I commit to sharing my priesthood with you, bringing good news to all people, setting people free. Ann, I give you this ring as a sign of my promise to you and a daily reminder of my love for you."

He put the ring on my left hand, and we hugged tightly, laughing, and then cried out with loud voices, "We now pronounce us husband and wife."

Afterward we toasted ourselves with champagne and made love for a long time. Every other day he was so scared to have sex. He kept telling me about all the distraught priests he had counseled and all the angry women who bore their children and received support payments but no husband.

That night, though, was different from all the other nights. That night Carter seemed to forget all about being anxious. He seemed to abandon himself to our pleasure and intimacy, to luxuriate in it. And I did the same.

When we had worn one another out from sex, we smoked a cigarette or two and toasted ourselves with some good, expensive Scotch we had bought for the occasion. Laughing and rolling around in bed, we ordered expensive room service, splurging on delicious shrimp, lobster, asparagus, wine, and French pastry. We both loved seafood, especially lobster, but normally neither of us ordered it because of the price. That night, however, was different from all others. We didn't even inquire what market price meant that night. We just ordered whole lobsters with everything we could want to go with them.

We spent the whole night curled up together. Sometimes I was asleep and other times I awoke and just lay there, my arms over Carter's chest, watching his quiet breathing. Once I woke him stroking his face and hair. We smiled at each other, made love one more time, and fell back asleep in each other's arms.

Everything was perfect that night, and it somehow felt as if it would never end because I was his and he was mine. Our hearts and our bodies were one.

We woke lazily in the morning and at the same time. Light was streaming into the room. Church bells were tolling gaily in the distance. To me, they sounded celebratory that Sunday. We made love again until a knock on the door informed us that the incredible breakfast ordered the night before had arrived.

I was happy. Carter seemed happy too. God seemed to bless us and pronounce, "It is very good."

Carter carried the huge tray to the bed, and we uncovered all the dishes: eggs, sausage, strawberries with whipped cream, paper thin French pancakes, bagels with cream cheese, coffee cake, all accompanied by a large pot of steaming, fragrant coffee.

We ate ravenously on that first morning of our new life.

Invasions, Robberies, Killings

It was the spring of 1970, and as the war in Vietnam escalated, so did the protests. On April 30, President Richard Nixon announced the invasion of Cambodia by American and South Vietnamese troops. Across the nation, men and women marched and rallied in opposition. Students everywhere held anti-war demonstrations and called for national strikes. College campuses were electric. Violence broke out.

At Kent State University in Ohio, 500 students demonstrated on May 1. The following day, officials made the decision to call in the National Guard. On Sunday, May 3, Governor Rhodes held a press conference, pounding his fist on his desk, calling the young protestors "un-American." Thousands of leaflets were distributed in an attempt to cancel further activities.

Nevertheless on May 4, 2000, students gathered to demonstrate against the war. Others stood in the background watching or walked along nearby paths. National Guardsmen began lobbing tear gas at the protestors in an attempt to disperse them.

And then Americans watched with horror as National Guardsmen opened fire: 67 rounds of ammunition. Four students were killed and nine wounded. Two of the dead students were participating in the protest. The other two were simply walking to their next class.

It was another watershed moment. How could this happen? Our country killing its own young? We were overwhelmed with grief and anger and took to the streets. I was among those weeping and marching, mourning and protesting the "Kent State Massacre."

The world seemed to be turning faster and becoming more and more violent.

One unusually warm night in late May, I returned exhausted from a protest march and fell into my small but comfortable twin bed in my beloved little studio apartment. My place of peace had been serving me well for almost two years now and still seemed wonderful to me. Since it was an unusually warm night for May, I left the window open and fell asleep to the song of a mockingbird in the apartment's serene little interior courtyard.

About 2:30 a.m., an unfamiliar sound broke through my dreams, and I sat straight up in bed, my eyes fixed on the window a few feet to my right. In the moonlight, I could see that the screen was gone. There, coming through the window, were a man's head and shoulders! I screamed.

The head and shoulders disappeared. Sounds of feet pounding the ground followed. Was he gone? Leaping out of bed to slam the window shut, I saw the cord of my television set trailing outside onto the ground and the screen on the patio lawn leaning against the building. A vase holding a single flower and a photo that had been on the window sill were outside on the ground too.

This was real. Someone had broken into the place that I thought was mine *while I was sleeping.* He had run away when I screamed and was now nowhere in sight. I quickly grabbed the vase and photo, yanked the cord in, and then shut and locked the window, leaving the screen outside. The intruder was gone, but his presence filled my small space, making it dirty, frightening. My belongings were all there, but what had once been my precious sanctuary was no longer beautiful and no longer mine. He had not managed to steal anything except a piece of my soul.

I called the police. Calling Carter didn't seem possible in the middle of the night; he didn't have a private phone in the priests' residence. An emergency call from a woman at that hour would raise questions. So I replenished the water that had spilled out of the vase with the flower, and then just sat on my bed, shivering in the heat, feeling very alone for about a half hour until two white officers showed up at my door.

One was short and very overweight with close cropped hair. The other was nondescript, average build and coloring, except for his hands, which I noticed were unusually small. On television the cops dust for fingerprints and things like that in these circumstances. But all that the tall one and the short one did was wander around my little room, picking things up, turning them over, commenting on them, and putting them down again.

The short one stood with the vase in his hands, tapping on it with his fingernails as he opened the window and gazed outside.

"Excuse me," I said, taking the vase and putting it back on the window sill.

"Hmm," the short one grunted, pulling the screen back into the room, turning it around to see both sides, and looking at the tall one.

"It's a break-in all right," his partner responded, belching softly.

I didn't have much: the vase, a couple of photos, a pile of books, a Christmas ornament from the parish. These seemed ordinary possessions to me, but the tall one and the short one stared at each one as though they were bizarre objects to find in a single woman's apartment. Their explorations of my things seemed without any good purpose and made me feel strange, foreign, and violated a second time.

Twenty minutes later, the tall one handed me a piece of paper and opened the door. "That's your case number there, Miss. Sorry for your trouble."

And they were gone. It was clear that nothing would be done to find the culprit.

The next morning at first daylight, I went to the manager's apartment.

"Someone broke into my apartment last night," I blurted out to the short, muscular man who opened the door drinking his coffee from a mug inscribed "Go Vikings!"

"Oh yah, Miss? Sorry about that. Terrible thing. Call the police, did ya?"

"Yes. They didn't do anything though."

"Oh yah. Say, any other folks see what happened?"

"No, I don't think so. Everyone was sleeping, I guess."

"Uh-huh." He took a large gulp of coffee, exhaling coffee breath in my direction. "You tell anybody?"

"No, Mr. Miller. I didn't see any reason to get other people upset."

"You betcha, Miss. Good for you, Miss. No reason to get anyone upset... So, how'd ya fancy a place up on the second floor? Got one nice place, bigger, got a separate bedroom."

I told Mr. Miller I didn't know if I could afford it.

"Well," he boomed, "given ya got such good reasoning and didn't get folks all upset, I'll give ya a real good price."

And he did indeed, only charging me $10 dollars more than I had been paying. I had the money. Now I had one room to sleep in and another to work or read or watch TV. The bathroom was big enough to turn around in and put down a bath mat. And there were two closets, one in the bedroom that was big enough for my still-small wardrobe, and a small one for coats in the living room. And I had two windows now, both 12 feet above the ground. It was furnished like the other apartment, which was good because I couldn't afford much furniture yet. But this apartment had a full-sized couch. I was moving up in the world. And I had learned an important lesson - never rent a first floor place!

By this time, I had been working at Our Lady of Cana for almost two years, and things were going well. The teachers and parents were pleased with the religious education program, which was now running itself. The racial integration work was going well too. There were, fortunately, no repeats of my experience with the bogus traffic stops. Parents were much less apprehensive. Women from the parish—white like all our parishioners—were involved on a routine basis with black women belonging to an inner city organization. Most parishioners were happy, and the parish priests had very nice things to say about my work.

One wrinkle was a surprising bit of news brought to me by young Father McMalley. He was about my age and came to me one day with a strange confession.

"Ann, I have to tell you something," he said, putting his hands in his pockets and then pulling them out again.

"Sure James." I was sitting at my desk but got up and moved around it to one of two chairs, motioning to him to take the other.

James closed the door before sitting down and speaking. "Well, it seems some parishioners are gossiping about me. Ummm... I guess they think I might be involved with a woman."

"Oh, wow. Sorry, James."

"And some are saying it might be you. I guess because they see us working together sometimes."

"That's crazy." I was getting nervous now; what if they had seen me with a priest? I kept talking to cover it up. "I hate gossip in churches. So what are you going to do?"

"There's really nothing I can do. Just think maybe we should not be quite so close."

"Okay. Sure. I don't know what that would mean though..."

"I don't know... Anyway, let's be aware." He got up hurriedly, left the office, and pulled the door too hard on his way out so it banged shut.

James never explained more. In fact, he never talked about it again. He came around to my office less often and seemed just a little on edge when he did. Perhaps it was because he always left my door open and his voice seemed louder than before. Or maybe it was my imagination. Was he perhaps actually involved with someone? It didn't seem right to ask.

If he only knew about me and Carter...

In any case, I was thinking of taking another job. St. Albert's, located in a suburb north of the city, was advertising for someone. The money would probably be better since it was a bigger and wealthier parish, but that wasn't the tempting part. I felt my work at Our Lady of Cana was done.

I was coming to realize I didn't like the routine of maintaining programs. Boredom had started to seep in.

Keeping something going year after year bores me. It actually deadens me. I'm always dreaming of new possibilities. And I love challenges. If there's a problem or a new possibility, my mind starts flying. All kinds of ideas rush in: new perspectives, new ways of doing things. Then I start pondering, imagining them, how they might look, how they could work. Pretty soon it all comes into focus, and then I start talking about my vision, seeing how others respond, tweaking it. I'm a visionary.

The program at Our Lady of Cana would keep running. I just was no longer the best one to be at the helm. I was ready for a new challenge. The volunteer teachers were well trained and equipped. I had great confidence in them. They would hire someone to manage the program, interface with the priests, order books, and other necessary tasks. The work would be in good hands.

St. Albert's on the other hand held new challenges. They had not had a Director of Religious Education and wanted to hire someone to develop their programming. They were eager to bring their teachers to a more up-to-date understanding of their faith and encourage trying new things. I sent in my application and quickly got a call back. They wanted to meet with me.

And so after some interviews and thought and prayer, I accepted their offer and handed in my resignation at Cana. Everyone understood, and they arranged a nice party for me. My last day would be June 15, and then I finish out the contract year with my two weeks' paid vacation. My first job in the church was coming to a very happy ending.

But there was still the interracial picnic, a final activity I needed to attend. It would be for elementary-aged children and was scheduled for mid-June. Fortunately I could plan my departure to come after the picnic because I would not have missed it for anything.

The picnic was at Estabrook Park. Parents from Our Lady of Cana drove their kids, and Ezekiel, a member of Father Groppi's Commando's Project 1, brought a busload of African American children from the inner city. I parked my car in the city and rode on the bus with them. Leaving the park that afternoon, I knew all the parish children had been picked up by parents. I was a little worried that Ezekiel was too casual about counting children climbing back on the bus. I didn't challenge him though; this was his responsibility, and besides, I suspected myself of being too uptight about it. I have a tendency to be overly compulsive and careful.

It was about six o'clock. Ezekiel and I chatted on the way back about how well the children had gotten on and how much fun they seemed to have when he turned to me and said, smiling, "If some mother calls tonight and says her kid never got home, we'll have to go down there and look for him."

Smiling as though it was a joke, I said, "Okay. I guess so."

I felt very uncomfortable immediately. I didn't really know Ezekiel; we'd just been at some planning meetings together. Yes, he was one of the young men working with Father Groppi, but I also knew a lot of those young men had been recruited from very troubled lives on the streets. The idea of getting a call from Ezekiel at 2 a.m. and having to go down to a park—known for some troubles itself—did not feel good. In fact, I felt afraid. By the time I got home, I realized that I never would have agreed to meet a white man in a park at 2 a.m. Since he was African American and since we were trying to work on racial reconciliation, I had felt obligated to say "okay." I was being patronizing and should have said something like, "I don't think so, Ezekiel. I'm not going to any park in the middle of the night." And that, I realized, was a kind of "inside out" racism.

It reminded me of a time years ago in the '50s when Baltimore buses were first integrated. I was coming home from a music lesson, and a black man sat next to me. He smelled terrible, but I just sat there not wanting to offend him. If he had been white, I would have moved. Remembering that day when I was just a teenager, I saw my own brand of racism pretty clearly. I wasn't ready to hold African Americans to the standards I had for whites, betraying the reality that I didn't really see them as equals.

Ezekiel had taught me another lesson. Whether he did it on purpose or not, I don't know. I suspect because of his smile, he amused himself by observing my reaction. Maybe he just wanted to have a plan if a child was missing, which none was, thank heavens! Or maybe he was just testing me to see my reaction. In any case, I was grateful. From that day on, I related to African Americans more respectfully — I would now respond the same way I would to whites, and at times that means saying "No way."

The goodbye party at Our Lady of Cana was great. There were at least a hundred and fifty people there, and I got lots of hugs and people told me how I had made their lives brighter and richer by talking a lot about how much God loved them and by helping them get to know and care about people different from themselves. I had a separate celebration at the Welby's home. All seven children sang a song they had made up together to the tune of "Mary had a Little Lamb." We all agreed our friendship would continue and ate lots of chocolate cake!

Then my two-week vacation began. I was eager to start the next challenge at St. Albert's and even started to do some work to get ready. And I waited for my final check...which did not come. That check was important because even though I had started my new job, I wouldn't get paid until I had worked for a month. A few more days passed. Still no check. Finally I called, and spoke to Cana's head priest Father Blakely.

"Well, Ann, no, we weren't planning to send you another check. You left on the 15th."

"But Father, I had two weeks' vacation pay coming at the end of the year."

"Well, that would have been after completing a contract year, Ann, and you left two weeks before that. I'm sorry if there has been a misunderstanding."

I was flabbergasted. There seemed to be nothing I could do however.

Another lesson learned? I prayed, "I give it to you, God. Do something good with it, please."

Words of Challenge

St. Albert's was a round stone edifice sitting on a pleasant, neat suburban two acres. Compared to Our Lady of Cana, it was about the same size but was a newer parish, attended largely by upwardly mobile families. Almost all were white. This congregation had more money and education. They were more sophisticated and emotionally guarded, but they too cared about the children and about the poor and were open to new ideas. The somewhat sterile building acquired warmth and heart when filled with about 1200 men, women, and children on Sunday mornings.

Father McCormick, the older of the two priests, was a tall, kindly man in his late 50's with an open, smiling face. In his own gentle, easygoing way, he promulgated the theology of Vatican II, opening minds and hearts to a modernized Catholicism. Father McCormick trusted me, gave me great freedom, and often expressed appreciation for my work.

The young priest Stew Wilson was more involved with the people, especially the children. Stew was a short, round-faced, cheerful man who was enthusiastic about his own vocation and about the work we were all going to do together. He supported my desire to teach the teachers and give them free reign to use classroom skills. These men and women were all volunteers. When they themselves were children, they had been exposed to a very conservative belief system and a punishing face of God.

Now they loved being liberated from images that had often made them afraid of God. They wanted their children to learn about the God of Love.

As they left behind former ways of viewing God, they needed fresh perspectives, more contemporary theological understanding, and new ways of experiencing God. They welcomed my classes on Scriptural interpretation, understanding that the Bible was not history in our modern sense of the term but rather collections of rich stories with great meaning. Genesis was not about eating a piece of fruit and falling far from God, but rather an acknowledgement that we are all pretty messed up and God is present to heal us and help us grow.

I loved the idea of passing on to them the open ideas I had learned in graduate school and was confident I would be able to communicate these in the language of the people. Jesus talked about "setting prisoners free," and that was how I saw my impact on the teachers and the children they in turn would influence.

By this time, I was not the only Religious Education Director in Milwaukee; I now had more than twenty colleagues. At first we made contact one on one, then got together in small groups, and soon we formed a Religious Education Association. Our backgrounds were quite different. Many came with an educational background, which I certainly didn't have. Most were women, but there were four men. Some of us became not just colleagues but friends.

I met Bryan Henderson at the first meeting in September, and we soon discovered we had a lot in common. Bryan's background was also in theology, not education. Both he and I were much more interested in ideas than in classroom methodology, activities for children, and curricula, although we should have been since we knew so little about such things. We wanted more conversations about interpretation of biblical passages, how much we can know about God, the essence of Jesus' teachings and way of life. Bryan told me he worked at St. John's, a very progressive parish with plans to develop a whole Religious Education department with several people.

He also told me he was an ex-priest and married. He and his wife Pat had been part of the same religious group—he in the men's order, she in the women's—sharing the same medieval tradition. And that is how they met, doing the work of the order at the same location. They fell in love and both left the order within a year.

After the September meeting, some of us went to a nearby restaurant to grab something to eat, and Pat joined us. I liked this quiet lay couple, both rather studious, introverted, and around my age. Bryan was handsome with tall, sandy-colored hair, although I personally didn't find him attractive; he was too thin and a bit passive. Pat was not memorable physically, being of average height and weight with blondish hair and unremarkable features. But she was feistier than Bryan, more direct with stronger opinions. She had been a nurse in the order and continued to work in public health after she left.

Over the rest of that school year, the three of us became friends, and I longed to tell them about Carter but was afraid to risk exposing him. Bryan and I had some interesting theological debates. I liked Pat's directness even though it could also have a cutting edge. She could go right to the core of an issue quickly, and often did so if Bryan and I whined about some of the down sides of parish life like complaining parents, tedious meetings, priests who sometimes needed convincing to try new things. We began to get together on most Friday evenings, meeting at Bryan's church and getting something to eat at one of the nearby neighborhood restaurants.

It took me six months to reveal my secret. Finally, still nervous for Carter, I took the risk of trusting this couple. After all, they had similar histories, and they were trained to keep confidences. It happened one snowy March evening after my children's programs were over and the last tired parents had collected their chattering offspring.

I drove over to St. John's as usual. The place was empty except for Bryan, who was just finishing cleaning off his desk, and Pat who sat patiently watching him. Everyone else seemed to have gone home long before. We were all tired and collapsed into some comfortable visitors' chairs in the office to relax before heading out somewhere for dinner.

"So, what are you doing this weekend, Ann? Are you dating anyone?" Pat asked, hunting for something in her purse. "Oh, I'm so glad I didn't have to go through all that dating ordeal."

"Well…no, I'm not really dating." My eyes were on my hands, which twisted a Kleenex in my lap, and I noticed my gold ring on my right hand.

"Actually, I know you'll keep this to yourselves…I'm in a relationship… it's with a priest." Looking up to search their faces for reactions, I couldn't tell what they were thinking. They both simply waited for me to continue. "It was part of the reason I left the convent — but only part — I'm sure I would have left anyway. He feels he has to stay though. He's in a position to have a lot of influence. He's in charge of a lot of priests, encouraging them to do new things, to be where the people are. We're in a time when a person like him can make a huge difference." My words were coming quickly now.

"How does he see you fitting in?" Bryan asked, opening a pack of cigarettes.

I reached in my purse to get my own but pulled out a limp, empty cellophane-wrapped package. "Can I bum one of those?"

Bryan reached over and handed me his lighter too. I flicked it open, hesitated for a moment, ran my thumb over the wheel a couple of times until the flame burst out, brought it up to the cigarette in my mouth, and inhaled deeply. The exhaled smoke rising around my face, I leaned over and returned the lighter.

"Thanks. He thinks he can be a much better priest with me in his life, that priests have lived in ivory towers too long, counseling people about challenges they know nothing about really. He says priests are reading papers at national meetings he attends about new kinds of relationships. It's called the Third Way. His name is Carter. I think you would really like him."

Bryan smiled gently at my confession and crossed his legs. "It sounds as though Carter is having a very big struggle with his vocation."

"Well, it doesn't sound that way to me," Pat retorted. "I don't hear that he's struggling at all. Seems to be pretty comfortable. How is this working for you, Ann?"

"It's really hard, but I understand him. Priesthood, his work, is so important to him. He wants to share that with me too. Still, I wish we could be together more. It is so good to be able to tell the two of you. You are the only people who know."

"How does he share his priesthood with you?" Pat prodded.

"Well," I said, rummaging in my purse for a mint and wishing we would go and get dinner, "we lead a home church together. He shares a lot about decisions he has made, and difficult decisions, where he's stuck. He really wants my advice." My anxiety rising, I began talking too fast, and my voice crescendoed. "And it's just so important to me to stand with him, be there for him, support him.

"And does he support you too?" Pat pressed on.

But Bryan intervened, standing and stretching as he spoke. "What if we all go get a beer and something to eat? My cousin Nick can meet us there." Bryan moved to his desk, dialed Nick's number, and quickly told him where we were going. "Thanks for sharing, Ann. I'm sure we'll talk more about this, and I hope we get to meet Carter. Time to get out of here."

I was glad Nick would join us. His inclusion would steer the conversation to less difficult topics. He was there waiting when we reached the restaurant, where we ate burgers and talked about nothing in particular.

My friends were tremendously important to me. And fortunately for my sanity, work and Carter were not all I thought about. But I also needed to make music again. Even without the lost vacation pay, I had a little nest egg by the time I started at St. Albert's. Since then, I had been putting some money into my savings account every two weeks, 10 percent of my check. It wasn't much; my salary was only $10,000 a year which meant $385 per pay check minus $40 or so for taxes. But I still decided to spend a little on something my whole being needed, body and soul.

So with $250 in my wallet, I headed toward a reputable music store downtown on Wisconsin Avenue that sold both new and used pianos.

"I need a clunker," I said, looking round the dozens of pianos in the showroom.

The salesman steered me over to some beautiful grand pianos with price tags in the thousands.

I held firm. "I need a clunker."

"Let me show you these uprights. They are more reasonable."

I could see the large white cards with prices in bold black ink - $800, $1000, $2500.

"I'm sorry, I can't afford those. I have $250. All I can afford is a clunker."

"Let me just show you this one upright. It sounds just like a grand piano." He extended his arm, aiming it in the direction of a tall upright with a label I had never heard of — Yamaha. The price tag said "$2000."

"Just try it," he urged, lifting the lid off the keys.

Why not?

I pulled the bench out, sat down, and ran my hands over the keys randomly, playing a few scales, then some chords, and finally launched into a Brahms Rhapsody.

"Well," I spoke declaratively, "it doesn't sound like a grand. No upright does. It does have a really lovely tone. But this tag says $2000. I have $250."

The salesman didn't hesitate: "The way you play, I'll give it to you for $650. Just put down your $250, take it home and then pay me $50 a month. I won't charge you interest. After eight months, it's yours. Oh, and there'll be no delivery charge."

Ecstatic, I pulled my wallet from my purse, took out a wad of $20, $10 and $5 bills and dumped them in his outstretched hand. A day later, a truly good instrument was sitting in my apartment, and I sat down and played for two hours, starting with what was already in my mind, my heart, and my fingers. The haunting, turbulent opening theme of

Brahms Rhapsody in G minor flowed seamlessly into a lyrical passage full of longing and then turned angry, forte, and rapidly percussive, rushing finally back to the original haunting melody.

Memories of my adolescence came flooding back as my hands moved effortlessly across the keys. How many raging passions had flowed through my fingers in those days? And what would have happened to me without that repository for my teenage turmoil? Oh, I played Mozart and Bach and even Chopin, all the repertoire of the conservatory student. But it was Brahms and Beethoven, the "sturm und drang"—literally the "storm and stress" of German romantic composers—that became the acceptable unrestrained emotional expression in my youth lived among restrained academics.

Playing the piano was also my way of praying. The dining room with its upright piano was my sanctuary. There, through my hands and a manmade instrument of strings, sound box, and keyboard, my soul left the modest room and connected with the Divine. I wandered into a different land through the music, becoming quite unconscious of the world around me. This could create a problem when I played formal recitals. I sat down at the piano, began, and then came to the end, almost not knowing where I had been or what I had played. I was simply lost in what transcended me, the instrument, and my surroundings.

When in recital, being abruptly dropped back into reality when I had finished, having to bow, and return to my seat looking calm and collected was sometimes difficult and even a bit disorienting. Once when I was fifteen—a very self-conscious age—I was selected to perform with a few other students at a special concert at Baltimore's Peabody Conservatory. All recitals were held in large imposing concert halls accommodating several hundred people. The audience sat flanked on both sides by tall statues set in niches in the walls. Generally students sat with the audience, walking up the long aisle, and climbing the steps of the stage to play. But on this particularly formal occasion I was seated backstage with the other performers. When my turn came to play, I walked through a heavy, red velvet curtain onto the large stage high above the audience who all sat staring at me.

I played a three movement Mozart piano concerto, lost in the beautiful music. When I had finished, I rose, bowed deeply to the audience, and turned toward the massive heavy curtains to exit. But where was the break in the curtains? I faced a wall of red, and I had no idea where one velvet panel gave way to another. I couldn't get offstage. Panicked, I walked the whole width of the stage, trying to feel for a break with my hand. Unsuccessful, I turned back and retraced my steps, but I was still unable to find the opening among the many heavy folds. Finally I fled to the far end and climbed over the ropes to exit. Fortunately they were close to the ground, and I didn't trip.

There was no such red velvet curtain in my apartment, no high stage or staring audience. No one to call me to do my homework. No complaining neighbors. My sanctuary was undisturbed. While I played, I returned to that other land I had known years before. It was the same promised land into which I had been lifted years before as an almost nineteen-year-old, that time during an incomprehensible Latin Mass when God simply embraced me at communion time. My soul was at rest, my happiness complete.

The piano was not the only thing that enriched my spiritual life. I was having a good time. Making friends. Enjoying each new challenge on the job.

And yet I often felt sad, lost among the myriad of conversations, feelings, dissonances, and explanations.

Pat's pointed comments about Carter kept replaying in my head.

Nothing had really changed with Carter and myself.

We're having sex, but that's so rare. He is still so afraid I may get pregnant. What could he do if we had a child? Marry me legally and take care of the baby? He couldn't do that.

Is that really the only reason? Doesn't he see I long for more closeness. Doesn't he? Hardly having any sex doesn't seem to bother him. Maybe there's something wrong with me?

He's a great priest and a great leader of priests. Be understanding. Support him. And he is fantastic with his brother George. Yes, Carter is a gentle soul.

Well, sometimes I wish he was more caring with me. Sometimes I wonder if he cares more about George than about me.

I climbed into bed and tried to lie very still without tossing or turning. I tried to breathe deeply, to think of rolling ocean waves. I closed my eyes. But my mind did not stop moving until the sun was almost coming up again to make another day.

Dodging Death

Bryan and I both signed up for a Religious Education conference in Detroit the following January. We bought tickets on an early morning flight, but at the last minute, Bryan suggested, "Let's leave around 11 instead." He didn't need to work to persuade me. We were both exhausted.

"If I never see Milwaukee again it will be too soon." My voice conveyed relief as I flopped into the middle seat next to Bryan the next morning, January 22, 1971. Relieved to be away for a few days, I looked forward to sitting through the conference on Religious Education with absolutely no responsibilities. No one would even notice if I skipped most of it, though I was far too responsible to do that.

"It's been some month all right. Christmas is barely over, and I've had to rush into all those classes for parents who want their children baptized," I exclaimed, buckling my seat belt and taking a deep breath.

Bryan was having his own experiences with some of the parents. "They aren't used to having to take these classes. It used to be that the church just baptized babies without requiring anything of parents. Yesterday two couples went to Father Edwards so angry that they were supposed to be practicing Catholics to have their baby baptized. They hadn't had anything to do with the church for years and didn't intend to raise their children as Catholics. They just wanted the baptism to avoid an inevitable fight with their own parents." Bryan groaned, turning to look out the window.

He seemed to want to forget about it all. So I busied myself extracting my Agatha Christie mystery from the bag under the seat in front of me. Bryan was right; we should leave all that ruckus behind and enjoy the brief, trouble-free interlude offered by our flight.

Settling in to read, I glanced up briefly as the final passenger in our row dropped his full weight into the aisle seat on the other side of me. He was tall and bulky with a barrel chest and muscular arms that intruded beyond the arm rest into my space. Being small, I always seemed to end up scrunched in the middle; no window opened up the expanse of the sky, and there was no aisle to give my legs that little extra bit of space. Instead, my arms were forced to remain close to my body, and my feet abutted the bag shoved under the seat in front. Perhaps because I so disliked these confinements, I felt a need to protect what little space I had. And when newcomer on the aisle said "hello," I answered with my head stuck in my book, putting up my own boundary. He apparently gave up any ideas of conversation, and he took out his own reading material, some magazine put out by the U.S. Marines.

Ten minutes and several announcement's about emergency exits later, the engines started, we taxied a short distance, and then lifted into the air. Immediately the blue waters of Lake Michigan were below us. I admired their beauty momentarily over Bryan's folded arms and then returned to my book.

Strangely though, ignoring the seat belt sign, a young man from the rear of the plane walked past us, heading toward the first class cabin. He startled me; everyone knows to stay seated during takeoff. So I looked up and saw he was carrying a briefcase in the hand closest to us, and something shiny in his far hand. No one, including Bryan and the ex-marine, seemed to pay any attention to him as he proceeded forward, passing through the curtain separating us from the wealthier passengers ahead.

First class leads to the cockpit...

"Bryan, did you see that guy?" I whispered, prevented from turning toward him because I didn't want to alert the marine whose muscled arm now almost poked me in the ribs.

Opening his eyes and yawning, he said, "Hmm? What guy?"

"The one who just walked past us and into the first class cabin. Didn't you see him walk up? He came from behind us?"

Bryan sat up straight. He was alert now, and his eyes flashed toward the curtain about 15 rows ahead of us. "What's he doing walking around? You don't think..."

"I think he's going to the cockpit. He's got something in his right hand, looks sort of like a club...but it's...shiny? An ax?

Even though Bryan and I had been whispering, the Marine finally snapped out of his magazine and was sitting muscles taut and fists clenched. "He walked right past me," he muttered under his breath to no one in particular. "I should have done something!"

By now I had concluded the young man was going to hijack the plane with us on board. And the muttering, fist-clenching marine only raised my fear.

The last thing we need is a would-be hero attacking this man, escalating the situation. That could get us all killed right now!

But the marine took no action, and there was no confrontation. In fact, nothing happened. No shouts or gunshots. Only silence, the whirring of the engines, and the rustling and coughing from the other passengers who seemed blissfully oblivious, content as they munched on snacks, turned magazine pages, read their business reports. No cart appeared, no coffee, tea, water, little snacks of cheese and fruit. But of course, it was only a one hour flight.

Eventually the calm voice of the flight attendant came over public address system. "We are beginning our descent into Detroit. Please fasten your seat belts and remain in your seats with your seat belts fastened when the plane has landed."

That seemed a little different from the usual speech, but maybe I was imagining things.

The plane's nose dropped, and we landed fast, screeching to a halt before a big, red brick building. On the other side of the plane, a little boy stared out onto the concourse at the other planes. Following his gaze, I read "Lufthansa." We were on an international airstrip! I was not imagining anything.

Then came the pilot's voice. "Ladies and gentlemen, please remain in your seats."

I looked out Bryan's window. The plane had pulled alongside a long, one-story building with a flat roof. And when I ducked down and twisted my neck I could see them: a whole row of men on top of that roof, each with his rifle aimed at us.

"Ladies and gentlemen," the pilot continued. "A young man is on board who has seized control of the plane. But everything is all right. We have persuaded him to go to Havana, not Algiers because of the limited fuel capacity of our plane."

Passengers sat up straight, straining pointlessly to obtain more information. No one cried out, not even the children. No one spoke at all. No one wanted to draw attention to themselves.

"Please remain calm. Airport attendants will refuel our plane, and we shall depart in approximately 20 minutes. Thank you." The time was 12:30 p.m.

The marine gripped the arms of his seat, but he did not stand up, nor did he speak. His magazine lay unattended on his lap. A tall, willowy flight attendant appeared, smiling, carrying a large basket filled with magazines, playing cards, coloring books, and crayons. She walked down the aisle holding out her placating distractions. Passengers took what they wanted. Still no one spoke, even as we lifted off, flying south.

Silence consumed the cabin. There was no movement. No one coughed. Even the pages of books and magazines seem to be turned soundlessly. Although smoking was allowed on the plane, passengers did not light up. We were all part of two worlds: the land of escape and the realm of near death. The important thing was to vanish into the nameless, faceless crowd, to do nothing to become visible as a person to be reckoned with.

We all seemed to know some things instinctively: we could be killed any second and the hijacker probably had a bomb. So we shut ourselves down and acted as though everything was normal. But of course, nothing was normal: no passengers climbing over one another to go to the bathroom, no intoxicated rants, no fussing children. Just fear and motionless silence.

Everyone was present by being absent, like dinner guests who don't show up. All emotional expression, all conversation that existed was locked inside our beings. We knew to be still and silent to get through whatever time we were granted as well as possible. We existed in a kind of twilight zone.

And at the same time, there was this real world.

God, I may die. If I do, I trust you.

My life ran through my mind like a film on fast forward with my prayer as the internal soundtrack.

I've done the best I can, God. Now I put myself in your hands. 'Into your hands, I commend my spirit.' If it's your will, help us all get through this safely. Keep the hijacker calm. Don't let him hurt anybody, and don't let anyone provoke him. If that's not your will, then I give you my life and trust you to welcome me into your arms.

After this relatively brief time of prayer, I took up my familiar coping mechanism: watching everyone else to see how *they* coped. The woman diagonally in front of me, travelling with her small son, quietly rubbed the child's back, pushed his hair back off his forehead, silently handed him a cookie. Two nuns across the aisle fingered their rosary beads, their lips moving soundlessly. A business man ahead of them worked intently on something, perhaps an upcoming presentation, scribbling page after page on a pad of paper. Next to him a priest bowed his head.

Across the aisle, a gray-haired woman knit furiously on a sweater, but when she ran out of wool, she just stopped. Out of the corner of my eye, I could see that she began counting the completed rows, not daring to hunt for more yarn in her voluminous bag. When my book slid off my lap, I pushed it soundlessly under the seat with my foot and left it there. The marine stared at his magazine, but his fingers held it too tightly and I never saw him turn a page. And I continued to observe and ponder, creating life stories from these moments of self-preservation.

Four long hours passed. "Ladies and gentlemen, we are beginning our approach to Havana. Upon landing, please remain in your seats with your seat belt fastened. Thank you for your cooperation."

It seemed we might survive the flight. But would we survive this communist country where we were about to land? We were going into the capitol of the enemy! The 1961 Cuban Missile Crisis was still fresh in our memories. It was the closest the Cold War came to becoming nuclear war.

Now there was activity among some passengers. Priests and nuns began removing their collars and veils. There were several of them on the flight, perhaps originally headed for the same Religious Education conference we were supposed to attend. They seemed also to be rummaging through wallets and purses.

Maybe they are afraid and looking for ID that doesn't indicate they work for the church. Cuba's government is anti-Catholic. Maybe I should do that too. No, none of my papers disclose my employment.

The priests opened the top buttons on their shirts. Unlike men who were very accustomed to being "out of uniform," the nuns appeared to feel a bit awkward without their veils. Their hair was not cut well or stylishly, and they did nothing to fluff it or smooth it down. They smiled bravely and shoved their veils into their carry-ons to hide them as best they could. We waited. The landing gear lowered with a clunk. The plane hit the ground, taxied, stopped. Silence. Then, from the rear of the plane like an orchestrated military parade, three Cuban police, dressed in green uniforms and carrying rifles, entered our tourist cabin. Soundlessly they glided through the plane and, mere moments later, exited via the front door with the young man, now handcuffed. Seamlessly they glided across the landing strip, opened the door of an old, battered Ford, climbed in with the young man and rolled away.

"We're okay, Bryan!" I took a deep breath. "I guess we will need some more fuel before we take off back to the States? What do you think?"

Before he could answer, the public address system sputtered: "Ladies and gentlemen, please unfasten your seat belts and deplane calmly and quietly. Once on the ground, please follow the officers into the building you will find there. Thank you again for your cooperation."

Why are we deplaning instead of heading back? Where are they taking us?

All the passengers grew silent once more. We did as we were told.

Maybe this is how a death march begins.

Slowly and in an orderly way, we entered the small one-story, white stucco building indicated by an official. Inside we lined up in a corridor and were told, in English, to proceed one by one through the door into the next room. We waited in silence, afraid to be overheard, afraid to voice our fears of what lay beyond the door. Somehow now that we had not died on the plane, I felt my fear like a powerful wave that might drown me.

But on the other side of the door we were simply asked some basic information—name, address, date of birth—and invited to take a seat on one of benches around the edges of the room. A smiling man with one tooth and a very large movie camera stood at a polite distance photographing us. Again, we kept silent.

Then a policeman appeared. Dressed like the others in military green, he stood tall and rigid, his hand on the rifle dangling from his shoulder. In a raspy voice, he uttered something I didn't understand. We passengers looked at one another for clarification, but no one spoke. The man then opened a door to his right which I had not noticed before. I could catch a glimpse of a staircase. Wordlessly, he beckoned to us to follow him up the stairs.

Fear slammed into me once more, this time full force.

Oh my God, where is he taking us? Maybe it's to the 'showers,' like Auschwitz...

I had no choice, and I did as he told me.

It was a short staircase, and at the top, to my relief and amazement, we emerged into a large dining room with tables for four set with white linen and real silver cutlery. Soon waiters appeared. They went first to the two women with babies, and I heard them asking in slightly broken English what they could get for these little ones. Soon one of them hurried in with bottles and what looked like some baby food. In the meantime, we started in on the beer; there was a bottle at each place along with a pack of Cuban cigarettes. And steak, bread, and potatoes began to appear.

Gradually, thanks to the smiles of the waiters, the good food and beer, we began to relax and talk. Bryan and I toasted our survival. I told him about passing the time by observing other passengers. He said he just tried to read the theology book he had with him and confessed to not having taken in a thing.

We talked to the waiters, asking them about how life was now in Cuba.

We asked one another, "When did you realize we were being hijacked?" Most people hadn't noticed anything until we landed in Detroit, then the announcements seemed a little odd.

"What do you think is going to happen to that poor young man?" a middle-aged woman asked.

"They'll probably throw him in some terrible, dirty prison," her husband guessed.

"Well, I hope they don't. I hope they take him to a hospital. He didn't try to hurt us," an older woman retorted.

"I agree. Actually, I saw his face when they took him off the plane. He looked really sweet."

We all seemed surprisingly concerned about him; I didn't hear anyone judging him. Then there was lots of talk about how soon we could go home and where we thought the crew had gone because they were nowhere in sight.

We had dodged death, and we were different. Nearing death had given me and others a new taste for life and an acute awareness of how everything can change in a moment. We had encountered another country and were engaged in different conversations. We had boarded the plane as strangers, hoping for enough space to sit comfortably, warding off unwanted conversations, annoyed by elbows and children's kicking feet. Now we were a family. Death had been close. And now we had more life.

Our plane took off at 10 o'clock and deposited us in Miami where we had to fill out lots of paperwork and dodge reporters. Then we took off again around one in the morning, landing about 2:30 a.m. in DC where we deplaned with glaring camera lights in our faces and more reporters shouting questions. Finally we boarded the third plane which took us to Detroit, where Bryan and I and others reached our hotel at 4 a.m.

The conference went on for three days. Every time I met one of the attendees who had been on the plane with us, we hugged and reminisced. We seemed to have endless stories, things we had noticed, ways to describe our fears and exaltation. We all seemed to be going through the motions of the conference in a sort of daze, waiting for it to end. Bryan and I ran into one another a lot. We would have loved to leave early, but our departure was dictated by our airline tickets.

When we finally flew home to Milwaukee, Pat met us at the airport and hugged Bryan for a very long time. She wrapped her arms round him weeping, looked deep into his eyes, laughed as she tussled his hair and let him go.

Pat gave me a hug too. It was brief and felt like an official hug, a polite hug, broken off as soon as propriety would allow.

Of course, Carter was not there.

I felt the absence of Carter so deeply. It seemed like a statement that I might just as well have died on the plane. Seeing Pat's affection— her warmth, her broad and brimming joy that Bryan had returned to her—followed the perfunctory hug she gave me, deepened my sense of loss. It wasn't just that I wasn't as important as Bryan; of course, that was true and right. No, something was different. Her hug that day felt different from any other hug. It felt cold.

Stop imagining things. It's been a long day.

Bryan suggested we all sit down and have a cup of coffee, but Pat jumped in with, "I just want to get you home, dear." And so we walked out to the parking lot together. Well, Pat was hanging onto Bryan's arm, their hips connecting as they hurried along with matching strides. I walked with them but at a respectful distance so as not to intrude. In other words, I walked alone, waving cheerfully as they turned toward Pat's car and I sought my own, tossing my suitcase in the trunk to drive home by myself.

By the time I reached my apartment building, an anticipated conversation with Carter was making about its twenty-fifth practice run through my head. I virtually ran down the hall, not caring how much noise I made. Turning the key in the lock, dumping my luggage on the bed, I picked up the telephone and dialed with one swift movement, only slowed when I was forced to wait while it rang.

Would he answer? That was always a question. This time he did.

"Hello?"

"Hi Carter. It's me."

"Hey." His voice was cheery. "Welcome home from Detroit via Cuba."

"You know, I have to tell you, I didn't feel too welcomed at the airport."

"What do you mean?"

"I mean you weren't there! I know you wouldn't usually come, but we were hijacked, for God's sake."

"I'm sorry," he said matter-of-factly.

"And there Pat was, all over Bryan. It made me feel very lonely, Carter."

"What can I say? I'm sorry." He sounded annoyed, harassed.

"Well, there's a lot you could say, I think. Like maybe you need to rethink how this Third Way thing actually works in real life. This isn't a seminar at your annual conference!"

"You sound pretty upset."

"What do you expect?" My voice was rising, and my right hand was clenched. "And you know Pat keeps after me about what I'm getting out of this relationship. She's sure to ask me how I feel about your absence at the airport. And by the way, here's something you could say. 'I'm coming over right away.'"

"I wish I could Ann."

"Well 'wishing' doesn't do me much good. So forget it. Good night."

As soon as I put the receiver down, I began wondering whether Carter would call back. The whole time I unpacked, brushed my teeth, washed my face, and checked that the door was locked, I kept hoping he would. Getting into bed, picking up the book I had retrieved from under the seat on our return flight, running my eyes over the marks on the page, I kept wondering. Finally, turning out the light, I let go of hope.

I am alive. Why do I feel dead?

Eventually, sleep seized me.

The next day I went over to St. John's first thing in the morning because Bryan was taking his turn hosting the monthly Religious Education Association meeting there. Everyone around the place—his cousin Nick, the priests, the receptionist—wanted to hear about the hijacking. None of our other colleagues had been able to get the funding to go to Detroit, so as they came in for the meeting, they rushed over to the two of us to hear all about our adventure. Some of the people had already talked to one or the other of us on the phone while we were in Detroit attending the conference. But now the real live survivors were present, and everyone wanted us to tell the whole story again with all the details. People from the parish dropped by for business of some kind, and they got in on it too, causing us to repeat some things several times.

It was late when the meeting finally began and we got down to work. At noon, the parish sent out for some food, and Pat dropped by to join us. She did this often, and sometimes I thought she hovered over her husband. That day she went straight to Bryan, who was standing in the food line behind me, and conveyed some message in hushed tones. They laughed at some little inside joke. Then Pat turned toward me and, without leaving Bryan's side, asked "How are you doing today, Ann?"

"Doing fine, Pat. It's good to be home," I looked up and smiled.

I made attempts at conversation with attendees at the table to be polite, but everyone seemed paired off and involved in deep discussions.

"I guess the conference wasn't too interesting after the hijacking," Pat continued. "You didn't get to Detroit 'til four in the morning. A long day and a pretty scary one. Bryan said you saw the hijacker coming up the aisle." She brushed cookie crumbs into her hand and tossed them into the trash barrel behind her. "Then all that time on the plane not knowing if you'd survive. And then Cuba! Who knew what would happen in that place? Bryan said the media was so insensitive when you got back to the States. Quite an adventure the two of you had."

"Yes. But we were lucky. I saw the guy's ax, although at the time I wasn't sure what it was. Some people are sure there was a bomb in his briefcase." I put my fork down and started opening a packet of cookies. "But he didn't want to hurt us, really. Just a mixed-up young man with some fantasy of a better life somewhere else. And the Cubans were actually great."

"Well, that's just propaganda, I'm sure." Pat was leaning back in her chair.

"They seemed very genuine. Anyway, none of us were hurt."

"Well, I imagine you won't forget this easily." Pat continued, picking cookie crumbs off her sweater. "By the way, where was Carter last night? I thought I'd finally get to meet him."

"He couldn't come."

"Pressing business of the Lord, I'm sure," Pat sniped.

I tried to ignore her sarcasm, but it cut me. And her whole tone was cold. I began to realize she was threatened that Bryan and I had this life changing experience together without her. She could never know what it was like, could never share the memories. She hadn't been there, and

I had. I suspected that made her feel like an outsider. But of course, she and Bryan shared so much more. Still, he had broken a commitment when he left the priesthood. Was she afraid he could abandon her too? I was no threat to her at all. Bryan was a colleague and a friend, but I had no desire for anything else. Still, Pat seemed paranoid about our relationship. And yet she continued to point out to me how little Carter was giving me? I didn't understand why she had become so cold and distant, and it hurt.

Bryan was saying goodbye to those who had come for the meeting, and I was anxious to leave. I had had enough of Pat's comments for that day. I still hadn't prepared for tomorrow night's class with the parents of kids making their First Communion. I was tired, having slept neither long nor well the night before. I said my goodbyes, retrieved my coat, and walked out to my car.

Even before I got the key in the ignition, I realized I wasn't just tired. I didn't want to hear Pat's comments about Carter over and over in my head; they drained the energy out of me. And when I forced my mind to turn to preparation for the class time with the parents, I honestly wasn't sure what I had to give them.

Graduate school had taught me that Scripture is a matter of interpretation and church history is a lot about who won the theological power battles and got to call their perspective the orthodox one. Working in the church had taught me what a flawed institution it is, even on its best day. Vatican II had brought life-giving innovations, but already some of my colleagues were finding that what it took them years to accomplish could be—and often was—demolished overnight by the arrival of a new priest.

So what was I teaching people once I had freed them from bad theology? *Maybe my parents are right.*

I was thinking about them more and more. When I visited them the Christmas following my departure from the convent, they had been gracious. They neither said nor implied a "we told you so." But I knew they thought it, even though they were mostly just glad to have me back.

Now I thought of them and wondered not just about the convent, but my whole search for God.

Maybe the path I've been following is just a dream, a fantasy. My mother often said 'Just because it feels good doesn't mean it's true.'

And then there's Carter...

Determined to cut off my ruminations which were going to a dismal and lonely place, I parked the car and marched into my own office. Since I was at the meeting most of the day, my assistant had gone home after lunch and volunteers had not come in. I was glad there was no one and no need to tell all the hijacking stories yet another time. That would come tomorrow. For now, I had to work.

But death was hovering around. Closer perhaps than on the plane. Yet there was no ax here, no bomb, no hijacker. Four hours later, I walked out into the dusk.

Less than two weeks later, on February 8, watching TV on my couch, cigarette in hand, I learned that United States bombers and South Vietnamese troops had invaded Laos in an attempt to destroy North Vietnamese supply routes.

Less than a year ago President Nixon ordered the invasion of Cambodia. Now Laos.

Nixon took this action without consent of Congress.

Presumably we were not at war.

Costly

Out on the lake in their sailboat, Deep River and Flying Bird lay on their grown-up-sized sleeping bag, gazing at the sky. A star twinkled in the East. A cloud passed over the moon.

"Look, Deep River." Her finger pointed ahead. "There is pale light in the East. A new day is coming. One we have never seen before."

"And will never see again, Flying Bird."

A wave made the sailboat jump up and bump down.

"Just a little turbulence. We'll be all right, Flying Bird." She took the little one's hand, held her close, was silent for a while.

"Flying Bird," she asked finally, "I know you said you want to fly, go everywhere, learn from all people. It has cost you much. Is this still your desire?"

Flying Bird propped herself up on her elbow, "Of course, Deep River. And you? It has been hard going so deep. Can you go on? Go deeper? Do you want to?"

"No one can reach the deepest place of all. I hope to come close. Where else shall I go, Flying Bird? Where else is Love?"

New Horizons

Carter thought I should move. He urged me to rent something in a huge, modern, steel and stucco building on the East Side; I agreed to take a look. The manager showed me a vacant apartment on the eighth floor.

It was much nicer than my current place, which Carter emphasized. It was also much more expensive—more than twice as expensive—which made me nervous. But it was also bigger; the living room and bedroom were both larger than what I had, and there was a real kitchen with a breakfast nook and a washer/dryer.

Although Carter never mentioned it, I knew he was thinking that the new apartment offered more privacy. In the old place, someone might recognize him coming or going. Since there were only about fifteen apartments, they might connect us. In this huge new structure, he could have been visiting anyone living in this bustling beehive with nine floors, elevators, and countless anonymous inhabitants. Those who lived there were fellow renters, not neighbors.

The soundproofing was better in this very solid building too, and the bedroom was further from the front door. There would be very little chance of anyone overhearing our conversations or even our lovemaking—which was rare and not very noisy—but still a bit risky where I was living.

My budget would be a little strained. I was taking home $900 a month. Conventional wisdom was that rent should be no more had one third of one's earnings, and the rent here was $400. But that was manageable and decreasing Carter's stress made it seem worthwhile.

Maybe he will come more often.

So I concurred with Carter, signed the lease, and moved in.

Despite my initial reticence, I loved my new place. From my eighth floor window, the view of the city at night was magnificent. Milwaukee has tall buildings, but it's not a city of skyscrapers, and it is very flat. At night, a whole ocean of light spread before me: some steady, some seeming to dance as they blinked on and off, some soaring high enough to touch the sky with its moving airplanes and stars and moon.

It was great to say goodbye to trips to the Laundromat too.

Not much had changed between me and Carter. He still came over only a couple of times a week. I still longed for more sex and more time together. Holidays were still spent far apart. At one time, this relationship had been new and fresh and more than I was used to. Now it was becoming less than I wanted, less than I needed. I spent a lot of time anticipating our next meeting and too little time loving and being loved. But I now knew things weren't going to change, so I focused on what I had and what I was giving him, and on what I would do next in my ministry.

By the spring of 1971, my vision at St. Albert's was in place. They hadn't needed much. The volunteer staff had a good curriculum and lots of professional teachers; I only needed to free them up a bit theologically. They welcomed this new freedom. I was happy imparting it. But I knew I had accomplished all I could and all the parish wanted.

So when a new position opened up at St. John's parish, I jumped at the opportunity. I was known there, of course, as this was Bryan's church. The sturdy, red brick building stood on the central square of a bustling working-class parish, occupying most of a block, its spires stretching up toward the sky. Father Edwards, the tall, jovial middle-aged priest, was an intelligent and very progressive man who loved his parishioners and took Vatican II very seriously. He seemed to support Bryan's work and give him great freedom to innovate. His assistant, Father Patrick, was a younger man, shorter, more rotund, with a freckled, round Irish face dominated by a broad smile. He loved working at St. John's.

Convinced of the importance of leadership shared by clergy and laity, and impressed with what Bryan had brought to the parish, they envisioned a whole Religious Education department. Bryan was Director, and now they were looking for an additional person whose primary focus would be on families, children, and the elderly. I applied and was hired immediately.

As usual, I would start on July 1, the beginning of the year for every parish in the archdiocese. That was a little more than a month off, which gave me time to resign my existing position, and participate in the search for a replacement. So I shared my plans with the priests at St. Albert's. All went well. They too agreed we had done good things together and the next person would be hired to carry on the program as it had been developed.

When it came to the question of my last day, I had not forgotten the lesson learned a year before at Our Lady of Cana. This time I would not leave before the end of the contract year and lose my vacation pay. This time my last day would be June 30. Everyone was fine with this. We had a great party with lots of food, kind words, and hugs. They wanted to give me a gift and asked what I would like. So at the party I got my very first kitten, an absolutely gorgeous Maine Coon, along with some cat food, a litter box, and litter.

The first night with "Alfie"—a name I took from Burt Bacharach's hit wondering about the meaning of life—was a bit harrowing. My new furry companion spent the night hiding behind the refrigerator, impossibly out of reach. By the second night, I had figured out that if I stopped pursuing him and went to bed, he would emerge, hop up on the bed, and spend the night curled up around my head. And he did. Carter wasn't there, but Alfie and I had many happy, intimate, unforgettable years together, and I became convinced there are animals in heaven.

At St. John's, my new adventure began immediately. Around July 15, I started looking for a check for the two weeks of vacation pay I had earned at St. Albert's. No check arrived. When there was still nothing after a few days, I called the priest in charge of education. After some pleasantries, I got to the point.

"Father, I thought you would want to know I haven't received my two weeks' vacation pay."

He got back to me two hours later with an answer.

"Ann, I spoke with our financial person. He said that you left us on June 30th, the day your contract year was completed. So as of July 1 you were no longer under contract and therefore owed no vacation pay."

I was dumbfounded. Once again, despite all the hours I had spent and the work I had done above and beyond the requirements of my job, despite all that I would get no paid vacation.

We ended on a polite but chilly note.

The more I thought about it, the more angry and agitated I became. This was the second time a church had cheated me. I had to do something; this was just wrong. So I sent a rather blistering letter to the Parish Council, the group of priests and lay people in charge of running the parish. I wrote about "Christian institution," "un-Christlike behavior," and things like that. In response I got a letter and a check not for two weeks' pay, but at least for one. And the lesson?

Beware, Ann. The church is, of course, not divine, but it is also not just human. It is sinful and likely to betray you.

I had lost some illusions about the church but was nonetheless excited about St. John's. I was involved in an exciting new church venture, and I threw myself into it wholeheartedly. Priests and staff functioned as a team. Together we were out to develop a new, dynamic kind of Catholic parish.

Some important changes had already been made. Parents were preparing their own children for First Communion with the help of the parish staff. When a child was ready, whenever that time came, he or she came to the altar surrounded by the entire family, proud grandparents included. And everyone wore whatever clothes they chose. This was different from just a few years before, when children were herded into classes and presented for communion as a group, regardless of their readiness.

Mass at St. Johns also showed a church on the move. Priests' vestments were modern, tending toward rough cotton rather than silk, modern symbols and bright colors rather than medieval embroidery. Lay people, not just priests, were involved reading Scripture, distributing communion, and occasionally a nun would give the "homily;" it was still only called "sermon" when delivered by a priest.

Since Nick was a gifted, well-trained musician, the Masses were greatly enriched by a mix of interesting music. Contemporary chants and songs mixed with classical renditions replaced tired 19th century hymns. The Beatles "Let It Be" might be played by guitars and sung at the same service honoring Mary alongside Schubert's famous "Ave Maria," soaring out from the organ and the throat of a soloist. Easter season's Alleluias might come in the form of peaceful Gregorian chant or a rousing contemporary urging the people with guitars, drums, tambourines, and full-throated praising of praise God: "Alleluia!" The more music opened up, the more talented instrumentalists and singers from the parish emerged, sharing their talent.

This working class parish of open-hearted, simple and straightforward people also fed the hungry, hosted days for seniors, and worked to increase awareness of racism, religious intolerance, and other social problems.

Taking a position at St. Johns was a big step forward for me. Here was a place where I could flourish; I could use my knowledge and sensitivities while being nourished myself. Working with Bryan was going to be fun. I would have a colleague with a shared progressive theology, and he was a friend. My hope and expectation was that my own spiritual life would gain substance and solidity.

But despite all of these enriching and nourishing new experiences, my own theology, and indeed my faith, were slowly drifting away that summer and fall, drifting off like falling leaves swept up by lazy breezes.

I could talk about some of this with Bryan and Pat, but she wasn't particularly interested in theological debates and, after all, he was my boss and my job involved the responsibility of teaching parishioners.

Graduate school had taught me to read and analyze Scripture through the lens of history. Vatican II brought the church into the modern and perhaps even postmodern way of thinking and doing. I loved reading Scripture in its historical context. I loved the reliance on personal conscience rather than declarations of church authorities. Faith was no longer blind; it was reasoned. And that also meant it wouldn't be the same for everyone.

I felt alone in my faith journey. I loved questioning, thinking things through, having a wide horizon of possibilities before me. But I felt like any explorer without companions. I couldn't share my questions with those I was teaching; that would just be confusing. Carter and I had conversations about faith, of course. But we didn't have that much time, and our conversations usually turned to more immediate concerns like how our day was going, or what we were worried, sad, or happy about.

I am someone who cherishes time alone. But too much time alone with a lot of heavy questions isn't necessarily good. I became increasingly aware of living in an echo chamber, of rattling around in my own head. Alfie was my faithful companion in the evening, curling up beside me or on top of the book I was trying to read. But Alfie's theological understanding was limited.

If the story about Adam and Eve is not history, if sin didn't come into the world when they ate that forbidden fruit, if it's a drama about how mixed up we human beings are, then what is the reason? Is God good? Did God create everything? Then why is there so much suffering?

I had to find another place of worship. And more ways to do priestly work. The home liturgy with Carter was only once a month. Maggie, a friend I had met when she made retreats at my convent, suggested I visit a very experimental liturgy happening on the East Side of the city. I loved it from the moment I walked up the stone steps into the church, saw all the diverse colors and ages of people, and heard Bob Dylan's music coming from the sanctuary.

It took only about two weeks for me to join the leadership team, which was made up of four lay people: two men and two women. This lay group, not priests, led the service from the altar. This could never have happened prior to Vatican II, which is not to say that the Council made it permissible, only it encouraged involvement of laity and experimentation. And experiment we did. We were, of course, pushing the envelope.

There were always priests present, usually stressed out looking men struggling with whether or not to leave the priesthood. They did not preside. We, the lay team, preached, presided, pronounced the words of consecration over the bread and wine. Hundreds of people came, from the rich Milwaukee's wealthy Lake Shore Drive residents to the mentally ill homeless. Many had not been in a church for decades, having been wounded or simply bored by intolerant institutional realities, turned away because they wanted to think for themselves, ask forbidden questions. We sang folk songs, read Scripture passages together, shared our thoughts, encouraged questions, embraced communion together as a real community. We were free and we were joyous!

I told Bryan and Pat all about it, and they were excited for me.

"It's important to have a worship community outside of the people you work with," Bryan responded. "And this gives you opportunities that even St. John's isn't ready for."

"I'm not sure I'm ready for it either," Pat added, leaning a bit pensively on Bryan's desk. "But I'm really glad you have it."

I was too, and I counted on this new opportunity to sustain me for years to come.

But wherever I was and whatever I was doing, whether leading liturgies or eating good food, I always made sure to be home by 10. I would jump in my car and hurry across town, unlocking my apartment door by 9:58. Carter called sometime after 10 when he was able, which was most but not all nights. Usually we didn't talk for too long. His day had often been stressful. He would be tired, too tired to tell me much about it.

Generally I am a good sleeper, but on some nights, I slept fitfully. Those were the nights when pictures and words and silences—Pat kissing Bryan after the hijacking, Carter's absence, Pat's sharp words about him, the sound of a phone that didn't ring—spun round and round in my brain.

Alfie was not enough. I would wake and feel Carter's absence in my bed.

Voices of the Cathedrals

I was good at it. I loved listening to people's heartfelt stories. And I heard many because, for some reason I didn't understand, people trusted me. They wanted to tell me their secrets, their pain, and their steps forward. I seemed able to let them know I understood what they said, and that made them feel alive in a new way. We walked together on holy ground, the holy ground of the cathedrals of their hearts.

For the most part, this came to me naturally. In the convent, I had gotten some training in counseling at the University of Chicago. Now I heard Dr. Stadler speak at a local conference. His workshop was interactive and fun. I knew his skills were laid on the bedrock of his own personal suffering as a child who was mute until the age of five; his sensitivity to suffering was palpable and moved me. So I signed up when he told us about his training sessions in Green Bay, Wisconsin.

Every week for a year I drove to Green Bay, which is about 120 miles from where I lived in Milwaukee. And every week I made the same long trip back, most of it in the dark. It was a long, lonely expressway trip with very few possibilities along the way for any kind of break. All around me were endless, flat fields of once-white, now-gray snow.

The sky was gray one Monday evening when I starting my 120-mile drive home. Thirty miles later, snow surrounded my car as though someone had opened a giant pillow case and poured feathers directly down on me. The wind began to swirl and howl. Soon, I could barely see two little spots of red somewhere in front of me. Actually those tail lights were reassuring. They were the only way I knew what lay ahead.

If someone gets between us with no lights on, I may just crash into him.

Clenching the wheel tightly and leaning as far forward as I could as though a couple of inches would help me see better, I crept forward.

And who's behind me? They can't see me either.

I could almost hear the horrible bashing of metal on metal and feel the impact of a car—or even a truck—hurtling into me.

My tires were beginning to slip on the snow-turning-ice.

I've got to get off. Wait it out. Maybe even find a restaurant or a motel somewhere around.

There were no tiny red lights ahead now.

Is the road clear ahead, or is there a car I can't see? Where am I? How far have I driven?

I could vaguely see a big sign by the road; it was covered with icy snow.

Frantic by now, I tried to find an exit, any exit, leading anywhere. Anything to get off that road. But huge mounds of snow—fresh snow on top of gray, icy old snow—were all I could see. There was no way to find an exit ramp.

If I take a guess at where it is, I'm liable to end in a ditch or crash into something I can't see. Or even slide into a frozen pond.

The sky was completely dark now, and suddenly the snow became less dense. Visibility improved, although it was still impossible to see any exit ramps or read any signs.

And then lights pierced the dark, glaring in my rearview mirror. They were high off the road.

A truck! A really huge *truck!*

He was close and then closer. Much too close. The roar of his large engine bore down on my little Chevy. Lights blinding me, he tailgated me for miles, driving too fast and forcing me to go faster than I wanted on the slippery road.

Oh my God, he's doing this on purpose. He's terrorizing me.

I tried moving as far to the right as I dared. But he wouldn't pass me, not even when the road widened. I thought about stopping and letting him go by, but I was afraid. What if he attacked me?

There were 50 miles on that road that were almost totally deserted: no civilization in sight, only fields. I drove at least 25 miles with the truck tailing me before I saw a coffee shop not far from the road and could vaguely make out the way to reach it. Cautiously I turned off, going very slowly in case I veered off the paved ramp. Then I pulled right up in front of the coffee shop, which was lit up with people inside and looked like heaven to me. I was shaking as I made my way over a mound of chunky ice and pulled open the heavy door.

Thank you, God. Thank you that I am safe, for the coffee shop and the people here. I thought he was going to kill me.

It was very late when I finally reached my apartment that night. I was exhausted and cold.

Other really bad storms engulfed me on that barren stretch of road with unpredictable winter weather, but I continued with the training. I was scared but not deterred, because I had discovered a new way to run and perhaps fly. Even in the midst of storms, I was excited by my experiences in the training and by how intuitively I took to psychotherapy. And every time I got to hear people's stories, the stories that came from their hearts, I was filled with sheer awe. It reminded me of encounters in the New Orleans Quonset hut. Being invited into a person's heart was like gaining entrance to a great European cathedral and being met by the presence of God.

Of course, like just about every other student of psychotherapy, I worked on my own stuff too. Maybe it was my own untold stories that most motivated me to engage in this discipline. They were often sad and frequently troubling. In fact, what lay under the surface of my ability was a good deal of depression.

It was not just the situation with Carter. It was also that I had seen too much good work in churches destroyed overnight by the arrival of a new priest, too many people shut out, too much fear of new ideas. It wasn't the parishioners; they might move cautiously or even just resist, but most people were willing to give new ideas a try and generally were pleased in the end. Most people I worked with loved their new freedom. No, it wasn't the people; it was all too many of the clergy. A parish might have a very progressive, loving priest for a few years and then be taken over in one day by a newly assigned man who was fearful, rigid, and determined to grant power, choice, and meaningful activity only to priests.

My friend Alice saw all her hard work undone in 24 hours. She had developed a wonderful, alive program for children. Now it was all gone. No more imagination, no more questioning, no more fun activities. Just dull, boring memorization of the old catechism. I sat with Alice most of one night as she talked and talked, crying most of the time, telling me that it wasn't just the children's program. The parish council, where lay people had been making important decisions about parish life, was also virtually dismantled, reduced to meal planning and cleaning schedules.

And then there were the questions all this raised in my mind about God: was there someone out there? If so, did that someone care? Was the Bible just one more series of stories written by men to explain the mess of the world to other men and perhaps to supply some hope? I knew those who wrote Scripture lived in particular contexts, and those historic and cultural atmospheres influenced what they intended to say and how they said it. Moses was not floated down the river in a cradle of reeds; reeds didn't exist where he was born. And we don't know what words ascribed to Jesus were really spoken by him.

Stories were passed down in communities and written down decades after the events they described. And ancient peoples did not have the same ideas about history as modern people. They didn't view accounts as detailed factual accounts. Not only did they not follow Jesus or other biblical figures around with note pads, they didn't want to. They told stories because they were rich in meaning, full of divine breath and truth through drama.

And then of course, we read translations. Translating is a great art. If you translate literally, word for word, you do not convey the meaning well. But it you go too far from the literal translation to give the sense of the passage, you risk telling your own story, not the original one. So how were we to read Scripture? What could we believe to be true?

And as for churches, with their rules and doctrines, was the church just a way of controlling people? And what about all the awful things the Catholic Church had done: the Inquisition, forced conversions round the world, anti-Semitism? And other denominations were guilty too. How many people had died in wars between Catholics and Protestants? Were my parents right that organized religion is a prison?

I was indeed depressed. I couldn't share much of this during our training sessions. I felt alone with my questions about God, which I didn't think many would understand. And I certainly couldn't talk about Carter. Everyone would be appalled by the thought of that relationship. Either they would be shocked by a priest sleeping with a woman, or by a woman—me—who could remain in such a relationship.

Not being able to talk with anyone about Carter made me feel more than alone. I was fenced in, imprisoned by secrecy and deceptions. I couldn't speak freely; he and I couldn't move about freely. I dared not lose control, allow my inhibitions to loosen for a minute, lest I tell all and destroy him. I did not feel I was dying. No, I was living—living in a coffin.

With warmer weather came construction on the roads. Hurrying down the expressway from Green Bay, my eyes grew tired of the endless strip of pavement, the yellow lines, the stopping and going. The concrete barriers seemed to gaze at me from the edges of the highway. At moments, they seemed to beckon to me as though they were doorways out of my stifling coffin. Doorways to another reality. Frightened by my thoughts, I picked up my primitive Motorola mobile car phone.

"Hello Dr. Stadler. This is Ann Temkin. I'm driving home from our class and scared. I keep looking at the concrete walls on the expressway and feeling drawn to them, like I might drive the car into them and leave this miserable world behind."

His voice was calm and reassuring.

"I think you're going to be all right, Ann. The fact that the idea frightens you tells me that you don't want to drive into the barriers. That's good. Turn your mind to some other things. You did great work today in class! Enjoy it. Do you have a radio in your car? Yes? Well, you might want to turn it on, find some good music."

His voice, the connection to a live human being, did more than calm me. That connection landed me back on earth, grounded me.

Of course, I don't want to crash into that concrete thing and die. I just want to be free!

But I couldn't think what being free might mean. So I took Dr. B's advice and turned on some Bach.

What was really going on, of course—the thing Dr. Stadler knew nothing about—was that everything we studied pushed me up against the reality of how miserable I was with Carter. I tried to just drive and listen to the peaceful Bach cantata. But my mind kept replaying the conversation from the evening before. Carter had been sitting calmly on the sofa smoking a cigarette. I, on the other hand, was bringing plates and silverware from the kitchen into the living room, where we usually ate, slamming them down on the coffee table.

"You are never here when I need you. Yesterday, work was *horrible*. A kid's father came to the office and yelled at me about our first communion program. He was all red in the face and almost screamed, 'You're going to tell me my son can't receive his first communion unless I go to your stupid classes? I paid my dues when I was a kid. I'm not about to do it again.'

"I tried to calm him down, to explain things to him," I had continued, standing in front of Carter who was finishing his cigarette. "'Well?!' the guy yelled at me. 'We'll just see what the Bishop has to say about all this. As a matter of fact, he and I are having breakfast together in the morning. I plan to tell him all about what you are doing to my son, and *you* can expect to hear from him shortly thereafter.'"

Carter had stubbed out his cigarette in the ashtray, I had flopped down on the other end of the sofa. Tears threatened to emerge, but I had shut them off; I had lots of practice doing that. For a moment, I had just sat silent and rather crumpled up.

"Bryan told me the father's a big donor. I'll probably get fired."

"Sounds rough," was all Carter had said, just looking at me.

I had gone to the kitchen and returned carrying pork chops and salad, talking as I handed them to Carter to help himself.

"In the afternoon we had our staff meeting. Bryan backed me up when we talked about this guy at lunch. But when we met with the priests, he just left me hanging out there, swinging in the wind, not a word out of his mouth."

I had exploded then. "I needed you *here* last night, Carter, *for me.* But I always seem to come last, if at all, after all your priests and your mother too." I remembered stabbing a piece of pork chop with my fork and almost throwing the dressing at him.

"This just isn't what I thought we were about!" had been Carter's response, beginning a conversation we had had a hundred times before. We might as well have playing the tape recording. The words were always the same. Carter went on about the Third Way, how important I was to him, the demands of *his* busy life. I tried to talk about *my* needs, my voice escalating as though that might make him hear me. Then I just shut down...on the outside. On the inside, all kinds of words boiled up.

Finally he had put out a last cigarette, gave me a peck on the cheek as I turned slightly away, and left.

Getting closer to Milwaukee, Bach was still playing on my car's tiny radio, but it wasn't helping a lot. I had been pretty close to telling him to go to hell the night before, and he knew it! I still felt that way and gripped the steering wheel as though I had my hands around his throat.

But every time I got close to telling Carter to go to hell, he turned into Father-Larger-Than-Life. So sure enough, when I finally arrived home after my long drive, the aroma of steaks grilling wafted down the corridor. Wondering which neighbor was preparing to feast, I opened the door to find Carter standing at the stove, looking very relaxed with a long cigarette in his right hand, dressed in a blue sports shirt open at the neck, an uncorked bottle of wine on the table, and the unmistakable sound and smell of sizzling steaks coming from my kitchen. He smiled, rested his cigarette in the ashtray, came over and kissed me. "Can I stay over tonight?" he asked.

And when we had sex after feasting, all thoughts of sending him to eternal damnation vanished. And so it was whenever I got close to breaking loose.

The next day around four o'clock when Pat showed up in the office as usual, I told her Carter and I had this great evening and I thought he had heard me the night before when I really stood up to him. Pat looked down at the floor and seemed to be making an effort to weigh her words carefully.

"Well, Ann, I hope you're right."

Carter had been encouraging about my counseling training. Sitting on the edge of the bed smoking slowly after we had sex, he suggested, "Maybe you should get another degree. I've got a friend, James Lee. He's a psychologist. He's good and a really nice guy too. Would you like me to give him a call? Sort of introduce you to him and get him to agree to meet with you? Give you some advice?"

Of course, I jumped at this. I had thought about going back to school too. Things I saw happening around me, plus my own questions about God and the joy of hearing hearts, had all combined to make me think there might be a new path ahead. And I was so grateful that Carter was offering to help me like this. Of course, he wouldn't tell Dr. Lee who I really was. It would all stay very professional. Still, he wanted to help.

He cares. I always knew he cares. I'll go meet with this James Lee. Ask him what he thinks about my becoming a professional counselor.

Sure enough, early the following week I got a call from Dr. Lee, and we set up an appointment for the next day. His office was in one of those small houses turned into a warm, client-friendly counseling center. Pressing the doorbell resulted in a sweet chime coming from behind the mossy green front door. The door opened almost immediately, and a tall, lanky, sandy-haired man appeared in the frame. His clothes were professional but very casual, geared to put the client at ease, and his smile exuded warmth.

"You must be Ann?" he asked, opening the door and waving me in. "I'm Jim. Come on in. My office is right here." He indicated a medium-sized space furnished as a living room with a sofa, three armchairs, and a colorful woven rug and coffee table drawing the furniture together into a harmonious whole. "Have a seat wherever you like."

I chose one of the armchairs, and he sat across the small table from me. "Carter tells me you are a very special person and also a natural counselor. So how can I help?"

That beginning confused me. I had been certain Carter would share nothing about the personal nature of our relationship with Jim. This "very special person" thing caused me to wonder because I didn't know whether Carter had said anything about us. And I certainly won't be the one to blurt it out, I determined, taking out a cigarette and lighter from my purse. I realized right away that I had Carter's lighter. It was bigger and heavier than mine, but flicking it open with studied casualness, I lit my cigarette and inhaled deeply.

"Yes, Carter said you might be able to give me some advice in case I decide to go back to grad school and get a degree in therapy. Could you tell me a little about what my options would be? I don't really know what programs exist, how long they take, you know, what's involved, and of course, what they cost."

And so we talked for about an hour. Jim recommended a Master's in Social Work with an emphasis in Clinical Work. "That's the fastest. It takes two years, generally, and includes a couple of internships, which are where you learn most. There's a pretty good program at UWM, right in the city. You're a Wisconsin resident, so you would get resident tuition, and they have loans you could apply for. Then after you graduate, you would need to work under someone's supervision for a couple of years before being independent. You won't get rich as a counselor, but it's a decent living and a really rewarding one."

Leaving Jim's office about an hour later, I felt greatly encouraged and lucky that I knew Carter and he knew a lot of people. We were having dinner that night, so I hurried home to get everything ready. I was excited and eager to share everything I had discovered. Maybe a new door was opening…

Carter was coming around eight. That was the earliest he could make it, he said, and I just hoped he would be on time. I wanted to share how well things had turned out with Jim, but I was also nervous. Debbie, to whom I owed my very first apartment, was in town to see a show, and I had promised she could crash at my place afterwards.

I wasn't sure how long her thing would last. Surely she wouldn't get to my place before 9 or 9:30. Maybe later. All I knew was Carter, our dinner, and his cigarette butts all had to be gone by the time she rang the bell. It was almost eight o'clock. I listened for Carter's footsteps.

Please don't be late.

The Bells Toll

It was a funeral.

People kept stumbling out of the church, holding tight to their kids, weeping. Hundreds of people outside, all up and down the wide steps, spilling onto the sidewalk. Everyone seemed to be clutching someone else. Whole groups of people stood wrapped together in a clump. Arms—dark almost black skin, brown skin, pale skin with freckles—all mixed and mingled. The two grandmothers, Betty from the wealthy lake shore and Cora from the inner city, the ones who shared stories of their grandkids every Sunday, stood just outside the church doors with their five little ones safeguarded between them. The children were crying as well, looking up at the grandmamas, bewildered.

One of the schizophrenic young men wandered around the edge of the crowd muttering to himself until an elderly woman led him gently by the arm to her family. She had known him for a year of Sundays and had always spoken to him, always treated him as one who belonged, sometimes brought him a small bag of homemade cookies.

"We are family," she always said to him.

The young man mumbled, "I'll tell you what it really means to worship the Lord."

"Tell me what it means, son."

"It means share your food with everyone who's hungry."

"That's right, son. It says that in Matthew's Gospel. You've got it exactly right. We're all family." She smoothed his tangled hair.

"Ann," a woman with two small children clinging to her cried out, pressing close to me. "Isn't worship supposed to be about setting prisoners free? Healing people? That's what it's always been like here. Isn't that what God says?" Her face was wrinkled together and bathed in tears.

"Yes, Emma, it is. That's what Jesus said he was all about. What just happened in there was not of God. Jesus wouldn't do this."

"What did happen? Why weren't you and Ben preaching the way you always do? Who were those priests all dressed up like they did a hundred years ago?"

Some couples standing nearby overheard her question and moved to join us.

"Yes. What the hell was that?" Jonathan asked. His face was angry, and his right hand was beating out a rhythm on his thigh. "The nerve of that guy, whoever he is, reading that Scripture about having a millstone round your neck and drowning if you mislead people and looking right at you and Ben." Jonathan's voice was deep and booming, and more people began to gather round us.

We were moving further out toward the street, making room for the crowds still pouring out of the building, crying, pulling frightened children close.

We stood outside on the steps on the church, the sidewalk, some even in the street, a mass of humanity huddled together. We stood in one intertwined clump of grief: weeping, angry, distraught.

The anguished priests who had been part of our congregation seemed to shrink further into themselves. Struggling over their own vocation, they seemed ashamed of it, not wanting anyone to associate them with the silk-draped men in the building.

Jonathan, the angry man was still standing there waiting for an answer to his question about why Ben and I were not preaching.

I had to give an answer and was struggling to find words to explain everything. The truth was that it was gone, lifeless, over. A terrible disease had entered the body the day before. It all flashed through my mind like a scene from a movie speeded up and hurling across the screen in my mind. It had all happened so fast.

Less than 24 hours before, in fact, the telephone had rung. "Come to the rectory. Father Johnson wishes to speak with you." We three—Ben, Carol, myself—all got the call. "Four o'clock." The voice was male, low, and lugubrious in a gothic sort of way.

I had hurried to get dressed since I was lounging around in pajamas that Saturday afternoon.

What would happen if I said, 'I cannot come at four. I have another commitment?' Never mind, what's the point of a question like that? Just remember your place. Better wear a skirt to the rectory after all...

The fatal encounter had only lasted ten minutes. There were no explanations, no discussion.

"This liturgy will stop immediately. You people will never be on the altar again."

Yes, we had wept and wailed afterward, for all the good that had done. We had been accused, tried, and sentenced.

And the next day? Three priests came to the altar; we were in the pews. They read the gospel about not misleading the sheep and glared pointedly at us. They told a young man who asked a question to sit down. They had not thought about contacting the musicians, however. As the ninth verse of "The Times, They are a-Changing" was almost shouted by those in attendance, listing all the people who should get out of the way, cacophonous chaos broke. Desperate, they asked Ben to restore order. He refused.

After the twelfth verse, there ensued a moment of silence, just a blink of an eye. I stood and simply said we had been informed the day before that the liturgy could not continue. I added that I could no longer take part and walked silently down the long center aisle toward the big doors. As I walked, I heard rumbling, some banging, and then footsteps. I pushed open the large, wooden doors and walked out into the dusk. Outside, standing on the steps, I turned around. They had followed me; women, children, and men flowed out the doors.

I tried my best to answer Jonathan's question. I do not remember what I said. Everything had turned upside down so quickly. Some eventually left to finish the liturgy at a big house on the lake front. I did not have the heart to go along.

The smell of death hung heavy in the air.

I had to talk to Carter. I just had to.

But that night after 10 p.m., my phone did not ring.

Paradox

Flying Bird was asleep. Deep River sat at the kitchen table staring at the blank sheet of paper. She needed to write to settle her heavy heart. But her mind was distracted by the news she had waited for all that day. Her eyes drifted again toward the phone in the bedroom. She picked up her pen. Words were coming quickly now.

> There is nothing quite so loud as a telephone that does not ring.
> I don't mean a pay phone out on the street,
> belonging to no one because it belongs to everyone,
> attached to the wall of a narrow glass booth.
>
> No, a telephone in someone's home with a cord that goes into the wall.
> A telephone that belongs to someone and lives in a bedroom or
>   a kitchen.
> A telephone like that, sitting there in attendance, not ringing.
> There is nothing louder.
>
> I see a telephone just like that.
> It is black and shiny like other telephones in other homes.
> It lives all day and all night on an oak nightstand next to a lamp,
>   a clock, a small pile of books.
> It sits waiting for someone to make it ring and for someone to
>   pick it up.
> It waits in vain.
>
> The guest who doesn't arrive is the person most on the host's mind,
> the empty chair the most visible to every person present.
> The telephone that does not ring is the loudest.

Bitter Truths

Breathless on a hot August night, I ran down the hall toward the door of my apartment. It was 9:58. Fumbling with the key, I could hear the telephone ringing and yanked the receiver up just in time.

"I was just about to hang up, Ann. Figured you weren't home."

"I am, Carter. I rushed away from the party and just made it. You know I always am home at 10 because you call between 10 and 10:30, hardly ever later."

"Yes, well, that's something I need to tell you about. When I'm able to call, it really needs to be right *at* 10 now. After that won't work."

I tried to ask him the reason for the change. He rattled off some things about new responsibilities and getting more rest. Nothing he said made sense to me, but I gave up trying after a few attempts at a clearer rationale. What I understood clearly was that Carter would now call at 10 o'clock or not at all.

I responded instead by making more excuses to leave restaurants, parties, and meetings, getting up even more abruptly and rushing home faster. So often I left people I loved only to sit by a telephone that did not ring. But sometimes it did, and we would talk for a half hour. So I kept racing home, standing by my man.

When there was no ring, I would sit, just staring at it for another half hour or so before heading for bed, disconsolate. This seemed to happen more and more often. Carter and I were still seeing each other, but our contact lacked the ease that comes with warmth.

Meanwhile the country was in turmoil. It was 1973. Troops were being withdrawn from Vietnam. Even the most hawkish Americans were beginning to face the futility of that war. Those of us who had signed petitions and marched began to hope for peace. We hoped we had made a difference, but napalm still fell from the skies destroying innocents, blood still flowed, and our mood remained dark.

"Why did we ever get into that war?"

"So much senseless killing, maiming, and destruction."

"It's all so crazy, so damn foolish."

Richard Nixon, our President, was in serious trouble. Our leaders were criminals; they had tried to fool a whole country. The Watergate scandal was well underway, the *Washington Post* exposing the entire story of the break-in at the Democratic Party Headquarters, the cover up, the conspiracy, the tapes of conversations between the President and his aides. All this plus the profanities, vulgarities, and paranoia of our chief leader got transmitted piece by piece into the living rooms of shocked Americans. Finally one day, they would see the disgraced Nixon grimly waving goodbye, standing by the helicopter that would remove him from the White House and from Washington.

Millions of Americans had lost trust in our leaders. We would not easily trust again. "Fool me once, shame on you. Fool me twice..."

I had come close to the end of the road as far as the church was concerned, having lost trust there too. The annihilation of our beautiful liturgy had hit me very hard.

What's the point?

In addition, I was no longer sure what I believed, I didn't trust myself to have much to give.

How can I speak to people about God when I'm not sure God even exists? If you do exist God, where are you in the midst of all this pain, all this evil?

The church offered me no venue to search my own heart or explore my own questions. The church was not safe. So many walls, walls that locked some people in and locked others out. If you doubted, if you were too innovative, if you really believed in setting prisoners free, you found yourself locked outside all too often.

I stopped going to services except those I couldn't avoid because of my job.

And I was making arrangements to leave that and head back to graduate school full-time. I had saved some money, and my parents offered to help out a little. They were glad to see me returning to academia.

My last day at St. John's was June 15, and my departure was friendly on all sides; goodbyes were warm, and there was a big party in the evening with good food and some funny songs set to tunes like "Home on the Range," rewritten just for me: "Oh, home at St. John's, where the priests and directors do roam. Where seldom is heard, a traditional word..."

Only Pat brought a chilly breeze to the party with her. I knew she saw me as a fool or worse for putting up with Carter. Ironically, I knew she was also threatened by my close working relationship with Bryan, especially since the shared hijacking experience. She didn't say anything that was mean or hostile. It was her silence. It was what she didn't say. It was the silence of her body: tight, smile-free. It was the absence of any of the spontaneity that friends share. It was her stoic silence.

That same month I had moved from the magnificent high rise into the newest apartment: a remodeled attic. It was tiny but had character, so it suited me well. Joe, one of the homeowners, showed me around, which didn't take long. We climbed up the stairs to the third floor of a large and very solid Milwaukee brick home near the lake and walked into the apartment's sole room, narrow with attic walls that rose vertically about three and a half feet and then sloped the rest of the way up. Light came in through a window at the far end and a leaky skylight in the ceiling.

The minute bathroom, which I could fit into only because I'm small, was right at the apartment entrance where space had been made by closing off part of the landing. There was no kitchen really, but enough space next to the bathroom to fit a tiny fridge and a hot plate. A bright red shag carpet ran from start to finish and added a touch of pizazz. It was tiny and humble, but artsy and a perfect sanctuary.

Joe explained that he and his wife had bought the house together with another couple, Nick and Jane Anderson. Joe, Betty, and their three children were on the first floor and the Andersons on the second. They all knew one another from their Presbyterian church. I hadn't met any of these people before but had been introduced to Joe by Ben, who attended the counselor training classes in Green Bay and knew I needed a new and inexpensive place to live.

Joe and I stood by the bathroom door when he explained why the couples bought the house together. He was so tall and had such long arms and legs he could barely fit his frame into the small space. He stood up straight when walking through the center of the room, but had to bend over to avoid hitting his head on the sloping walls if he veered to either side.

"We want to have a real community here," Joe told me, staring up at the skylight and feeling the walls for dampness. Stretching out his arms, he could almost touch both side walls at the same time. "Our idea is to eat together at least three times a week, share tasks, pray together often, and play together a lot. We also have a meeting once a month to talk about how things are going, share any concerns, and appreciate what's going well. We would love to have you join our little community if you decide to take the apartment. Ben told me about you, and I think you would be a great fit."

I hadn't expected this, and immediately pulled back inside at the idea of community. "Oh, thanks, but I don't think so, Joe. I've kind of done the community thing. We Catholics did that earlier than you Protestants."

I laughed lightheartedly, not wanting to offend. "I think I'll pass. But thank you for inviting me." I hoped I sounded polite and appreciative; I wasn't sure of that since the idea of being in community with two families made me feel imprisoned. I had left one convent and had no desire to join another.

"That's fine. No problem. Just know you are always welcome."

And as it turned out, I became a big part of the community, eating with Joe and his wife often, babysitting for their kids, and becoming good friends. It was the Andersons who turned out to have less interest in togetherness as time went by.

I started school that September. My goal was an MSW, Master's in Social Work with a Clinical Emphasis, which would enable me to earn a living doing what I loved so much: sharing the deepest kinds of human experiences and passions with my clients, and healing wounds. This would be priestly work!

I had not been allowed to be a Catholic priest because I had no penis. But I shared Carter's priesthood, and now walking with the depressed, the anxious, and the broken-hearted would become my priestly work.

But even as so much changed, one thing had remained the same: the relationship with Carter.

Well, actually nothing remains the same. Relationships, like everything, either grow or decline. We had been a couple for five years now, and our relationship had not been growing since we married three years ago. And although I put a lot of energy into not seeing what was happening, the relationship was definitely declining. All the telltale signs were there to be seen.

The indicators all seemed small though. Some phone calls that didn't happen, but there had always been some of those. Fewer dinners together, but how many fewer? The signs were not so dramatic as they were cumulative. There were just a lot of little things, mostly present by virtue of their absence. And the silence was growing louder.

And then there were stranger things that started happening.

"Did you bring the book with you?" I asked when Carter came over one summer evening just after I had moved into my new place. He had settled down on the sofa and was smoking a cigarette.

"What book, Ann?"

"You know. Rollo May's 'Love and Will.' You said you'd finished it and would bring it for me to read."

"No. I actually haven't read anything by Rollo May," Carter responded, crushing his cigarette in the ashtray as he rose and sauntered toward the refrigerator.

That's odd. Maybe I'm going nuts. Was sure I remember a conversation about the book.

"Oh well," I told him casually, "guess I thought you said that."

"So you want a sandwich?" Carter asked, pulling some bread and cold cuts out of the fridge for himself. And so the conversation veered off in the direction of the televised pictures of troops leaving Vietnam.

I just let the topic of the book drop like a lot of things, like his not bringing any food with him.

Later, after Carter had left, I lay in bed reading, but the conversation about the book kept getting in the way.

Was he lying? Why would he lie about having read a book? I'm being ridiculous... imagining things. So what if he forgot about the book? Or maybe it was Joe who talked about it...

And so I turned out the light, rolled onto my side, and eventually managed to silence my internal conversation and fall asleep. But in the morning, I saw the sheets were all messed up, and I had obviously slept restlessly. I don't do well with things that make no sense.

I remembered the day a month ago when Carter told me he had to go to his mother's. She was having a party. But a week later, he said "My mother called today. She asked how much time I was spending with you and complained that I never visit her anymore."

And there was the new tie, or was it new? Or was it really one his uncle gave him for Christmas five years ago?

I had used a lot of energy to deny what I saw or heard or felt. Carter lied to me, and I lied to myself, but it took more and more effort.

I had finally confided my confusion to Carol, who was also involved with a priest and with whom I kept in contact after the liturgy was shut down. She was the only person other than Bryan and Pat who knew my secret.

"He keeps saying these things that contradict something he told me just a week or so before. Is he lying? Why would he do that? These things, likebooks and ties, aren't even important. Why would anyone lie about things like that?"

It was helpful to confide in Carol. She was not judgmental like Pat; her lover hadn't left the priesthood either. Her situation was a bit more straightforward. From what she told me, her friend Roger was sweet and rather naïve. He didn't talk about papers about the Third Way, though he may have read some. But he had entered the seminary as a young teenager, had no experience with dating, and had no idea what involvement with a woman would look like.

Roger, apparently unlike Carter, was very conflicted, actually drowning in conflict. He realized Carol's needs were not being met and felt terrible about it. He just didn't know what to do. He had no one to confide in or receive advice from. He couldn't leave the priesthood and didn't know how to extricate himself from the relationship. Because he was drowning in the swirling waters of conflict, Carol was too. We were not able to be of much help to each other, I'm afraid.

It was good to share, to have a sounding board, but a sounding board that has been warped by being in the water with a near-drowning person cannot give a clear sound. Sound is mysterious and all around us. The softest sound can draw the soul most persuasively. The loudest can overwhelm the ear. The gentle notes of the wind chime enchant us. The roar of the ocean calms us. A ringing telephone demands our attention. But it is the silent phone, the phone that does not ring, which is the loudest.

How many hours had I myself to be battered by my telephone's silence? How many people had I said an early good night to, only to rush home to blaring silence? The telephone on my nightstand was so loud so often that I could no longer bear it.

One night between Thanksgiving and Christmas, the phone had not rung for days. I was angry and crying and bewildered. I thought about calling Carter; I often thought about calling him but had never done so. That time I wanted to more than ever, but was afraid as usual.

What if someone recognizes my voice? I've met some of his colleagues, 'professionally,' of course. What if he is mad that I ventured into his world?

After an hour of *Yes/No/Yes* circling endlessly, beating my brain up from the inside, I was past caution and perhaps past caring. Certainly I was distraught enough to take a risk.

And so I called Carter. Lying on my bed holding on to my pillow, I dialed the number of his residence.

On the other end, the receiver was picked up. A man answered, but it wasn't Carter's voice that said "Hello."

I thought I must have misdialed, still I blurted out "May I speak to Father DeLuca, please?"

"Father Carter isn't here anymore. He moved some time ago."

I just sat there, breathing fast. Finally I asked "Well, where can I reach him?"

"He's living in one of the priests' residences downtown."

"He is? Well...can you give me the number there?"

Now I didn't give a damn what the person on the other end of the line thought. He had been living somewhere else for who knew how long and never told me. Now I was going to reach him no matter what, and I dialed the number the man gave me.

Carter picked up after the second ring.

"Carter! What the hell is going on? You've moved? When? It's the first I've heard of it! You've been lying to me about a lot of little things lately, things there's no reason to lie about. And now this? We need to talk. Come over tomorrow night. And don't tell me you have some important meeting! I'll see you at eight." And I slammed the receiver down, sobbing, my world spinning off its axis.

The next night, Carter arrived at eight looking a little pale. By nine o'clock, I was on my third scotch, hurling accusations, crying, beating the pillow on the coach. It wasn't that he was living somewhere else. It was that he hadn't told me. Now I realized why he could only call at 10 o'clock. He didn't have a phone in his room anymore and had to use a community phone.

I was drunk, out of my usual controlled self. My British genes, which usually served me so well in the stiff-upper-lip department, had given up. Finally, after numerous attempts to return me to my normal contained state, shut me up, reassert his control, Carter walked out.

I fell asleep eventually, not knowing what I had done or what I was going to do...

And then it was only a couple of days later that Carol casually mentioned as we were talking on the phone that she had seen Carter—at Marquette—at a lecture by the famous Dutch theologian Hans Kung.

"Really? He said he wasn't going to go to that lecture. We talked about meeting there and agreed neither of us was going." I was trying hard to keep my voice calm. I wasn't ready to say too much and certainly not ready to lose control again. What I needed was more information.

"Well, I saw him. He was there with a blond woman."

"Really? What did she look like?"

"In her mid 30's probably. About your size, I guess. Straight hair hanging shoulder length."

Barbara Wells! That psychologist Carter encouraged me to befriend. Said we could support one another.

"Well, I've got to go, Carol. Have to make another call." I spoke calmly and gently hung up the receiver. A few deep breaths, and I picked it up again. Indeed I did have to make another call.

"I thought you weren't going to that Hans Kung lecture."

"Right."

"Well, you were there. A friend of mine saw you!"

A long pause followed.

"Well, I just changed my mind."

"Uh-huh. And when were you going to tell me that?"

"I don't know. It didn't seem important." He paused again. I could hear him breathing fast.

"You mean you didn't think I would know. And you didn't think I would find out that you were there with Barbara Wells!"

"I...I don't know what to say."

"I can only imagine. You lie all the time, don't you? You lie for no reason at all...and you lie for big reasons too, like having another woman."

"Look, Ann. I...I have a lot to think about. Tomorrow I'm going to make an appointment with Jim...see if he can help me sort some stuff out...I'm sorry. I just can't talk anymore tonight...but I promise I'll get back to you—"

I hung up before he could. There was nothing more to do. I looked at my hand which was still resting on the phone, looked at the little gold ring on my right hand. Slowly, deliberately, I took it off. And then I walked across the room to my file cabinet and dropped it purposefully into the file labeled "History."

Carter did get back to me about ten days later. At his request, and for the first time, we met outdoors, in a carefully groomed park. The grass was perfectly cut to a height of one and a half inches. The paths were all scrupulously cleared of debris. Flimsy, drab bits of color showed from a few plants surviving but not flourishing in the northern clime. A small brook gurgled nearby. We sat as far apart as the green bench for two could allow, huddling down in our coats. The sky was overcast. It was winter. The temperature was falling fast.

"After our conversation the other night, I called James Lee and asked to see him professionally," he told me, his voice rather grim. "I asked him to give me the MMPI."

Of course I knew what that was: the most commonly researched and used psychological test of the day. The answers to almost 600 questions resulted in an assessment of personality and psychopathology. Here was science, standing separate from psychological theories; its greatest claim was objectivity. I just sat there, saying nothing, listening, but staring at some birds flying in the distance, dark specks moving across a mottled gray sky.

When I finally looked at him, Carter looked me straight in the eye and said, "I scored very high on Scale 4 of the test."

He's telling me he is a sociopath!

Sociopaths lie routinely, break all kinds of rules of behavior because they basically have no conscience. They often belong to groups with rigid rules, groups like the mafia or the Catholic priesthood. They feel fine about their own behavior, they don't respond to treatment, they don't change. And they don't tell people they are sociopaths...

Carter is saying, 'This is who I am, and I can't help it. I am incapable of changing.'

He was summing up our seven years together with a confession of unconscionable behavior white washed by medical diagnostic terminology, sterilized of moral impact. He had conducted himself abusively but was not guilty because he was just "that way."

Then without a word or a nod, he got up and walked away.

I watched him go down the road to the parking lot, saw him get into his car, and drive away. I lit a cigarette and stared at the path he had trod. The sun was sinking. Some of the grass seemed to have turned brown while we spoke. Leaves on the trees were going dry. Soon they would fall. Clouds were gathering. It was getting dark. I suddenly became aware of feeling very cold and pulled a shawl out of my purse, draping it over my shoulders and arms. Summer seemed to have ended prematurely.

So it's all clear and neat now. I know why he lied. I know how he always knew instinctively when I was about to throw in the towel and how he turned himself into 'Father Magnificent.' I see that his mother spoke truth years ago when she told me he was a womanizer.

Carter did not just lie. Carter is a lie—a lie parading in a collar...

What does a person do who has been proven a fool? I got up slowly, crushed the butt of my cigarette under my foot on the once-perfect path, found my car, and drove home. It was already dark. Once home, I undressed, brushed my teeth mechanically, wrapped myself in a blanket, and turned on the TV. That night I stared at it until the signal was gone and there was only the circle on the screen accompanied by the loud buzzing sound.

For a week, I walked around in a daze, putting one foot in front of the other, numb. Stunned. Totally shut down.

The following weekend, I forced myself to attend the 40th birthday party of my internship supervisor. She served sangria, not the usual kind, but sangria with whiskey hidden under the wine in the fruit. I only had two. But they landed on a deadened brain. I ran home, rushed to the bathroom to be sick.

It was while I rested, lying in a heap on the cool bathroom floor waiting for the next wave of nausea, that the thought entered my mind.

Is Carter really a sociopath? And if he is, would he admit it? He, who lies so easily, why would he reveal such a damning thing about himself? Sociopaths don't go around talking about their diagnosis, do they? I wonder whether Carter was lying when he told me about his score on the MMPI? Wonder if he even took the test? I am a problem to him by this point, a problem he probably wants to get rid of. What better way than to say he is a sociopath? One final lie? A diagnostic pretense served up as an excuse?

I spent the night leaning over the toilet throwing up.

Darkness

The sky was dark. The air silent. It was like being in nothingness, perhaps in that which is in-between. Deep River started reading out loud. She wanted to believe some light would rise. She wanted to hope—for something—she didn't even know what.

> Lord, God of my salvation,
> when, at night, I cry out in your presence,
> let my prayer come before you;
> incline your ear to my cry.

> "For my soul is full of troubles,
> and my life draws near to Sheol.

Flying Bird asked, "What is Sheol?"

"I don't know, Flying Bird. I think it is a gray place full of shadows. I do not know whether the gray will grow lighter or turn to blackest night."

She picked up her Bible again.

> I am counted among those who go down to the Pit;
> I am like those who have no help,
> like those forsaken among the dead,
> like the slain that lie in the grave,
> like those whom you remember no more,
> for they are cut off from your hand.
> You have put me in the depths of the Pit,
> in the regions dark and deep...

> "You have taken from me friend and neighbor—
> darkness is my closest friend.
> (Psalm 88:1-6, 18 NIV)

Thunder crashed into the stillness, sending it scattered like shattered glass. Lightning dashed across the sky. A mighty blast replaced the stillness of the air, sending the Bible careening down the hill.

Judgment Day

When the communist North Vietnamese Army captured Saigon, the nation's capital in April 1977, the Vietnam War was finally over.

Saigon was in chaos. South Vietnamese citizens, Americans, and other westerners were desperate to escape, and US helicopters attempted hazardous evacuations. The number of dead and mutilated was estimated by some to reach four million.

In the United States, an entire generation had been torn apart by this conflict. Some young people had fled to Canada to avoid the draft, others returned from combat psychologically and morally devastated by what they had seen and themselves done. Returning home to anti-war demonstrators who often treated them as pariahs only increased their anguish, flashbacks, and, on occasion, delusional violent behavior. As someone who had been on the streets with anti-war protestors, I was relieved the war was over, but I knew that the fallout from what seemed like futile horror would be long lived.

Seeds of destruction would last for decades. Men, women, and children dying, stepping on landmines, blown into pieces by bombs still lying in fields. Cluster bombs sending bits and pieces of metal and human flesh and bone flying through the air. There seems no answer and no end to the question, "Why? Why this war?"

In 1977, we were simply relieved it was finally over; there was hope for going forward at last.

My own personal world had moved forward in those four years since the breakup. I received my Master's in Social Work in December 1974 and was among the very fortunate who almost immediately got a really interesting job in a mental health clinic. I was in my third year there. My career as a psychotherapist was well underway, and I counseled a very diverse clientele of individuals, couples, families, and a few teenagers. Life no longer revolved around Carter, although I thought about him frequently. Still, I no longer deceived my friends to hide my secret, and I no longer left restaurants and parties abruptly to arrive home by 10 o'clock. But I still kept my secret.

That particular Thursday, I had worked a 10-hour day and seen fourteen clients, including a group of teenagers over the lunch hour. This was an experiment. My friend Frances and I wanted to try working four days a week instead of five. Could we see the same clients in four days and enjoy three-day weekends? The answer was "no," and became obvious very soon. I felt as though I was working in a factory with clients parading past me on a conveyor belt like cans of tomato soup.

A pile of charts on my desk matched the sequence of people in my appointment book. I always knew who was at my office door each new hour.

Who are you now? What's going on in your life? Are you the person with the dying aunt?

I felt like a perpetual motion machine: Open door. Smile and greet. Listen. Say something. Stand. Close door. Open chart. Open door... It was terrible.

"This is definitely not the way I want to practice," I told my supervisor after two weeks of this mind-scrambling routine. And I quickly returned to the usual five-day work week.

But that Thursday night, Frances and I had not yet abandoned the idea of a shorter week, and we were in it together. The experiment was Frances' idea originally. She was the more experienced therapist. Thin, large-boned, platinum blond, and in her late 40's, Frances had been doing this work for ten years. But Frances was also a published novelist and wanted more time to write. She was also an ardent feminist, a survivor of three divorces, and a fighter. Coming from her, the ten-hour days had sounded doable. She was tough.

We had both started at 10 that morning and had worked straight through until 10 that night. Well, Frances actually took a lunch hour while I spent mine with eight teenage girls who whined about their parents and sniped at one another for an hour and a half. By ten o'clock, we just about fell out the clinic door, stumbling toward our cars.

It was only a six block drive to Pete's Bar and Grill, a small, independently owned restaurant. The red brick building stood on the corner welcoming us with a warmly-colored neon sign advertising "great food, full bar, friendly staff." And we also knew it would still be open.

Frances and I parked next to one another and close to the front door. It was a cold night in Wisconsin. Pulling open the door, we were greeted by warmth, tempting aromas, and a cheerful hostess who showed us to a quiet booth about halfway back along the right wall. Exhausted, I sank into the comfortable, padded red benches facing the door with Frances across the table.

"My name is Cindy. May I bring you something to drink?" asked the waitress as she handed us menus and poured our water.

"A scotch, please, with a twist," I responded without hesitation. Frances ordered a Manhattan.

"Right away," said the young waitress. She indeed returned almost immediately, our drinks in hand, asking what we'd like to eat.

"Thank you." Our gratitude was heartfelt. "We'll wait a few minutes and relax before ordering."

"I'll be on the lookout. Just give me a signal," she said, and hurried cheerfully to another table.

I gazed a moment appreciatively at my scotch and then lifted my eyes and my glass toward Frances. "Cheers," I said. "Here's to surviving!"

Frances raised her glass too, and we were about to clink when, out of the corner of my eye, I saw a left hand extending from a table across the room with a cigarette grasped between the index and middle fingers. And I knew...and all the pain I thought was safely in the past came rushing back.

All I needed to identify him was that one hand and the way it held the filtered cigarette. Not that I needed any further proof, but now that I looked at the man, it was Carter all right. He was sitting with Barbara, the social worker he was with at the Hans Kung lecture years before. I saw her just before she rose and walked rapidly toward the back of the restaurant, to the rest room, I imagined. I don't think she noticed me. I had been too cold, hungry, and eager to get a table to have looked across the room and spotted him when we came in.

My mind was immobilized, and my hand put my drink down. I neither thought about what I was going to do, nor was there a moment of conscious decision. My legs decided for me, immediately carrying me across the restaurant to Carter's table. Seated with his back to me, he didn't see me coming, and then I was standing before him, my arms crossed over my chest.

"Are you still into this shit?!" I shouted, looking down at him.

Carter said nothing, just stared at me like a drunk driver staring into the glare of a cop's flashlight. Fear doesn't need words to communicate itself. His large frame seemed to shrink until he looked like a third grade boy facing an angry teacher.

I glared, and he gaped. A long minute passed.

Then his arms pressed against the table and his long legs pushed him to his feet. Tossing some uncounted bills on the table, this six foot four inch tall man began to walk backwards away from this woman a full foot shorter than himself. Not taking his eyes off me, he backed all the way to the door. And reaching it, he turned and fled.

But it was not over.

Again it was my feet, not my head, that took me back across the restaurant to the table where Frances stared at me, her glass glued to her lip.

"Who was....?" she began.

Flinging myself into the booth and staring at my friend, I burst out, "I've got to get out of here!"

"Well, you can't go home like this." She saw how flushed and jumpy I was. "Better come to my place. It's just four blocks away."

Frances waved her hand at the waitress and made a sign about needing the check.

"Okay." I took a gulp of my scotch.

"Just follow me. Do you think you can make it? Can you drive?"

"Yes." I was already standing.

The waitress arrived with the check. Frances already had her wallet out of her purse, looked at the bill, glanced for an instant at the ceiling while she figured out the tip, and tossed bills on the table.

"Thanks," she called after the startled waitress, picked up her coat and purse and stood herself.

I reached down for my own coat, gulped one more swallow of scotch, and followed Frances as she advanced with determined strides toward the door.

Outside, the weather had changed abruptly the way it sometimes does in the Midwest. The night had turned coal black and windy. The temperature had dropped, and the clouds hung low and menacing. We walked to our cars, and Frances began the slow parade: turn left, two blocks straight, turn right, pull into the apartment complex on the right. She pulled into her reserved spot, and I screeched into the empty visitor's space just behind her. Pulling our coats round us against the wind, we hurried up the walk to her building. We just flew in, stepped into the waiting elevator, and rode to the third floor.

Frances opened the door to her apartment, and I saw it. Right in the middle of the spacious room, sitting there, just waiting on the snow white shag carpeting all alone, was a very bright, very red telephone. No table, no chair nearby keeping it company.

Without saying a word and without taking in anything else about her place, I marched straight toward the phone and sat down on the white carpet in front of it. Lifting the receiver, I dialed Carter's number. This was done with no advance planning; my body simply enacted the precise sequence of movements.

Rrrrrrrrrrrrrrrrrring.

"Hello."

"You bastard. I thought Barbara went to the bathroom, but she went out the back door. She walked out on you, didn't she?" I paused to catch my breath. "Good for her. Smarter than I was!"

Silence resounded. Silence from Carter. Silence from myself as the words I had just uttered echoed through my soul—*"smarter than I was"*—and then a deep breath.

"How many women have you used? Did you tell them all about your fucking Third Way? That they would be part of your priesthood? Doing so much good for the world?"

I picked up the phone and started to pace a few feet to the left, a few feet back, stretching the cord tethering it to the wall as far as it would go.

"Did you take them all to visit your mother? And did they all think what I did? That doing that was pretty unique and special for a priest? And of course, when she told them you were a womanizer, I suppose they all thought she was just trying to break you and them up. Like I did."

I stopped pacing and stood straight, staring at the floor, base of the phone in one hand, receiver in the other.

"You never gave a damn about me!"

Silence, again silence. I had said it—for the first time—not just the first time to Carter, the first time to myself. Painful truth, searing deep into my flesh.

"Not about any of my needs. Not on holidays or after tough days at work, not in the bedroom, not even after I was hijacked!"

I choked down a sob. I *would not* cry!

"Oh, no! It was all about *your* schedule, *your* work, *your* fear of getting a woman pregnant."

Frances had walked out of the room, and I heard her bedroom door shut as I continued, louder.

"And you, who did that training at Johns Hopkins, that great psychiatric place. Did you ever take five minutes to think about what keeping this secret did to me? Yes, I know you kept a secret too. But in your world, people didn't talk about dating or marrying or their husbands and wives. None of those forbidden things. In your world, people don't come to parties or other events with a partner. In your world, everyone just assumed, or pretended, those things were not part of their life or yours, and there were no questions, no awkward conversations."

I was screaming now, a long, high scream of pain.

"Well, you can go to hell! You can take all your papers about the moronic Third Way and shove them up your ass. It's nothing but a lie. You lie to the world about being celibate. You lie to women about how important they are. You lie to yourself!"

There was still only silence on the other end of the line.

"You call that love? It's more like abuse!"

I was coming close to exhaustion, but after a few breaths, yet another volcanic outpouring of hot rage spewed out like lava. I had to defend God, the God he had defamed.

"And you use God as your authority. 'God wants this,' you tell us. 'God is using you.' Well, I don't think so. I think we are just used by selfish cowards like you..."

For exactly 45 minutes, I vomited every poisonous truth that had been bottled in the dark, hidden places of my heart for seven years. One after another the pain and anger I had not been able to look at tumbled out, the words pouring over one another until they crashed at the bottom of the waterfall in a foaming, swirling vortex.

Silence hung in the air for just a moment. Silence turned to ice. My voice turned calm, low, dangerous.

"And what's this confessional about being a sociopath? Don't tell me this is just the way you are. Don't try to say this wasn't your fault. It was your fault!"

My thoughts turned for a flash to my parents. I saw my father's face, an honorable face. The face of a true "Mensch," a man of character and worthy of respect.

"And furthermore, if you don't return the book you borrowed a year ago, the book my father wrote and inscribed...if you don't return it by Tuesday, I am calling your superior."

My whole arm slammed the receiver down on the phone, and I collapsed to the floor and rolled up into one exhausted ball. I had finally— finally—puked out all the pain, all the anger, all the self-deception of seven crazy years as I lay on the white shag carpet. My world went black.

I don't know what happened then. I suppose Frances came back into the room. She must have heard every screamed word. Knowing Frances, she probably congratulated me, saying, "Well, you got him by the balls." I don't know how long it took me to get off the floor. Frances no doubt offered me her couch for the night, and I no doubt accepted. I certainly could not have driven home. And I suppose that three-day weekend was spent in a formless cloud of depression, the clock ticking away the hours.

The following Tuesday, I picked up all the charts of clients I had seen that day. The day had gone by in a blur. One client after another, coming and going. Still, I managed to listen, respond, ask questions, smile. And I had gotten through the pile of charts on my desk. They all had the appropriate notes inscribed within: what we had discussed, the client's mood, progress toward goals, and so forth. All charts had to be refiled each day in the huge floor to ceiling files behind the receptionist's area. She would be the first one in the office the next morning, and when the clinicians arrived, we would find a new pile on our desks. My pile was heavy. Everything felt heavy that day.

Drawing near the receptionist's area, I saw it: a hand with a book, an arm. Then all six feet four inches of him followed, seeking invisibility, slipping sideways through the front door, moving just close enough to the receptionist's desk. Still a couple of feet from her, still believing himself unobserved, his arm shot out and tossed a book onto the desk. The arm retracted. Carter turned and was gone.

Finally! Finally it was over. Finally, for once, I had made him do what I wanted!

There is New Life after Death

A telephone rings. Except this time it is my iPhone, housed in a pink OtterBox case, alerting me with the jumping "Spanish Flea," courtesy of Herb Alpert and the Tijuana Brass. This phone, now called a "cell," has a caller ID too. Right now it's telling me that Luise wants to speak with me.

A few months ago, I had one of my regular conversations with Luise. I first met her in a church we both attended. Her husband was in the hospital, and I brought communion. She is now a widow and has moved to an assisted living facility where I visit her regularly. Luise is 92 years old, was born in Germany, and grew up in New England with her siblings and immigrant parents. A small woman with beautiful white, wavy hair, her mind is sharp as a tack, and her opinions are clear and boldly expressed. Our conversations range from her latest encounters with healthcare professionals to theological topics. Our discussions are always interesting. Most important, we love each other.

This particular morning, Luise called to let me know her thoughts about our conversation the day before. I had told her, sitting by her bed because she was having some dizziness that day, that I rarely participated in any way at her church. She has known for quite some time about my activities elsewhere, but now I had left the community she still considered her own. She didn't like that idea and said as much, frowning.

Luise is not one to chit chat. So when caller ID identified her, I anticipated she had more thoughts on the church matter.

"Hello. This is Luise, Ann. I want to talk about our conversation yesterday." Her voice was strong and clear, with a hint of brisk, no-nonsense New England.

"Oh, that's great, Luise. What are you thinking?" I responded, sitting down at my kitchen table ready for a serious exchange.

"Well, I've been thinking about what you said. I just think that at your age you should settle down and be satisfied with the church you are in. That's what Bob and I did. We tried a couple of churches, settled on one, and stayed there. Lots of times it wasn't perfect, but we were satisfied."

"I hear you, Luise, and I think I understand where you're coming from. For a lot of people that works. But it's just not me."

"I think it's important to be loyal. And no church is perfect, you know."

"I really believe in loyalty too, Luise. I think I'm a *very* loyal person." I am loyal to a fault actually, and bristled a bit at her suggestion that I wasn't. I poured some water in a cup and put it in the microwave with a tea bag. "I just need to keep moving forward."

"Well, you've been a Jew and a Catholic and a Protestant. You are an Episcopalian now. Maybe you should look inside *yourself.* You take yourself with you wherever you go, you know."

"You are right that I take my own issues with me wherever I go. Actually I do look into myself a lot, probably too much. I've asked myself whether I just jump around. But when I look at my life, that's not what I see, Luise. There's a process here, a journey. There's a thread to all these changes. I'm moving forward."

"Well, what are you *looking* for?" she pressed further.

"I'm looking for more of God. And when I search in a new place, it's not about throwing away what I found before. Not at all. I take it *with me.* I try to put it all together, integrate all my experiences and encounters with God."

This was getting intense, and I could see it was going to be hard to explain my journeying to Luise.

"You love music, Luise. I do too. What I'm talking about is like a symphony with themes and moods that appear, disappear, come back in different ways, rise and fall. I think of the different ways God touches me as a bit like a symphony.

"God is always more, will always be more, will be way beyond what I can grasp. I just want as much as I can. I want to be *connected* with God and grow from lots of people and their ways of connecting.

"'Nothing's wrong with the church you've been in. It's good. I just want more, Luise. I want to experience different ways of worshiping, different communities, different cultures. I just don't want to be limited to one church, to one institution. And I'll still go to your church sometimes, just not most of the time. I realize we have to have institutions. I'm just not an institutional person."

"I still just think you won't ever find what you're looking for and should just be satisfied. At your age, I think you should just settle down."

"It's just not me, Luise."

The microwave rang saying it had done its job. I took out the hot liquid, tossed the tea bag, and breathed in the fragrance of ginger. I could tell there wasn't much more I could say. Luise was just worried about me.

"Well, all right." Her reluctance was evident in her voice. "Don't think I love you any less now," she proclaimed with Germanic definitiveness.

"No, I know that, Luise. And I love you. And thank you for your thoughts and for being honest. I really value that. It tells me how much you care about me. So thank you."

"Don't wait too long to come visit me. Yesterday was the first time I had seen you in a long time. But I know you're busy, so I don't call much."

"I'm sorry. It was a long time. But please call me any time you want to, and I'll try to come again soon."

"All right then. Bye," Luise said wistfully, and the call clicked off.

I understood the questions Luise was posing. They are ones I have asked myself so many times.

A great deal has happened since that night with the red telephone on the white shag carpet. I quit smoking. I think Mark Twain said something about quitting being easy and that he had done it fifty times. That was me for a long time. One cycle after another of quitting—*smoking is bad for my health and costs more to get insurance*—followed by becoming convinced I could enjoy just three cigarettes a day, followed by two packs! Finally I heard about Nicorette. That worked, although I confess that if I were diagnosed with a terminal illness, I might just run to the nearest cigarette counter. Actually I can't stand being around people smoking. It's a kind of "hate the smoke or join the smokers" reaction.

I'm still smoking in other ways, still making waves, still getting in trouble. At 80, I am an ordained Protestant minister leading retreats, pastoring a congregation, building bridges between churches of different denominational and racial histories. More than twenty years passed between my departure from the Catholic Church and my Protestant ordination. During those 20 years, I followed my call by serving wounded people as a psychotherapist. For some years, I developed programs for persons with disabilities. Spiritually, those years were full of wandering in the desert, searching, feeling joy, and shedding tears, making my home in many different places both in and outside the US.

I am a published author. *Sight in the Sandstorm: Jesus in His World and Mine* shows the Jewish Jesus living in the world of his time with all its political, socio-economic, and religious turmoil. Dramatized Gospel stories are woven together with tales from my own life, including the day in first grade when I beat up the school bully, the December I brought my Jewish husband to my parents' home for his first Christmas, and the frightening experience of being detained and questioned by customs officials in Poland.

I have been happily married for over 30 years, 25 of which have been spent in Atlanta. I have three stepchildren and four grandchildren.

A decade ago, I began pondering my long and winding journey, and wondered whether I had just jumped around restlessly. I am very clear now that my path has been neither fanciful nor capricious. I have sought intimacy with God. I have tried to love people, ease pain, and release prisoners.

Wrestling is, in fact, my near-constant companion and personal dynamic. I have struggled with the reality of being part of many worlds, yet belonging to none of them. This has made me complicated and different, and I have been afraid of being simply weird. But the truth is I have never wanted to be ordinary. I love the wrestling, although it is often hard and painful. I love it because it is life giving. Through it, I live out, in my peculiar way, the journey from loss to gain, from night to day, from Death to Resurrection.

And at 80, my journey is not over. These days I choose to participate in a couple of different churches rather than just one. Two weeks out of each month, I lead the service and preach at a small church in West Georgia. Actually, I am connected with four small rural churches, helping them to stand with one another. We have multicultural services, show up at one another's events, and hold workshops in public spaces. When I am in Atlanta, I worship at a historic black UCC (United Church of Christ) church and sing in their choir. Through interfaith activities, I have friends of many different religious traditions. And I sing with The Trey Clegg Singers, a touring semi-professional, multicultural group whose mission is to bring hope through our journey together, sharing the music of many nations.

This works for me right now. I get to indulge my visionary self, serving in innovative and creative ways. I still have the privilege of hearing the stories of people from many nationalities and races, many ways of living, of thinking, of loving. And I can stay away from church politics and most restrictions. I am, in turn, nurtured by times of silence, the love of friends, and the beauty of music and glorious nature, breathing in the Spirit of God in all these cathedrals.

Pain and injustice persist in this world alongside great love and miraculous beauty. I continue to ease pain where I can and work for justice as I am able. I experience God there, as well as wherever people are curious, expand their visions, reach out loving hands. I find God in the blue sky, the purple flower, the rolling thunder, the song of the bird, and the delicate dance of a leaf moved by a gentle breeze. And I meet God in silence.

What lies ahead for me today is a mystery. I know there will be adventure. There will be new people to love, new worlds to enter, new opportunities to stand for what is right. I know there will be dark nights and bright days. I know that night will eventually overwhelm me and carry me off. And I believe that out of that very darkness will come a great Light.

As I write this, Flying Bird runs along the beach, splashing in the waves, hair blowing in the breeze. Deep River sits and watches the sun slowly rise, light spreading across the heavens. A new day is dawning.

"Flying Bird, how far will you run today? Won't you get tired?"

"I will run and walk and rest a bit. I will not stop, Deep River. There is still so much to see, to feel, to learn, to love. So many people I don't yet know, experiences I have not had. And you, Deep River? Are you still going deeper?"

"I hope to always go deeper, Flying Bird. Closer to where Love is. One day I will have gone so deep that all is dark. Then Light will surround me, the Presence will embrace me. I will be home, and everything will be all right."

ACKNOWLEDGEMENTS

First to my husband of 35 years, friend, encourager, and frequent cook Mort Josephson, without whom this book could never have been written. His unselfish willingness to share me with my many friends and activities, as well as with this manuscript, has manifested in so many things: long conversations, reading and commenting on manuscripts and revisions, cooking dinner more than I, and always encouraging me to be who I really am and do what I need to do. Thank you.

To my editor Wayne South Smith, who has walked with me through two books, connected me with other writers, brought me from the earliest experimental pieces through publication with honesty, gentleness, skill, and an ability to "get" this complex woman I find myself to be. You are my editor and my friend, Wayne, and I am deeply grateful.

To the members of my focus group, who read and reviewed my manuscript and whose comments were so encouraging and helpful: Roger V. Freeby, Karen Kroeger, Cristina Montesinos, Sami Payton, and Candice Rankin. Thank you for your time, your thoughtful input, and your honest and kind delivery. To Regina Kay, my voracious reader friend, who encouraged me throughout the writing process, took the time to read my manuscript, and provided important feedback. And to Mark Reeve and Connie Tuttle, both fellow writers, for their time, support, and detailed comments.

To Cristina Montesinos whose huge talent and great patience made working on the book cover a joyful and fun experience, and for whose work I have deep respect and am extremely grateful.

ABOUT THE AUTHOR

Ann J. Temkin is half Jewish/half Gentile, a former Catholic nun, and an ordained Protestant minister. Born into a family of many traditions, she was raised in none. Her long spiritual journey, which began in early childhood, has been marked by wrestling with hard questions, dissatisfaction with easy answers, and a deep yearning for the living God. Her passion for social justice and concern for the marginalized, the invisible, and the oppressed led her to involvement with the Civil Rights Movement and into careers as a psychotherapist and minister.

The Smoking Nun is a memoir covering the Catholic period of Ann's journey, exposing conflicting loves, difficult decisions, dark times, and new light and life. Ann's first book, *Sight In the Sandstorm: Jesus in His World and Mine,* is part memoir and part dramatic depiction of the troubled times in which Jesus lived.

Ann had a call to serve the wounded and marginalized and earned an MA in Theology from Marquette University. Because women could not be ordained at that time, she went on to earn a Masters in Social Work from University of Wisconsin-Milwaukee and worked as a psychotherapist for over 30 years.

In 1999 Ann was ordained to the ministry and served as co-pastor at an interdenominational church until 2010 and has taught in churches and seminaries. Today she ministers at small churches of different denominational and racial traditions, building bridges across historical divides. She also leads retreats, develops creative liturgies, and provides spiritual direction.

Ann believes that God is always more—more than we can understand, imagine, or experience. Her own journey has included the integration of portions of many traditions. Ann loves to hear people's stories because to her, human hearts are cathedrals. She is happiest among the questions and the questioners, walking with the wounded and shut out, testifying to both the depth of the human struggle and the extravagant love of God.

Ann is a complex person with academic credentials and a depth of understanding, but her books speak most strongly from her heart. Currently she lives in Atlanta with Mort Josephson, her husband of over 30 years. She has three stepchildren and four grandchildren. When not working, she loves to sing with the multicultural choral group The Trey Clegg Singers and to spend time with family and friends.

Ann can be reached at ajtemkin@comcast.net. Visit her website at www.anntemkin.com.

Made in the USA
Middletown, DE
13 March 2019